Enabling Consumer and Entrepreneurial Literacy in Subsistence Marketplaces

EDUCATION IN THE ASIA-PACIFIC REGION: ISSUES, CONCERNS AND PROSPECTS

Volume 12

Madhu Viswanathan
S. Gajendiran • R. Venkatesan

Enabling Consumer and Entrepreneurial Literacy in Subsistence Marketplaces

UNESCO UNEVOC INTERNATIONAL CENTRE

ASIA-PACIFIC EDUCATIONAL RESEARCH ASSOCIATION

Springer

Madhu Viswanathan
Marketplace Literacy Project
and University of Illinois
Champaign, IL
USA

S. Gajendiran
Marketplace Literacy Project
and SDV Educational Trust
Chennai, India

R. Venkatesan
Marketplace Literacy Project
and SDV Educational Trust
Chennai, India

ISBN 978-1-4020-5768-7 e-ISBN 978-1-4020-5769-4

Library of Congress Control Number: 2007937391

Printed on acid-free paper

9 8 7 6 5 4 3 2 1

springer.com

SERIES SCOPE

The purpose of this Series is to meet the needs of those interested in an in-depth analysis of current developments in education and schooling in the vast and diverse Asia-Pacific Region. The Series will be invaluable for educational researchers, policy makers and practitioners, who want to better understand the major issues, concerns and prospects regarding educational developments in the Asia-Pacific region.

The Series complements the *Handbook of Educational Research in the Asia-Pacific Region*, with the elaboration of specific topics, themes and case studies in greater breadth and depth than is possible in the Handbook.

Topics to be covered in the Series include: secondary education reform; reorientation of primary education to achieve education for all; re-engineering education for change; the arts in education; evaluation and assessment; the moral curriculum and values education; technical and vocational education for the world of work; teachers and teaching in society; organisation and management of education; education in rural and remote areas; and, education of the disadvantaged.

Although specifically focusing on major educational innovations for development in the Asia-Pacific region, the Series is directed at an international audience.

The Series *Education in the Asia-Pacific Region: Issues, Concerns and Prospects*, and the *Handbook of Educational Research in the Asia-Pacific Region*, are both publications of the Asia-Pacific Educational Research Association.

Those interested in obtaining more information about the Monograph Series, or who wish to explore the possibility of contributing a manuscript, should (in the first instance) contact the publishers.

Books published to date in the series:

1. Young People and the Environment:
   An Asia-Pacific Perspective
   Editors: John Fien, David Yenken and Helen Sykes
2. Asian Migrants and Education:
   The Tensions of Education in Immigrant Societies and among Migrant Groups
   Editors: Michael W. Charney, Brenda S.A. Yeoh and Tong Chee Kiong
3. Reform of Teacher Education in the Asia-Pacific in the New Millennium:
   Trends and Challenges
   Editors: Yin C. Cheng, King W. Chow and Magdalena M. Mok
4. Rasch Measurement: A Book of Exemplars
   Papers in Honour of John P. Keeves
   Editors: Sivakumar Alagumalai, David D. Curtis, Njora Hungi
5. Reforming Learning:
   Issues, Concepts and Practices in the Asian-Pacific Region
   Editors: Chi-Hung Ng and Peter Renshaw, *in press*
6. New Paradigm for Re-engineering Education:
   Globalization, Localization and Individualization
   Editor: Yin Cheong Cheng
7. Towards a Global Community:
   Educating for Tomorrow's World
   Editors: William J. Campbell, Nicholas Baikaloff and Colin Power

8. Educational Decentralization:
   Asian Experiences and Conceptual Contributions
   Editor: Christopher Bjork
9. Secondary Education at the Crossroads:
   International Perspectives Relevant to the Asia-Pacific Region
   Editor: Phillip Hughes
10. Alternative Education:
    Global Perspectives Relevant to the Asia-Pacific Region
    Editor: Yoshiyaki Nagata
11. Educating in the Arts
    The Asian Experience: Twenty-Four Essays
    Editor: Lindy Joubert
12. Enabling Consumer and Entreprenurial Literacy in Subsistance Marketplaces
    Madhu Viswanathan, S. Gajendiran, R. Venkatesan

Dedication

by Madhu Viswanathan

To Appa
for his service to India

To Amma
for her empathy

To Deepa and Sidanth
for their unconditional support

To Avinish Chaturvedi
for his eternal inspiration

Contents

Introduction by the Series Editors

In countries throughout the world, consumer education and entrepreneurship (or enterprise) studies are increasingly regarded as important. This is because there is a growing realisation that promoting consumer and entrepreneurial literacy is important if individuals are to be best able to effectively play their important roles in the economy and society, as both consumers and producers of goods and services. As such consumer education and entrepreneurship education are increasingly included as subjects in the school curriculum, and also in non-formal education programmes.

Today's consumer of goods and services faced a difficult task in conducting their economic affairs because they operate in an increasingly complex, sophisticated and confusing market place. This is true for those living in both developed and developing countries.

Although such difficulties are faced by all people to varying degrees, several groups of consumers can be singled out as being those who find it particularly difficult to adequately cope with these problems. These include low income earners, the unemployed, youth, the elderly, minority groups, the physically and intellectually challenged and rural consumers.

It is largely in response to such developments that individuals have organised themselves into associations which seek to protect the consumer interest through such means as distributing information that will assist in making informed decisions; forming pressure groups to help bring about the reform of undesirable business practices and encouraging governments to pass and enforce improved consumer protection legislation.

Unfortunately, most of these attempts to put consumers on a more equal footing with businesses have not been fully successful and it is clear from available evidence that the provision of more consumer protection information and legislations will not, by itself, better equip individuals to cope with the expanding range of problems and issues which confront them as consumers.

Research indicates that the most effective way to better equip people to function is to promote consumer literacy through such means as including consumer education as part of the core curriculum in all schools from the kindergarten through to grade 12, and (particularly in the case of developing countries where many learners do not have an opportunity to participate in formal education) in non-formal and informal education programmes. Consumer education refers to the development and refinement of the concepts, knowledge and skills relating to the role of the consumer in contemporary society. It includes more than understanding areas such as good buymanship and effective money management. The definition includes a consideration of what some may regard as non-market consideration such as the environmental impact of consumer considerations, and the social and political role of organised consumer groups.

Consumers are also producers and so education programmes to promote entrepreneurship education are also of importance. The purpose of developing and strengthening entrepreneurship literacy is to assist individuals to be enterprising not just business but also in their daily lives. It encourages them to develop the necessary skills to be innovative while at the same methodical in establishing and operating successfully (for example) small or medium sized business enterprises. What makes entrepreneurship education distinctive is its focus on the realisation of opportunity, mainly but not exclusively in the area of business opportunities.

Entrepreneurship education not only helps learners to 'acquire the mindset and know-how necessary to make self-employment a viable career option' (UNESCO, 2006). It also equips them 'with the skills they will need to be successful in a complex world. Creativity, innovation, independence, initiative are essential attributes for personal fulfilment and success.' (Website of the European Commission, 2008).

Although the terms entrepreneurship education and enterprise education are often used interchangeably, there is a subtle distinction between these terms, with the latter being broader in scope, to refer to most areas of life, not just those which are business related. 'Enterprise education is learning directed towards developing in young people those skills, competencies, understandings and attributes which equip them to be innovative, and to identify, create, initiate, and successfully manage personal, community, business and work opportunities, including working for themselves. The development of enterprising skills in young people is important preparation for work and life.
Both entrepreneurship and enterprise education seek to foster:

- Creativity, innovation and self-reliance;
- The ability to generate, recognise and seize opportunities;
- Greater appreciation of the need for lifelong learning; and
- Personal development that will help them to be more adaptable.'

(Website of the Australian Department of Education, Employment and Workplace Relations, 2008)

This important and timely book examines consumer and entrepreneurial literacy with regard to meeting the needs of low literate and low income adults in India. As such it deals with an area about which there has been a paucity of research, particularly with regard to consumer and entrepreneurship literacy in developing countries. The book reports on research conducted to identify learning that can best assist such population groups operate most effectively in the marketplace. As such it has implications that go well beyond India.

Rupert Maclean
Director of the UNESCO-UNEVOC International Centre for Education, Bonn, Germany;

and

Ryo Watanabe
Director of the Department for International Research and Cooperation, National Institute for Educational Policy Research (NIER) of Japan, Tokyo

Preface

This book is the result of several years of research, curriculum development, and testing of a consumer and entrepreneurial literacy educational program for low-literate, low-income adults in India. Whereas there has been considerable attention on microfinancing in recent decades, we describe an educational program that focuses on enabling generic skills about the marketplace and complements these important efforts. We conducted research aimed at understanding lives and marketplaces in subsistence contexts in urban and rural parts of a state in South India. We used the research as a basis for developing a consumer and entrepreneurial literacy educational program. This program uses the "know-why" or an understanding of marketplaces as a basis for the know-how of being an informed buyer or seller. Despite the difficulties with abstract thinking that low-literate individuals experience, we enable deeper understanding of marketplaces by leveraging the social skills that participants bring to the program and relating educational content back to their lived experiences. Such understanding can enable individuals to embark on a path to lifelong learning. A detailed explanation of the evolution of this work follows.

My previous research on the study of low-literate consumers in the USA, which commenced toward the end of 1997, was expanded to the study of low-literate consumers in an Indian context in 2001. I used qualitative interviews and observations of low-literate, low-income individuals in urban and rural Tamil Nadu, India, to educate myself and gain a broad perspective. To accomplish this, I was assisted by the third author of this book, R. Venkatesan, who was recommended to me by a nonprofit organization in Tamil Nadu. Whereas my experience related to broader perspectives on business education, consumer behavior, and research methods, Venkatesan's insights and experience from having lived and worked in the communities we studied were a perfect complement. He is extremely knowledgeable of families in the communities where we conducted interviews. Being an employee of the organization I worked with and in charge of these communities for delivering services, he had personally interacted with some of the individuals we interviewed. Over three months, we conducted many interviews. He observed the process during the initial phases of research and took on increasing responsibilities over time until he was able to conduct his own data collection and report to me. Very soon, the research objectives expanded to understanding buyers, sellers, and marketplaces in low-income communities. Venkatesan and Gajendiran, the second author, also recommended to me by the nonprofit organization I had contacted, continued interviews and observations throughout the year. Our analyses of a total of 60 interviews conducted in the first year of a variety of buyers and sellers and ongoing research with additional interviews provided the foundation for the educational program we developed.

The trip to India intended for research was a transformational experience for me personally. The dedication of individuals who work for nonprofit organizations and the courage and honesty displayed by low-literate, low-income individuals in the face of the worst of adversities was truly inspiring. Toward the end of the trip, I began thinking about possible ways of disseminating our research to benefit the people we had studied. This idea took shape over the next few months and, in early 2003, I visited India again. Over several discussions with Gajendiran and Venkatesan, we planned a curriculum for a consumer and entrepreneurial literacy educational program for low-literate, low-income individuals in the state of Tamil Nadu. My coauthors, who have experienced subsistence contexts first-hand and possess several decades of experience in social work and community development between them, provided a bottom-up perspective, which complemented my experience in business education, with our local research providing the third key element in our foundation of knowledge. Our curriculum focused on conveying some basic concepts for buyers and sellers assuming that our audience was low-literate, essentially not able to read or write. Therefore, both the content and the form, or the "what" and the "how" were challenging issues. Through detailed brainstorming and discussion, we developed a 5-day educational program for consumer and entrepreneurial literacy.[1] Our approach was simple, that we draw on the lived experiences of participants and build on their social skills to convey basic concepts and encourage continuous learning.

Our philosophical orientation is to enable participants to learn how to create their own opportunities. The foundation for this learning environment is absolute respect for the inherent dignity of each individual who participates in our program. Our approach is discussion oriented, with the participants providing much of the material that we organize and summarize from the bottom up rather than use a top-down lecture-based approach. A guiding orientation here is that buyers and sellers are two sides of the same coin.

Our 5-day educational program uses teaching methods such as picture sortings, group discussion, and role-playing, and assumes that the typical participant cannot read or write. Day 1 focuses on the process of exchange and its evolution over time. We focus on marketplace literacy and cover the concept of a value chain from production of products to consumption. In Day 2, participants assume the role of customers. We focus on consumer literacy by using simulated shopping environments with common traps that our previous research has identified low-literate consumers as being vulnerable to. We use the notion of value for an exchange as the guiding concept to communicate the importance of informed consumer behavior. On Days 3–5, participants assume the role of entrepreneurs. We emphasize a customer-oriented philosophy of doing business that makes a profit on the bases of satisfying customer needs and providing valuable, mutually

[1] We have now developed other configurations from this program including a 1-day marketplace and consumer literacy program and a 2-day entrepreneurial literacy program as well as a 2-day combined marketplace/consumer and entrepreneurial literacy program.

beneficial exchanges. This orientation flows from the customer orientation of Day 2 and the importance of value in a product. We start Day 3 of the educational program with participants now in the role of sellers and a discussion of how business opportunities can be evaluated based on customer needs, competitors, and strengths and weaknesses of individual entrepreneurs. Over the last three days, we cover several specific areas of business, such as production and product design, distribution and management of the supply chain, pricing and related financial issues, and promotion. We end the educational program with a discussion of ethics and the need to balance societal concerns with profit making and customer needs and the importance of sustainable production and consumption. Although we start out with a 5-day educational program, several variations are possible to fit different durations, such as a day-long or half-day-long marketplace and consumer literacy educational program or a day-long entrepreneurial literacy program.

I remained skeptical of the benefits of this program until actually observing and participating in it for the first time and receiving feedback from participants. It was difficult to believe that we could provide a new and beneficial educational program in light of the dedication of volunteers and employees of existing nonprofit organizations. Nevertheless, our pilot educational program in June, 2003, was as close to perfection as I have seen in terms of plans for a new educational effort unfolding. This was most encouraging in addition to being a testament to the sincerity and dedication of the teachers. We used our first experience to make changes to the program and offered it several times in urban and rural settings.

We also followed up with our participants 3–6 months later to assess their progress. The feedback was overwhelmingly positive. Participants reported making considerable savings as customers and grouping their resources to buy staples, such as rice, wholesale. For instance, one group reported savings of thousands of rupees by buying rice in this manner. About 4–5 individuals in each group of approximately 20 individuals reported having started small businesses. Participants reported conveying the essence of the educational program to many others in the neighborhood. We understand the need to use more structured, quantitative assessment and are currently implementing it. Preliminary results of our quantitative assessment are presented in this book.

Over the years, we have gathered experience in offering different configurations of the program to urban and rural audiences. We provide a 1-day marketplace and consumer literacy program, a 2- or 3-day entrepreneurial literacy program, and a combined 2-day marketplace, consumer and entrepreneurial literacy program. We are now working to have the benefits reach a much wider audience in many villages. After several years of offering and customizing our program, it is currently being adopted by a large nonprofit organization that provides a variety of services to hundreds of villages in India. We have also customized the program for specific audiences, such as entrepreneurs attempting to run computer kiosks as sustainable businesses. We are also exploring opportunities to customize the educational program to other countries and contexts.

The book is organized as follows. Chapter 1 provides a detailed discussion of the research on buyers, sellers, and marketplaces in subsistence contexts that formed the basis for the development of the educational program. Chapter 2 describes the process of developing the 5-day educational program as well as details about its implementation and assessment. Each of the next five chapters describes the educational content for specific days of the program in the form of a manual. This is followed by four chapters that discuss implications for nonprofit organizations, for education research and practice, for business research and practice, and for academic and applied research, respectively. Our book will be of interest to a wide audience spanning basic research to practice in a range of disciplines and functions, such as education and business.

A set of chapters in the book are in the form of a manual. To make this material user-friendly, we do not include extensive citations in the body of Chapters 3–7, but footnote a few key citations. However, our thinking has been influenced by a vast literature in a variety of areas including management, education and social work. It is perhaps impossible to do full justice to the articles and books that have influenced our thinking either directly or indirectly. A few books from which we have adapted material for our purpose are *Marketing Management* (Prentice-Hall, 11th edition, 2003) by Philip Kotler; *The Theory of Buyer Behavior* (Wiley, 1969) by John A. Howard and Jagdish N. Sheth; *Consumer Behavior* (Harcourt College Publishers, 9th edition, 2001) by Roger D. Blackwell, Paul W. Miniard, and James F. Engel; *Competitive Strategy: Techniques for Analyzing Industries and Competitors* (Free Press, 1998, 1980) by Michael E. Porter; and *Pricing: Making Profitable Decisions* (McGraw-Hill Higher Education, 2002) by Kent B. Monroe.

Each chapter is described in more detail below. Chapter 1 provides a summary of our basic research. The discussion is organized by first describing the method we employed. We then present a background of the individual context and the larger marketplace context. This is followed by brief profiles of a buyer and a seller that put human faces to our research. We then provide discussions of product interactions, of marketplace interactions, and of unique characteristics of the product and market interactions we studied. The final section focuses on the development of consumer and entrepreneurial skills in the subsistence marketplaces we studied. Our research provided insights into the individual and larger marketplace context, product and market interactions, and the development of consumer skills in the subsistence marketplaces we studied. It provided a window into the strengths and vulnerabilities of subsistence customers and entrepreneurs, thus enabling us to design the educational program in terms of content and instructional methods.

Chapter 2 outlines the development of a consumer and entrepreneurial literacy education program based on the research described in Chapter 1. We describe the need for such a program, and the philosophical orientation, content, and instructional methods relevant to the development of the program. The details of the 5-day educational program are presented. Piloting, implementation, and assessment of the program to date are discussed.

Chapters 3–7 cover the part of the book presented as a manual reflecting the 5-day program discussed earlier. Chapter 3 covers the first day of the educational program and focuses on marketplace literacy. Chapter 4 covers the second day of the educational program and focuses on consumer literacy. Chapter 5 covers the third day of the educational program and focuses on entrepreneurial literacy. Chapter 6 covers the fourth day of the educational program and continues the focus on entrepreneurial literacy. Chapter 7 covers the fifth and final day of the educational program, which includes miscellaneous issues, such as ethics and societal responsibility and the importance of sustainable consumption and production, and costs and accounting.

Chapter 8 summarizes the implications of this educational approach for social initiatives by nonprofit organizations. These implications extend to both governmental and nongovernmental organizations. We begin by emphasizing the distinct aspects of our program in terms of a focus on the know-why followed by the know-how. We then discuss how consumer and entrepreneurial literacy programs can complement other initiatives, such as microfinancing. We discuss operational aspects of our program. The chapter concludes with a discussion of scaling and customization issues based on our experience to date.

Chapter 9 presents a number of issues that are relevant to education. These issues are important in placing this educational program in the context of the literature and practice in education in general. Our discussion in previous chapters is grounded in the research and development of the educational program. In this chapter, we draw out some broader issues relevant to education and discuss them in the context of the literature where relevant. We start out with a brief discussion of linkages with research and practice documented in the literature. We then emphasize some of the key distinctions in our program. This work has a number of implications for educational research and practice particularly for areas such as nonformal education, adult literacy, and educational programs in subsistence contexts that are discussed in this chapter.

Chapter 10 discusses a number of implications for business in subsistence marketplaces. The educational approach in itself has direct implications for business practice. The translation and modification of generic business concepts to an educational program focused on subsistence contexts highlights a number of issues of relevance to business education, research, and practice. These issues are directly relevant to businesses that work with individuals in subsistence marketplaces as part of the value chain, both as entrepreneurs and as customers. The research underlying the educational program also has broader implications for business, in a variety of areas ranging from product design to distribution to marketing communications. Unique to this research in distinguishing it from other approaches to studying poverty is the bottom-up focus that can be contrasted with a macro-level economic focus or a medium-level business strategy focus, such as the base of the pyramid approach. The lessons learned in subsistence markets can extend to all markets, in terms of doing more with less or finding sustainable solutions.

Chapter 11 discusses a number of lessons learned and insights generated by this process of moving from basic research to education. This chapter explores these implications for basic and applied research in the social sciences, including a focus on research across literacy and resource barriers, research methods, treatment of human participants, the iterative process between basic research and the development of an application for societal welfare, and synergies between research, teaching, and social initiatives.

A brief discussion of terminology is relevant here. Terms such as base of the pyramid, and poorest of the poor have raised awareness across the disciplines of the potential for improved social welfare and profitability. Our term, subsistence marketplaces, reflects a somewhat different although highly complementary bottom-up orientation of buyer, seller, and marketplace behavior, in contrast to macro level economic approaches or mid-level business strategy approaches. "Subsistence" describes the phenomenon on which we focus, and is intended to convey being resource-poor, barely having sufficient resources for day-to-day living, yet perhaps rich in other dimensions, such as social networks. This terms is intended to be descriptive but not patronizing. Likewise, "marketplaces" signifies that these contexts are and have been often characterized by vibrant exchanges and market activity, whether they are acknowledged or ignored in relatively resource-rich settings. The choice of the term, "subsistence marketplaces", also reflects the purpose of this work based on the need to understand these marketplaces in their own right, and to view them not just as markets to sell to, but as individuals, communities, consumers, entrepreneurs, and markets to learn from. We hope that an optimal combination of governmental initiatives, social enterprises, business efforts, and local enterprises can enable subsistence marketplaces to become sustainable marketplaces, i.e., marketplaces characterized by sustainable production and consumption that conserve natural resources and enhance individual and community welfare.

Also relevant here is the need to delineate our coverage of the literature. The topic of poverty has been examined in several disciplines, such as anthropology, by many great scholars and social enterpreneurs (e.g., Amartya Sen, Mohammed Yunus) and by organisations of global scope (e.g., United Nations Development Programme). Research in consumer behavior, marketing, and management has focused on a variety of disadvantaged consumers and in subsistence contexts and researchers have highlighted the need for businesses to serve consumers at what has been referred to as the base of the economic pyramid. Research has also been conducted on various aspects of poverty and literacy in India. Our focus was distinct; examining how individuals living in subsistence interact with the marketplace and how the the realm of marketplace activities interacts with their larger life circumstances. We aimed for a deeper understanding of buyers, sellers, and marketplaces in subsistence contexts. Such understanding based on research can be critical in aligning the design of educational programs with the needs of the target audience. Similarly, there are many examples of innovative educational programs in developing contexts such as India. Our focus was on the development of educational programs based on our research that would benefit individuals living in subsistence in terms of their marketplace interactions. Our intent here is not to provide an exhaustive review of the literature on poverty in terms of research and practice, but rather to provide a grounded description of the subsistence contexts we studied with particular emphasis on the realm of marketplace activities. We have strived to represent past literature of immediate relevance to the specific orientation of this book. Despite our best efforts, we hope that there are no significant oversights.

The topic of consumer and entrepreneurial literacy in subsistence contexts is broad, with implications for a number of areas of research, teaching, and practice. We should emphasize that our work, conducted in urban and rural South India, should not be assumed to reflect the many and different subsistence contexts in the rest of the world, and generalizations should be made cautiously. However, the marketplaces we studied highlighted central issues in consumer and enterpreneurial literacy in subsistence contexts. In closing, we hope that this book delivers what is promised here and contributes in a small way toward the betterment of the lives of individuals living in subsistence and toward enabling them to participate in sustainable marketplaces.

Madhu Viswanathan
On behalf of M. Viswanathan, S. Gajendiran and R. Venkatesan

Acknowledgments

This book reflects a fascinating journey over many years that has enriched me in innumerable ways. It has been supported by many individuals and organizations. I am grateful for the intellectual environment at Illinois that enabled my endeavors. I thank the Marketing Group, the Department of Business Administration, and the College of Business at the University of Illinois for their encouragement and support. I hope this effort is fitting and worthy of the great interdisciplinary traditions of the University of Illinois. I am very grateful for the support I received for basic research as well as curriculum development and assessment from the Center for International Business Education Research, University of Illinois. Their support over several years has been invaluable to this endeavor[1]. I have always been encouraged by my colleagues to pursue new avenues of research, no matter how different from the mainstream.

I thank Springer and UNESCO for the invaluable opportunity to publish this book. Harmen van Paradijs and Marianna Pascale of Springer, supported my efforts every step of the way. I thank Padmaja Sudhakher for her tireless efforts through many iterations during the production of this book. It has truly been a privilege to work with the Springer team and I cannot imagine a better experience for an author.

Several individuals have supported this project. Jose Antonio Rosa (University of Wyoming), my coauthor in work on literacy and subsistence marketplaces, has been a constant source of encouragement and advice over the years. Dr Balgopal (University of Illinois) provided valuable advice and encouragement and took a keen interest in this project. R.N. Subramanian, an entrepreneur, encouraged and facilitated our work, going beyond the call and being ever-willing to do what it takes to help us. Robin Orr (University of Illinois) encouraged our efforts and provided an inspiring example through her work in alleviating poverty. Their sincere interest and constant encouragement have

[1] I wish to acknowledge the financial support of the Center for International Business Education and Research at the University of Illinois, which is funded by the United States Department of Education (award numbers P220A60003-98, P220A020011 and P220A060028). This material is based upon work supported by the National Science Foundation under Grant No. 0214615. Any opinions, findings, and conclusions or recommendations expressed in this material are those of the authors and do not necessarily reflect the views of the National Science Foundation. I wish to acknowledge financial support from the Department of Business Administration, the College of Business, and the Campus Research Board, at the University of Illinois.

meant a lot to me. Five of my students, Susan Byrd, Avinish Chaturvedi, Ayush Choudhary, Roland Gau, and Karthik Rapaka, have supported my efforts and inspired me through their own interests as well as their assistance with this book. I also thank several of my colleagues at the University of Illinois and in the academic community who have collaborated with me or supported my research and teaching on subsistence marketplaces that were synergized with this initiative; Liora Bresler, C. Y. Chiu, John Clarke, Avijit Ghosh, P. R. Kumar, Tony Mendes, Gale Summerfield, and Ali Yassine of the University of Illinois, Urbana-Champaign, K. Chandrasekaran (RMK Engineering College, Kavaraipettai, India), Timothy Gonsalves (Indian Institute of Technology, Chennai), Ron Hill (Villanova University), H. S. Jamadagni (Indian Institute of Science, Bangalore), David Mick (University of Virginia), Julie Ozanne (Virginia Polytechnic Institute and State University), Robin Ritchie and Srinivas Sridharan of University of Western Ontario, London, Canada, Julie Ruth (Rutgers University), Jagdish Sheth (Emory University, Atlanta), S. Usha Nandini (National Institute of Technology, Tiruchirappalli), and Jayshree Suresh and M. J. Xavier (SRM University, Chennai). Krishnanand Maillacheruvu, Atul Prasad, Sridhar Ramamoorthy, and Ravi Sunderarajan have supported the efforts of the Marketplace Literacy Project and encouraged my initiatives. I thank Kumar Sarangee for his assistance in proofing this manuscript. I thank Kiran Kumar for his work as a translator when demonstrating our program.

Two individuals in particular deserve special acknowledgment and have been instrumental in this endeavor. My aunt, Jaya Sitaram, (Ex-President, Family Planning Association of India, Chennai Chapter) who has spent many decades in social service, introduced me to individuals at organizations with considerable experience and expertise when I first expressed an interest in this topic. Her wisdom and encouragement over the years and the inspiration she has provided through her own work have been central to this effort. One of the people she introduced me to was Shameem Siddique of Guild of Service. From the outset, Shameem took enormous interest in the project even when the objectives were exclusively research-oriented, and provided encouragement and guidance. She recommended Venkatesan and Gajendiran, my coauthors, to me. Her own dedication and enthusiasm toward social work has been a source of inspiration as well.

A number of nongovernmental organizations, Guild of Service, Chennai, in particular, and community-based organizations, have supported our efforts and facilitated access to the settings where we have experimented with our educational approaches. We thank these organizations and individuals for their encouragement and for believing in our work. We thank V. Shanmugam, V. Srinivasan, T. Baskar, and A. Selvarasan, previously of Guild of Service, and P. Mohana, V. Shanthi, D. Vishnugandhi, and R. Rolina Mary, Self Help Group Project, Guild of Service, Chennai. We thank the Byrraju Foundation in the state of Andhra Pradesh in India for their initiative to scale our program to reach a large number of villages. In this regard, we thank Verghese Jacob, Suresh Reddy, Rama Rao, and Yamini Veena for their encouragement and support. We thank a number of community based organizations and individuals associated with them: D. Jebamalai Mary, Annamaria, and their team of Annai Theresa Pengal Sangam, Ashok Nagar, Chennai; K. Pachayammal, S. Lalitha, N. Sundari, and their team of Kannigapuram Pengal Munnetra Sangam, Ashok Nagar, Chennai; P. Shantha, K.

Vijayakumar, and their team of Nungambakkam Mangayar Marumalarchi Mandram, Nungambakkam, Chennai; Nathan and his team of Vinayagapuram Narpani Mandram, CMDA Colony, Chennai; Regina Mary, Shantha, Rajeswari, Mala, and their team of Kasthuribai Magalir Sangam, CMDA Colony, Chennai; and Hemalatha, Radha, Annamma, and their team, Sogandi village, Kanchipuram district. We thank the SEED Trust, Villupuram, and Kalaiselvi Karunalaya Social Service Society, Chennai. We thank Dr Subramaniam (Tamil University, Tanjore), Zafarullah, (Community Development Officer, Tamilnadu Slum Clearance Board), and Raj Varadarajan and D.K. Raju, both of TeNET Lab, Indian Institute of Technology, Chennai. We also thank S. Mugundan, I. Emmanuel, E. Ravikumar, Munavar Shajahan, and Murugan for their help in piloting our program with organizations.

All the participants in our research and educational programs deserve special acknowledgment for sharing their life stories with us and for patiently sitting through many hours of educational programs and providing feedback. In some ways, the most fulfilling reward in conducting the research was to hear from participants that they had benefited from the experience. Similarly, the most fulfilling reward from conducting educational programs was to hear from women that we had educated their entire families through them.

I cannot express in words what it has meant to work with Gajendiran and Venkatesan. We have been a team in the true sense of the word: frank and constructive in our disagreements and mutually appreciative of our efforts. They have been central to the creation and development of the educational program. They have a number of exemplary traits, but none more admirable than their innate desire to learn. This project is the direct result of their talent, dedication, motivation, and honesty. They have been researchers, teachers, managers, computer specialists, and social workers, learning many new things along the way.

This book is dedicated to my dear student, Avinish Chaturvedi, who left us all so suddenly. Avinish was an extraordinary young man, a very special human being. He was a central contributor to our work and a constant source of encouragement and inspiration. He cared deeply about using research to address the most pressing problems of society. Avinish was passionate about educating himself, and in the process of doing so, imparted to me the most important education of all, about how to live life.

Perhaps the biggest investment I have made in this project is time. This would not have been possible without the unconditional support of my wife, Deepa, and my son, Sidanth. They understood what this project meant to me and supported me every step of the way. I am very fortunate to have such a family that understands me completely and encourages my endeavors. They deserve much of the credit for enabling my efforts. This book is dedicated to them.

This book is also dedicated to my mother whose words and actions taught me much about empathy and the importance of looking beyond one's own narrow self-interest. I learned a valuable lesson from her: that to give is to get. I am ever grateful to my father for his support, wisdom, and enthusiasm at every stage of this endeavor and for the time and energy he invested in taking care of administrative details and in participating in our educational programs. His belief that what we are attempting to do is truly beneficial to individuals and communities was validation of the entire effort. He has held many positions in government, and the private sector, and this book is dedicated to him for the integrity, initiative, dedication, and energy he has brought to his service to India.

Madhu Viswanathan
On behalf of M. Viswanathan, S. Gajendiran and R. Venkatesan

Chapter 1
Basic Research on Low-Literate, Low-Income Buyers and Sellers

This chapter provides a brief summary of our basic research. The discussion is organized by first describing the method we employed. We then present a background on the individual context and the larger marketplace context, followed by brief profiles of a buyer and a seller that put human faces to our research. We also discuss product interactions, marketplace interactions, and unique characteristics of the product and market interactions that we studied. The final section focuses on the development of consumer and entrepreneurial skills in the subsistence marketplaces we studied.

1.1 Method[1]

1.1.1 Overview

Data was collected in the city of Chennai (formerly Madras), the fourth largest city in India, located in the state of Tamil Nadu, and in nearby rural areas. The first author began the project by interacting with a community-based nongovernmental organization (NGO), which works for integrated family and community development and provides a variety of services to people in low-income communities. This NGO encourages its target beneficiaries to form neighborhood-based organizations to aid with the implementation of development programs and activities. These neighborhood organizations assist families through loans, financial assistance, tuition and nutrition for children, vocational

[1]The material in Sections 1, 2, and 3 including Table 1 and Figure 1 is reprinted with minor editing with permission from Elsevier from Viswanathan (2007). This article was published in Product and Market Development for Subsistence Marketplaces: Consumption and Entrepreneurship Beyond Literacy and Resource Barriers, Editors, Jose Rosa and Madhu Viswanathan, Advances in International Management Series, Joseph Cheng and Michael Hitt, Series Editors, Viswanathan, Madhubalan (2007), "Understanding product and market interactions in subsistence marketplaces: A study in South India," 21–57, Copyright Elsevier, 2007.

training for adults, and training and grants for starting businesses. Two employees of the organization with over 20 years of aggregated experience, who later became full time associates of our research project and the second and third authors of this book, assisted with recruitment and interviewing of participants, and with transcription and translation of the interviews. Unique to our data collection is that two members of our research team have experienced the subsistence context first hand.

1.2 Data Collection

Essentially, this research was qualitative in nature, involving interviews and observations of individuals with low levels of literacy in terms of their roles as buyers and sellers. Such an approach enabled understanding of a range of issues confronting low-literate, low-income individuals. The interview itself was an open discussion with few broad questions. Rather than using a structured approach, the format was unstructured, allowing people to inform us about their life experiences. Our interviews were designed to allow informants to share a broad range of information about their life circumstances. An overview of issues covered in interviews is shown in the Appendix. Although we attempted to cover the issues listed in the Appendix in each interview, these issues did not constrain the content or sequencing of questions. Rather than cover a set of questions in a particular sequence, the interview was unstructured and wide ranging, and in the form of a conversation.

The research process involved recruiting people from different communities based on the need to balance demographic representation as well as theoretical considerations. Individuals were interviewed, or observed in marketplace settings. Interviews were audio-taped and reviewed on an ongoing basis, resulting in methodological adjustments (i.e., adding questions) and in identifying emerging characteristics of informants for gaining insights into them. Final sample composition developed over time. Interviews were conducted in Tamil, the language spoken in the state of Tamil Nadu, and also the native language of the authors. Beginning with female customers who made most purchase decisions and had education levels of 8th grade or less, the sample was deliberately expanded to cover customers with different education levels, gender, income levels, and urban/rural residence, and a variety of different sellers. About 75 interviews of buyers and sellers supplemented with many observations were conducted and analyzed over a 5-year period.

1.2.1 Analyses

The process of readying interviews for analyses involved the tasks of transcribing interviews into Tamil, the language in which the interviews were conducted, translating interviews from Tamil to English, and then typing the material. A single interview sometimes resulted in more than 100 pages of handwritten text in the original language. The transcription was done in a form that remained very close to the original text, almost word for word. Other than correcting for grammatical errors, the quotes were not edited, in order to reflect translation that remained close to the text in the original language.

We used qualitative analyses, in accordance with standard guidelines for qualitative research (Strauss & Corbin, 1998), looking for themes in the data that informed us about low-literate, low-income individuals and the lives they lead. During data collection, immersion in the environment was combined with listening to interviews to develop field notes. As mentioned earlier, this process was greatly facilitated by two of the research associates having vast experience in their capacity as employees of a nonprofit organization and working with individuals who were similar to our informants in their income and literacy levels. In some instances, the informants were individuals who had received benefits from the nonprofit organization where our research associates worked.

1.3 Background and Context

This research was a fascinating journey into a marketplace of one-to-one interactions and exchange, rather than the customer to large organization interaction that characterizes much of the marketplace in the USA and the West. The typical low-income, low-literate individual lives in a very small, usually rented, dwelling and spends a high proportion of income on necessities such as food (rice, the staple in this part of India, lentils, vegetables, meat, and spices) and clothing, and unexpected expenses (usually for serious illnesses or family commitments due to traditions associated with death or marriage).

In terms of the family context, the woman is usually responsible for household purchases, with assistance from the husband on some big-ticket items or when considerable travel is involved. Husbands usually delegate most shopping decisions to their wives. Dysfunctionality due to alcohol addiction characterizes a sizable proportion of men. When men addicted to alcohol are the primary breadwinners, they may give only a small proportion of their income (or none at all) to their wives to run the family, while using most of the money for alcohol. Some men with an alcohol problem may just not go to work.

In terms of the nature of the work itself, individuals sometimes run very small businesses, such as street vending, or are employed in jobs, such as house construction or agriculture for hourly/daily wages, or as a painter or some other service provider for a fee. In addition to the normal uncertainties of obtaining a regular income, seasonality is a major influence, with the rainy season, in particular, severely affecting income. In terms of employment for women, the bottom of the pecking order is to work as a housemaid, with a very low salary, usually supplemented with food, clothing on special occasions, and help when necessary. Increasingly, women are employed outside the home and two-income families are becoming common. Educating children is a high priority. As an added benefit, literate children often provide help in computing and making shopping lists.

The typical individual in these communities has a primary economic relationship with one store. Usually, this is likely to be a small neighborhood retail store that buys generic products at wholesale rates and sells to the local community. It may also be a large seller[2] located farther away who sells to retailers as well as to individuals. Both retailers and large resellers are characterized by being responsive to customer needs and having detailed knowledge of individual customers, akin to, and in some ways better than, sophisticated databases. They usually accept product returns, allow exchanges for unsatisfactory products, adjust supply based on customer complaints, sometimes deliver products to homes, and generally strive to satisfy customers. For those with sufficient money at the beginning of the month, the large reseller provides practically all the necessities, and is responsive in terms of refunds/returns. However, the large seller is often not a viable alternative with weekly or daily incomes, or toward the end of a month with monthly income. Customers buy from a retailer, who usually charges higher prices, and offers credit. Thus, the customer is tied to the retailer who may ask for full repayment if patronage stops or decreases. The retailer is responsive to customer needs. The retailer may price higher for credit purchases, often without the knowledge of customers. By helping in times of need, being responsive, and providing credit, the retailer cements relationships with customers and elicits loyalty. Occasional purchases of big-ticket items may be made through installment plans. Individual sellers buy clothing and small appliances (big-ticket items in this context) from retail or wholesale outlets and sell on an installment plan, thus enabling customers to procure products beyond their immediate means, although often at extremely high interest rates. Companies offer much lower interest rates, but for much bigger purchases such as televisions. Thus, the installment seller, often a member of the same community, offers goods and services that cater to the needs of the community. The low-income, low-literate marketplace studied here in some respects reflects a truly free marketplace with sellers and buyers exerting balancing influences.

The balance between purchases from larger resellers versus neighborhood retailers, while triggered by income, involves other factors. Loyalty to retailers is also influenced by credit, which represents help in times of need, and by the need to patronize and encourage a local business. The retail shopkeeper provides more customized service than the large reseller in some respects. Purchase patterns are not just due to income management but also due to consumption management. Buying things in larger quantities may not be preferable when consumption may have to be restricted down the road.

1.4 A Low-Literate Buyer

Sumitra,[3] a 46-year-old woman with no formal education, provided an illustration of how low-literate, low-income individuals cope and how adult literacy programs can lead to quantum increases in consumer skills. She reported having been abused

[2]The term, 'wholesaler', may be some what misleading in that such outlets may be larger stores that resell to retailers and sell directly to end users, i.e., consumers, hence, our use of the term 'large reseller'. However, because our informants often refer to these large resellers as wholesale shops, we use these terms interchangeably.

[3]Fictitious names are used to protect the identity of individuals who are quoted.

and controlled by her husband over a long period of time. She was thrust into the role of primary decision-maker on her husband's demise, and subsequently enrolled in adult literacy classes that have had a transformational effect on her. Lacking the ability to read numbers, she would rarely travel. Due to very low literacy, she used pattern matching to identify bus numbers, at a great cost to her in terms of taking the wrong bus, or being treated rudely by strangers whom she approached for help. On such rare occasions when she had to travel by bus, her husband would write the bus number on her hand and she would try to memorize it. But when it was washed away by rain, she was left to depend on her memory or ask people around her or the bus conductor.[4]

Interviewer: Could you check the bus number before you attended the (adult literacy) class?

Sumitra: I tried to remember the number, otherwise my husband would write on my hand and advise me not to forget it. Sometimes it would be erased while washing the hand or washing the plate after serving the food. I would have forgotten to note it. I would notice it after reaching the bus stand, what do I do? I would ask the conductor to give the ticket for the Periyar road stop (nearest stop to her house), but he would drop me at Liberty (a stop next to the Periyar stop).

Sumitra was forced to travel often when her husband was in hospitals over several years preceding his death.

Sumitra: I took him (husband) there and admitted him in the hospital. 37D alone would go there, 37 wouldn't. I believed that 37 would go and caught the bus. He (conductor) told me that it wouldn't go and dropped me halfway. What do I do after getting down midway? When I enquired of people, they would advise me to go to next bus stop, where the 37D would stop. I would walk with the lunch boxes and luggage in the hot summer. I struggled like this and took lunch to my husband. I visited different hospitals for five years in Madras (name of city) for the treatment of my husband. If I have the money spent for him, I could have built a big building. I struggled like this without knowing the places and identifying the bus numbers. Now, it is okay (after attending an adult literacy program). Now, I go to Genjee (village located 140 km away). I visited Cuddalore (name of town) last Saturday and returned on Sunday. I went alone by train to Cuddalore. I used to be afraid earlier. I would be afraid to go alone at night after 9:00 pm and when it become dark. Now, I do not fear. …

I know the numbers and can speak well. I can say the address, my children's name, and other members' names. Now I know everything. Do I not? Suppose I go there, I could add the letters, read slowly and know the name of the place. I went to a temple. I don't recall the name of the place. It is beyond Cuddalore. Yes, it is Kurinjipet (name of town). After that, I read all the name boards on the way by adding the letters. I enquired there about how to go to Kurinjipet. They guided me and asked me to wait at the Cuddalore bus stand where the bus would come. I did so. The bus came, I caught the right bus, and paid the ticket charge of Rs. 8 and reached the place.

---

[4] Such pattern-matching is also used when determining whether medicines at the pharmacy match doctors' prescriptions.

Interviewer: You said that you could not read the number. How did you read, and know what he wrote when your husband wrote the number on your hand?

Sumitra: He wrote 20. He wrote 2 and 0 then the initial ...

I would show it (the number written on her hand) and ask whether this particular bus would stop here. ... Whether the 37 (bus number) would stop here or the 27 would stop here. I would show it (the number written on her hand) and ask the people in the bus stand, and then I would catch the bus. I didn't want to enquire of anyone in the middle of the journey. ... I wouldn't ask anyone who was standing in the bus stand. First, I would judge the people around, whether they were good, then I would ask them. I could identify the right people from their face and appearance. ... They wouldn't tell or guide, but criticize. So I would decide that we should not ask such people; instead I should catch whatever bus comes. I would catch the bus and enquire from the bus conductor in the middle of the travel. Suppose he was a good person, he would say that this bus wouldn't go on the route I asked and he would guide me to get down and show the proper stop to catch the right bus. Sometimes, the conductor was not in a good mood or was an irresponsible person, and he would shout at me in anger with filthy words and ask me to get down from the bus.

Having no formal education, very low income, and little experience as a customer, her role as a customer for many years had primarily been to buy basic necessities at the nearest retail store on instructions from her husband. She did not enquire about prices, did not compute her bill, and always shopped at the same outlet. She had been cheated on numerous occasions through unfair weighing and other means, but never took action either by switching stores or by arguing with sellers.

Sumitra: He (husband) didn't ask me anything. Yes, he would give me his weekly salary of Rs. 500 to Rs. 600 when he was alive. I would take all the money and buy the necessities. There wouldn't be any balance to spend or save. Sometimes, he used to shout. I used to tell him, "What do I do?," and check the bill if he needed any clarification. He (local shopkeeper) would have issued the bill with many mistakes. I managed my family in this manner in the past. Now, it is better. I ask him to give the right weight even when I go to the ration shop. I would fight. I would demand of him to give the full amount, otherwise I won't accept. Now I can speak all the rules....

It was the situation. What do we do? You have to simply accept whatever is given. Now (after adult literacy classes), that is impossible, I would fight. I used to tell him that I would complain to the appropriate authority. The ration supplier says that this is nonsense and that every month I have become a headache, whereas earlier I used to buy and go silently with whatever was given. He says now: "Okay, you take the full amount and don't shout."

The adult literacy classes have transformed Sumitra, increasing her skills and confidence. Before literacy, her children would check the bills for her, whereas now she feels empowered. Her consumer skills were previously extremely low. However, pursuant to becoming the primary decision-maker and attending adult literacy classes that her husband had forbidden her from taking in the past, the difference is night and day. Now, she argues, bargains, threatens action against sellers who engage in unfair practices, makes enquiries at several shops before buying, purchases wholesale whenever possible, weighs packaged products for accuracy, reads some information on packages, avoids high-interest loans, saves money, and takes actions, such as taking her business elsewhere. She is much more confident of her ability to create her purchase environment through conversation, argument, and action.[5]

Sumitra: He (shopkeeper) would give the bill; I would show it to my children to check it. My younger son doesn't know to calculate; my elder son would calculate the bill. If the bill total shows an extra Rs. 2 or 3, he would ask me why I paid more. I would tell him what I know! But now I am commanding the shopkeeper. I make the calculation the moment I receive the bill. The moment I calculated, I would recall the price for what I bought yesterday and check the discrepancies in today's bill....

Nowadays I am asking with a commanding tone. He (shopkeeper) would say that the drumstick is Rs. 2. I would ask him whether he is ready to sell it for Rs.1, otherwise I would go to next shop. I would ask everything very assertively and in high tone....

Interviewer: One month ago you didn't join the (adult literacy) course. At that time, you bought the same vegetables. The situation was the same as it is now. What would have happened?

Sumitra: Nothing. He had exploited me.

Interviewer: So, you wouldn't have calculated?

Sumitra: I wouldn't have calculated, wouldn't have calculated. I wouldn't know the price. It was just what he told. I just followed the same for the past 36 years. I was 13 years old, when I got married. Now my age is 46. I had been buying for the same price, that he fixed and stated. I paid the same.

Interviewer: Would you ask the price in other shops?

Sumitra: I wouldn't ask the price.

Interviewer: You wouldn't ask the price in the same shop too?

Sumitra: Now, it is okay for the past one month. I would check and verify as they coached me. I would verify the bill. I know all this. I would ask him why he cheated me? It is in the wholesale shop too. They (local shopkeepers) asked why I am not like I used to be earlier? They realize that I am changed. He asks like that. He is selling the soap for Rs. 11, which is sold for Rs. 10 at the wholesale stores. I would ask, how could he sell like that. I would ask him to justify. He would ask me to pay the wholesale price and not to shout there. He cheats well. It is the place for cheating. We earn hard money. Here, we could earn good money if we know cheating.

Interviewer: Now, you have learned within a month and you are checking the prices. When you look at this, there are people like you. Do you say that they are cheated always?

Sumitra: Yes, they (shopkeepers) are cheating. They cheat, even the weighing is not correct in the local shop. The person here has bought a new machine. I would check the weight because, sometimes, it was wrong.

In Sumitra's case, the adult literacy program has also had the effect of changing the way she relates to others.

Sumitra: Now, they (employers in the house where she works as a housemaid) say to me that I am confident after attending the classes; I may dominate them if I am a literate. Even this morning she (employer) told me: "You are performing at this level though you are unable to read and write well, if you were literate you would command us."

---

[5] The shopkeepers reportedly now complain about her!

> They should approach me in a respectable way and enquire politely, and then it is okay. I don't like indecent treatment or rough words. I would slap him whoever it is. I would get angry. Now I try to reduce it (anger) gradually. But, even now I have a little of a bad temper. My employer madam advises me to reduce my anger. I used to slap the moment anyone scolded me or disrespected me and warn him that he should not keep the shop in the vicinity. I did once. Now, I don't do it. I am quiet and calm, because I attended the classes. The people are wondering whether I am in the house or not, and that I was seen here but they couldn't hear my voice. Today, this is the first time I am talking much in the past one month. Madam has advised me to reduce my talking, especially in the summer, and suggests to me to speak selectively with good people. She told me to reduce the talk when I know well that they are not good people. She said that I have the capacity to analyze and understand whatever she says and adjust though I am low-literate.

Although she has completely transformed herself since her husband's death using the adult literacy program, Sumitra has not changed some things, living her life the way "her husband would have wanted her to." After her husband's death following a long and abusive relationship, she hesitates or avoids going to a restaurant to eat. She is sensitive to comments by others that she is now enjoying "luxuries" after her husband's demise. She states that she is living today the way she lived when her husband was alive and the way he would have liked her to live. This is a striking feature of many women we interviewed. Despite psychological and physical abuse, they have an idealistic notion of what it is to be a wife and live by it.

Interviewer: Would you go to restaurant or films? Do you visit hotels?

Sumitra: We visited, when my husband was alive. Suppose I go now, there are chances that my neighbors would notice it. If someone noticed me in the restaurant, they would come and tell others that so-and-so's wife is eating in the restaurant. They wouldn't say that I was in the restaurant to have food because I was hungry. But, they would pass sarcastic comments like "look at her, she goes to the restaurant instead of cooking in the house." I would get angry if I hear such comments. So, I won't even buy and have a snack from the shop nearby here. You could check with others. Even when I am hungry, I prefer to prepare rice porridge and eat it. I don't have the habit of eating in hotels.

1.5 A Low-Literate Seller

Velamma, a 45-year-old woman with a 5th grade education, provided an illustration of how adult education and business training empowered her to successfully run a business and support a family. Having no formal education, minimal experience as a customer and very poor consumer skills, she managed her household with her husband and two children for many years with next to nothing to eat and substituting regular meals with some very inexpensive alternatives,[6] never borrowing but living within very limited means. After 15 years of staying at home, she had to be the primary breadwinner because her husband became dysfunctional. She decided to start

[6] An inexpensive beverage rich in carbohydrates is often the last resort.

a business, buying utensils from stores and reselling them to residents in her community. Early in this endeavor, adult education, business training, and financial assistance from an NGO enabled her to buy a vehicle to transport products, and developed her ability to manage her business.

In one of her initiatives, she runs an installment plan wherein people pay a fixed sum each month for 15 months, at the end of which they choose a large utensil from an assortment, individual items being comparable in price. She offers free gifts to customers who sign up at the beginning of the installment plan and has a monthly lottery witnessed by some subscribers to give out a large utensil to a lucky winner. This is a scheme for customers to buy large vessels through installments that requires considerable skills to implement in a one-to-one environment. It requires witnesses for a monthly lottery, collection of money every month, and a free gift at the beginning of the scheme, as well as distribution of large vessels at the end. Various aspects of the scheme have to be designed before introducing it to many people.

Velamma: I introduced a chit (financial scheme) in which the members have to pay Rs. 20 per month. There would be 200 members in total. From that, I gained courage. I would give them a prize when they join the scheme. Apart from this, we would choose a winner per month through a lottery method. At the end of the 15th month, all members would be given the vessels....

Now, suppose you were selected as the winner of the month, you would be given the vessel in the same month. Finally, 150 members would be remaining, so they would be given the vessel in the last month. Through door-to-door visits, we would enroll. ... I enrolled those who trusted me or were willing to try. I have been steadily doing this from 1993 onwards. So, everyone joined and paid regularly.

She explains to potential customers the benefits of buying certain items that would be useful during important life events such as marriage.

Velamma: Without any knowledge of the item, they would ask what the price is. Some didn't know the price, so they would ask their husbands. If they asked their husbands, what would they say? They would say that it does not have to be bought. So I would explain to those who don't know anything. I would tell them not to consult their husbands. If they consult the males, they cannot add a single article in their house. I would tell them: "See, you should save Rs. 3 when they give Rs. 10 for the family expenses, you could pay me Rs. 1, and you save the balance of Rs. 2. You have children. Suppose they get married tomorrow. What would the others ask you? They should say: 'Okay, your talent has saved (the situation) though your husband is an alcoholic.'" When I talk in this manner, they get confidence and courage. They would decide that they should support the woman (me) and encourage me, who counseled them and gave them the courage. I have the skill (to do this). They would listen to my words and ask me to enroll them. They would appreciate me for encouraging them. They would support me in this manner.

Velamma counters what husbands are likely to say, discusses a hypothetical situation, such as a marriage of a child, and points out that others would commend the potential customer for having saved despite having an alcoholic husband. She is willing to discuss at length with individual customers, but maintains confidentiality. She expects potential customers who were encouraged to be courageous to then reciprocate and give her business for having counseled them. Velamma works within cultural norms, also managing potential communications within a family. Being a woman, she deals primarily with women in households.

Interviewer: You said that you wouldn't approach the males while enrolling members for the chit (financial scheme).

Velamma: Because women would buy the materials without the knowledge of the males. There could be confusion between them suddenly. Even if the men pay Rs. 50 in the absence of the women, it should not be a problem between them. It is okay if we collect the money when both men and women are in the house. The women would have bought the item without the knowledge of the men. … How can I collect the money from the men? It would become a dispute between them. He would ask her how she can buy? "I gave Rs. 50 to the chit women," he would say to her. The next day the women would come and ask me why I received the money? So, I won't collect the money. I would collect the money from the women.

Interviewer 2: So, if the male paid Rs. 50 first?

Velamma: I won't receive. I won't receive it. So far, I never receive from men. Because I should not give room for the problem between them. She would have bought it without his knowledge. You tell me!

Velamma points out the importance of dealing with the woman in the household and not the man. She notes that there may be disputes among couples and, being a woman herself who is dealing in household articles, feels comfortable dealing with the woman in a household. Relevant here is how her basic interpersonal skills blend into some business policies she adheres to. Her business policies reflect the day-to-day context where the separation between private individual lives and the marketplace is blurred, or even nonexistent. She is sensitive to potential family communications and problems that could be created between husbands and wives by some business practices.

She also adheres to a strict business code of not discussing her judgments of specific customers with other customers. It also gives the seller a sense of control, perhaps stemming from making individual judgments and not worrying about myriad opinions of individuals. She notes that customers may have bad relationships currently with someone, which may be resolved, at which point any of her opinions may be shared to her detriment.

Interviewer: You are selling to all?

Velamma: Immediately they would ask, how the chit woman (Velamma) gives always to you. A woman named (person's name) would ask, how is she giving always? She would ask me too on what basis I am giving to them (others). I would smile rather than responding. I would not reply.

Interviewer: Why?

Velamma: Because we should not discuss. They may have so many connections with each other. We should not discuss. I should see how I collect the money from them. So I would pass them with a smile.

Interviewer: When you are a customer, would you speak to others?

Velamma: I won't speak to others and outsiders.

Interviewer: (Questions about consumer issues like) "Where are you buying the rice?" …

Velamma: When we have exposure and experience, I would talk about the business with business people. If someone called and asked for an item, I would ask for an advance.

Interviewer: But you would talk to others when you are a customer and ask?

Velamma: Yes. I would ask.

Interviewer: But you won't ask (about others) while you are running the business?

Velamma: Wherever they can go, why do we worry? I would have this control. It is important (the business and collection). They may fight or quarrel with each other now and may join a little later. Then they would say that the chit woman said this and that against you. They may speak behind my back. Is it not a problem? So I won't ask anyone about anything.

A constant issue for sellers to deal with is judging creditworthiness and honesty. This is done in a variety of ways, essentially judging people based on apperance, familiarity, on the recommendation of an acquaintance, or from their dwelling. It is a highly personal, subjective judgment made on the basis of available information and, in many instances, recommendations from others.

Interviewer: How are you deciding that you can give (credit) to a particular person?

Velamma: Well, they work in the government with a regular salary on the 5th or 6th of every month. They would come to my house to pay or I would go and collect it. It is all based on my assessment and confidence. I won't give to all. ... Who can pay back? Who goes for housemaid jobs? ... I would first verify. But I won't really ask anyone. I would just make my own assessment.

Judgments of creditworthiness and honesty are made by Velamma while avoiding asking others, again because word can spread. Moreover, there are many motives for people to speak poorly of others, such as personal animosity. She believes in her judgment and in making it independently and sticking with it.

Velamma: I won't ask anyone (about creditworthiness of specific customers), any neighbors. ... I won't ask anyone. I would give (products) based on my assessment and confidence. They may tell me (if asked) but they may have quarreled (with the potential customers). So they would tell me not to give products to their neighbors and say that they would move out of the area. Even the people paying me now would say that they don't know, when I am asking about their neighbors. They would respond without any seriousness...

They would come and quarrel with me immediately. They are all fighters. They would ask me not to give to their neighbors. In the end, they (who asked not to give to their neighbors) would be the ones who won't pay regularly, but the neighbor would pay regularly. So I won't count on input from individuals. I would decide based on my own confidence.

Here, Velamma makes the point that others can be unreliable in their judgments of people, and that she prefers to depend on her own judgment and is confident of it. It appears that an integral part of business skills in this context is the ability to judge customers on such attributes as their ability and motivation to repay loans. Credit ratings are fluid, and have to be made through personal judgments. She maintains confidentiality in the case of individuals who have not made appropriate payments. She maintains cordial relationships and does not shout, although the threat of shouting is an effective mechanism that many individuals fear. For this seller though, moral fear, rather than anything else, is effective.

Interviewer: When you run the business, what are all the things they (customers) do to avoid the repayment ...

Velamma: They would do nothing sir. They would say that they will give tomorrow if it is not possible today.

Interviewer: You said that they would send you back by saying money is not available?

Velamma: Two such people are there. I would be alert in their case. But I won't ask them in public. I would tell them to say that she would give tomorrow if it was not possible today. "But don't do like this." They would say: "Okay, sorry I would give earlier." If I ask them in front of ten people, they would be embarrassed. You tell me. Is it not? I would talk to them individually. I would do so....

I would ask them correctly (strictly). If it is not possible today, give me tomorrow. But don't send the message while hiding. It will become a regular practice in your life. (They would say) "Okay, chit madam. I feared that you may scold me." I am confident because they have fear.

Interviewer: But you won't shout?

Velamma: I won't shout. However, they have (moral) fear.

Interviewer: They have a kind of fear? You have never shouted so far?

Velamma: I won't collect (payment) by shouting. Even my husband would speak sharply sometimes. But I won't speak (in this manner).

Interviewer: Two out of hundred have cheated you?

Velamma: Yes two (percent) only, not all.

Interviewer: Why don't you shout?

Velamma: I won't shout sir, I won't. I would keep the polite approach with them as much as possible.

Velamma functions in an environment where there is a constant threat of someone shouting and "creating a scene". Customers asking for refunds on product returns is another facet of running the business.

Interviewer: While you give products, has any one complained that you are not giving a product worth the Rs. 300 they paid for it?

Velamma: Few people are like that. ... I would ask them to check the products that were given to others. I would tell them that I gave them the same products that I gave to others. Some may accept what I said and leave quietly, some may shout. I may have to adjust to both situations.

Interviewer: How are you managing such situations?

Velamma: I would invite them to check the quality of products supplied to other customers. The other customers would say that the product given was good and useful. This feedback would cool down their temper and they would leave quietly.

Interviewer: Suppose they say even after the explanation and feedback that the product is not good and that they don't want it?

Velamma: If they don't want, they can choose any other product available with me. But I won't return the money. At any cost, I won't give the money back.

Interviewer: Your principle is not to return the money?

Velamma: I won't give (back money), only products.

Interviewer: Could you give them the costly item? Could you give the item worth Rs. 300 because they come and question you?

Velamma: We can't encourage this, others may follow it. They may go and announce to others that she got the money back from the chit woman (herself). So the others would follow suit. Hence, I would give the product only. Whatever item, they can ask, but no money. I would not give the money back.

Here is an example where there may be intense pressure to customize offerings for one individual. However, Velamma resists at all costs; the consequences if she accepts would be all buyers making similar demands. In fact, even if someone refuses to pay, the seller has to take a stand and insist that payment be made.

Whether payment is expected or is likely is a separate issue. The seller cannot be seen as wavering on the issue of payment because others will take the cue from it. The seller emphasizes the importance of adhering to the same price across customers.

As this entrepreneur demonstrates, managing a business in this environment is no small task. Thrust into this role while previously having almost no experience in the economic realm, she has managed a number of functions, such as negotiating and buying from wholesalers, identifying and appealing to potential customers, and coming up with innovative installment plans that make her products affordable to customers while providing liquidity for running the business and for additional income through lending. She has to manage relationships with customers and not cause problems among family members; hence, she only accepts orders from the female head of the household. She has to use the threat of public humiliation, without actually carrying it out, as a way to induce repayment of money. In an environment where dwellings are extremely close to each other, most, if not all, discussions may not be private, hence the importance of managing interactions with customers. She is careful not to compromise on price or the cost of the type of utensil that people get; otherwise the word would get out and cause myriad idiosyncratic requests and arguments. Yet she is flexible in allowing people to join later and catch up on payments; they are, however, given a utensil of lesser value at the end to compensate for their money being available for 'rotation' only later in the process. She also uses the money in hand to lend and collect interest. This seller illustrates the context for running a business as well as the unique skills that are needed to be successful.

1.6 Products and Purchases[7]

The set of products that subsistence individuals use is discussed, while also describing purchase options whenever they are difficult to separate from the product offering itself. A subsequent section examines market interactions in more depth. A rough category of needs, products, markets, and budgets for households in subsistence contexts is presented in Table 1 and our discussion is summarized in Figure 1.

---

[7] The material in Sections 6, 7, and 8 of this chapter including Table 1 and Figure 1 is reprinted with minor editing with permission from Elsevier from Viswanathan (2007). This article was published in *Product and Market Development for Subsistence Marketplaces: Consumption and Entrepreneurship Beyond Literacy and Resource Barriers,* Editors, Jose Rosa and Madhu Viswanathan, Advances in International Management Series, Joseph Cheng and Michael Hitt, Series Editors, Viswanathan, Madhubalan (2007), "Understanding product and market interactions in subsistence marketplaces: A study in South India," 21–57, Copyright Elsevier, 2007.

Table 1 Sample Needs, Products, Sellers, and Expenses in Subsistence Marketplaces.[b]

Categories of needs	Sample goods and services	Sample sellers/Providers	Sample expenditure break-up (for families with monthly income as listed below)[a]		
			Rs. 1,500	Rs. 3,000	Rs. 5,000
Housing	Mud huts, concrete houses	Homeowner, landlords, government programs	<Rs. 400	<Rs. 750	<Rs. 1,000
Sanitation	Sanitation service, water	Government services	Nil	< Rs. 50	< Rs. 100
Food and beverages	Rice, meat, vegetables, spices, grinder, stove	Neighborhood retail store, large reseller, mobile vendors, large markets, government ration shops	<Rs. 600	<Rs. 1,000	<Rs. 1,200
Clothing	Saris, lungis (clothing for men)	Larger stores, sidewalk sellers, door-to-door resellers	<Rs. 40	<Rs. 250	<Rs. 300
Personal care and hygiene	Soap, detergent soap, toothpaste	Neighborhood retail store, large seller	<Rs. 100	<Rs. 150	<Rs. 200
Health care	Consultations, allopathic medicine	Government hospitals, clinics	< Rs. 25	< Rs. 50	< Rs. 100
Education	Government schools, private schools, adult education	NGOs, government, private organizations	<Rs. 50	<Rs. 100	<Rs. 200
Entertainment	Televisions, movies, festivals	Theaters, cable stations	Nil	<Rs. 100	<Rs. 150
Financial services	Retailer credit, pawning jewels, noncollateral loans, savings plans with stores, chits (schemes)	Retailer, store owner, pawnshop, moneylenders	<Rs. 75	<Rs. 100	<Rs. 150
Transportation	Walking, bicycle, motorized two-wheeler, public bus, autorickshaws	Government buses, private buses, uto companies	<Rs. 50	<Rs. 50	<Rs. 400
Communication	Cell phones, land lines, phone centers	Private phone centers, cell phone plans sold through retail outlets	Nil	Nil	<Rs. 400
Energy	Electricity, fuel for cooking, fuel for two-wheelers	Government utilities, gasoline stations, retail outlets, wholesale outlets	<Rs. 160	<Rs. 300	<Rs. 600
Spiritual/Religious Needs	Fruits as religious offerings, new clothes, fairs and carnivals	Temples, retail outlets, community based organizations		<Rs. 100	<Rs. 200

[a] Families may receive material help from employers, other acquaintances and friends, and organizations. Examples include medical expenses paid by employers, educational materials for children, clothing, food, and other items, and gifts during festivals. The cost break-up shown above is for income received as money. The currency rate has ranged approximately between Rs. 40–45 to a US dollar in the past few years, and does not reflect the higher buying power of the rupee for daily necessities.

[b] The material in Table 1 is reprinted with minor editing with permission from Elsevier from Viswanathan (2007). This article was published in *Product and MarketDevelopment for Subsistence Marketplaces: Consumption and Entrepreneurship Beyond Literacy and Resource Barriers*, Editors, Jose Rosa and Madhu Viswanathan, Advances in International Management Series, Joseph Cheng and Michael Hitt, Series Editors, Viswanathan, Madhubalan (2007), "Understanding product and market interactions in subsistence marketplaces: A study in South India," 21–57 (Table 1 on Page 26), Copyright Elsevier, 2007.

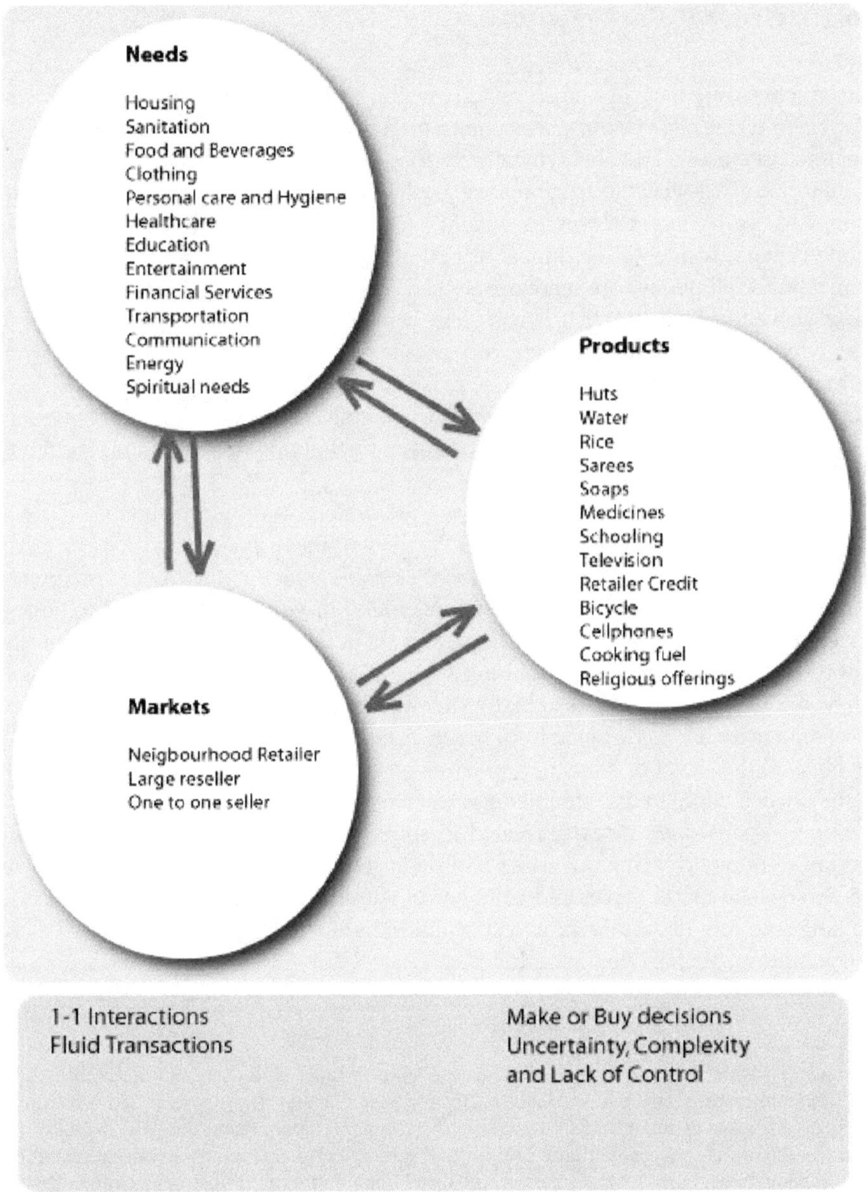

Figure 1 Product and Market Interactions in Subsistence Marketplaces[8]

[8]The material in Figure 1 is reprinted with minor editing with permission from Elsevier from Viswanathan (2007). This article was published in *Product and MarketDevelopment for Subsistence Marketplaces: Consumption and Entrepreneurship Beyond Literacy and Resource Barriers*, Editors, Jose Rosa and Madhu Viswanathan, Advances in International Management Series, Joseph Cheng and Michael Hitt, Series Editors, Viswanathan, Madhubalan (2007), "Understanding product and market interactions in subsistence marketplaces: A study in South India," 21–57 (Figure 1 on Page 27), Copyright Elsevier, 2007.

1.6.1 General Background

The typical family lives in a small rented dwelling, often with very poor infrastructure relating to electricity, water, and sanitation. Housing may range from mud huts to concrete structures.[9] Travel is typically by foot, by public transport, and by bicycle or by motorized two-wheeler. In rural areas, lack of access is characterized by few travel options to nearby larger towns for medical treatment and for other shopping needs. Phone centers, residental landlines, or cell phones are used for long distance communication. Cell phones are increasingly used and provide an example of technology being viewed positively when it has clear benefits, as well as an illustration of the adaptivity of users to new products. Individuals have increasing exposure to a variety of information and products through television and word of mouth and are willing to learn about new products. Energy needs for cooking include kerosene for stoves and gas cylinders for gas stoves. Electricity is used for lighting and appliances, although power supply is often not reliable.

Children's education is central to parents, with government schools or private schools being the alternatives. Individuals are willing to make sacrifices to enable their children to receive a good education. Schools with English as the medium of instruction are valued. Similarly, parents may also strive to send children to college. In rural areas, individuals may have access to about the 8th grade or so for basic education, with further education requiring travel to a larger town. This latter constraint can be difficult, or even impossible, for many girls to overcome, as parents are fearful of sending them a long distance from home. A generational difference that is noteworthy is the higher level of education in terms of grade completed for the younger generations when compared to middle-aged or older people.

Some expenses are directly related to spiritual and religious needs, such as for making religious offerings of fruits and other items at temples. Religious festivals are also occasions for travel and celebration with new clothes. Thus, they are often the single or few occasions in a year when individuals buy some products by way of celebration, such as new clothing.[10]

---

[9] Many individuals live on (i) encroached private lands without land titles and are not eligible to get basic amenities, (ii) encroachments on roadsides, canal boundaries, and government wastelands, treated as unauthorized habitat by governmental authorities, and (iii) the same land as in (ii) above that government authorities have subsequently deemed as authorized habitat by including locations under special schemes and developing minimum infrastructures and providing minimum facilities, such as electricity, water, and sanitation. Wherever the government does not allow individuals to live in a specific location, it may provide alternative settlement in exceptional cases. The first two categories are characterized by basic infrastructure problems in terms of electricity, sanitation, and water.

[10] Differences between urban and rural settings are significant and briefly mentioned throughout the book. Many of the people we interviewed in urban areas had migrated from villages to the big city. Rural settings are, indeed, striking in the lack of economic opportunity. Some who grow up in villages have experience from working in fields and from observing or participating in exchanges. The village often appears to be a place with strong human relationships and social

1.6.2 Food

Rice is the staple diet in South India. Rice has special meaning in being used synonymously with food, akin to the use of the term "bread" in other societies. Often, the focus of daily life is to have one square meal of rice a day. Even the poorest may pay a little more to get better-quality rice. Lentils are purchased to make curries with spices and vegetables or meat, to be eaten with rice. Vegetable and meat dishes are also prepared in a dry form. With relatively higher income, these liquid and dry dishes become viable. The state in India where we conducted interviews also has an extensive variety of snack items that can serve as regular meals. With extreme constraints, the diet may be a meal consisting of plain boiled rice with salt, or even more limited to a starch-based drink.

The quality of rice, as well as of other generic food items, is subject to many variations due to agricultural (e.g., quality of the soil) and other factors. Many products are generic, needing further processing, such as boiling. This is akin to making bread out of dough versus buying it directly. Trials are needed to determine whether rice boils appropriately. Some buyers may try out small quantities of rice before buying in larger amounts. The quality of rice is an important issue. There are many variables in how cooked rice turns out. Individuals manage the process of identifying the type to buy and complaining to sellers. The same rice can be perceived as being of different quality by different individuals based on such factors as the way it is boiled or the water used to boil it. Localized variations exist in such factors as water quality that affect the outcome. Many factors that may be assumed to be constants, or of minimal variation, in western societies can affect the processing of food products in this context.

Rice is sold by neighborhood retailers and larger stores who deal in both retail and wholesale distribution, heretofore referred to as large resellers. Moreover, a set amount of rice and other basic necessities may be available through government ration, which is generally of poorer quality. Rice may also be obtained in bulk from villages for some who either own land or have relatives in villages engaged in farming. Vegetables are usually sold by weight by neighborhood retailers, large resellers, street vendors, and larger markets, the latter being either just retail or both retail and wholesale. Often, lower-quality assorted vegetables are sold at a lower price, not by individual weight but as an assortment of vegetables with a specific price. Very poor individuals often opt for such a purchase. Vendors may offer lower prices later in the day to avoid inventory being left over.

---

support, despite severe economic adversity and lack of easy access to goods and services. The city in comparison can initially be viewed as being harsh and frightening, in several realms including the economic. A woman who migrates from a village after marriage may be trained for a year or so by a relative, often even staying in the same household and observing how to manage a household and buy products. Such a transitional arrangement appears to be an effective training ground for then independently managing a household in an urban area.

1.6.3 Health and Medicine

Medicine can range from homemade treatments, to relatively inexpensive folk medicine, to allopathic medicine based on advice from a pharmacy or neighborhood retail store, to consultation with doctors depending on seriousness and duration of illness. Government hospitals are the low cost option, providing free consultation and medicine, however they have restricted hours.[11] Private doctors, considered as offering better-quality health care, usually charge more (Rs. 20–30 for minor illnesses), with medicine being extra. Medical doctors are identified and assessed for effectiveness, with those perceived as being good or lucky developing a loyal following. Patients ask their doctors to check filled prescriptions for accuracy, reflecting the one-to-one interactional marketplace. In rural areas, lack of access includes distances to be traveled for medical treatments. Bicycles and public buses are possibilities but options are often restricted during the night, leading to individuals suffering through the night without medical attention.

Individuals often sacrifice their physical well-being, neglecting health concerns until it is too late. There is often a sense of resignation in health-related issues. Only when health is affected to the point of affecting earnings do some seek out medical attention.

Interviewer: Where do you go for treatment when you are ill?

Rani (female, 30 years, no formal education): I always go to the government hospital. But I would take the children to private practitioners when they fall ill. The treatment in the government hospital won't be effective. When I take the children to the government hospital, they would advise to take ¼ tablet or ½ tablet where we are supposed to take 1 tablet. So, it won't be cured. … But, I won't prefer (private practitioner) for me, I would compromise and go to the government hospital.

Interviewer: You visit the government hospital for treatment for yourself? Why are you going to private practitioners only for children?

Rani: We get treatment from the private practitioner only for children.

Interviewer: Is the private hospital located nearby or at some distance?

Rani: It is situated near my house.

Interviewer: How much do you pay as doctor's fees?

Rani: He would charge Rs. 20 and provide drugs too. When we go for treatment for cough and cold, he would give cough medicine, tablet (pill), everything. He would prescribe medicine, if we feel that the child is too ill and ask him to prescribe. Otherwise he won't prescribe. The drugs he provides are sufficient.

Interviewer: It would be cured? … if he prescribes? …

Rani: I would ask to prescribe, I can't tolerate when the children are affected by cough and wheezing. There would be high shivering due to fever. They will be crying. I am struggling completely for the children. I should take care of them, so I would ask the doctor to prescribe medicines and assure him that I would buy it outside. He would prescribe within Rs. 20 to Rs. 30.

---

[11] Although there are typically no consultation charges in government hospitals, fees may be charged for x-rays and other special tests.

Interviewer: Where will you buy those medicines?
Rani: Nearby, there is a medical shop. I would buy it there.
Interviewer: You will buy it at the medical shop? OK. Are you checking whether they are giving the same medicine prescribed by the doctor?
Rani: Yes. I would check. I would take it and show it to the doctor. "See, doctor, whether the medicines are the right ones." After checking, he would advise doses to be taken and timings in a day.

Here is an example of how things may work in a one-to-one world, with the patient taking the purchased medicine back to the doctor to make sure it is the right one. Here, this woman takes her children to a private doctor while she herself goes to the government hospital, which she views as being of lower quality.

Interviewer: Do you go to the hospital when you are sick?
Badri (husband; 37 years; 5th grade education): If I have money I will go to the hospital, otherwise, I will buy medicine from the shop.
Interviewer: Where do you go and buy the medicine?
Sivakami (wife, 30 years, no formal education): Medical store.
Interviewer: You buy it from a medical store when you have money.
Badri: If I have money I will take injection.
Interviewer: Whom do you go to?
Badri: Dr (name of doctor).
Interviewer: What are his fees?
Badri: Rs. 20 is the fees. I will go to him if I have Rs. 40, otherwise, I will get medicines for two times.
Interviewer: You will go and buy the medicines from the medical shop. Will you check the medicines?
Badri: I don't know all these things sir.
Sivakami: We don't know much about the medicine. We will take whatever medicine they give. We will take it, even for our children.
Interviewer: When do you go to the doctor?
Badri: Only when we are very unwell, we will go to the doctor. When we are attacked by fever and are unable to walk, we will go. If we get cough or slight fever, we will take the medicine from the shop.
Interviewer: Do you go to the government hospital?
Badri: We have no time to go to the government hospital.
Interviewer: You can't go on time?
Badri: Instead of going to the hospital I go to Dr (name of doctor) who will clearly examine (us) and give medicine duly, telling us how to take the medicine, but it is not so in the hospital where they will give the medicine without even telling us how to take it. But (name of doctor) will tell us to take porridge or bread and take the pills.
Interviewer: Will he use injection?
Badri: He will use injection and for that reason, I will go to him. The injection will make us all right.
Interviewer: In which shop do you buy the medicine when he prescribes?
Badri: Medical shop, sir.
Interviewer: Will they give the correct medicine?
Badri: They will give the same medicine which he prescribes.
Interviewer: How do you know that?
Badri: I will see the first letter sir. It will be in English. But there will be numbers like 550, 5500. I will see the first number. I will ask my children to see the number.

When going to a doctor, an injection is a hallmark of good treatment. As this person states, he goes to a doctor because the doctor administers an injection, sometimes even for common colds. An option here is to go to a government hospital, which has restricted timings and little by way of instruction when compared to a private doctor. In terms of medicine bought at pharmacies, some individuals do not check but take whatever is given. Others match the first letter as mentioned. Some individuals take the medicine back to the doctor to confirm that it is the right one.

Interviewer: Do you visit the same doctor?
Kavitha (female, 38 years, 5th grade education): We visit the same doctor.
Interviewer: Why do you visit the particular doctor?
Kavitha: We get cured when he administers the injections, it is healed immediately, and we get sudden remedy. He is a kind of lucky and auspicious person. We are cured if we get treatment from him, hence we visit him. Suppose it is other doctors, they would ask us to visit again and again. He won't do this; he would administer an injection and tell us that it would be cured in one visit.
Interviewer 2: Is there any difference in the fees between both the doctors?
Kavitha: All are charging the same fees of Rs. 20.
Interviewer 2: He too charges Rs. 20?
Kavitha: But, he charges Rs. 20 and prescribes medicines for Rs. 75. ...
If we go to another doctor, he would prescribe costly medicines for Rs. 100 and ask us to visit him again and again for 3 days. He would administer three injections too. The fees would cost around Rs. 60 and medicine would cost around Rs. 100, so it would cost a total of Rs. 160. But, we visit the same doctor here and try to finish it within Rs. 100.
Interviewer: Administering injection is ... for what kind of problems? Is the injection for fever?
Kavitha: He would administer injection if we go with fever or cough with cold. Earlier, he provided both the injections and medicines. Now, it is not like that. He would inject if we buy the drugs from medical stores and give it to him. It costs around Rs. 30 to buy the injection drug.
Interviewer: Now, which medical shop do you buy in?
Kavitha: There is a medical shop on the main road; we buy there. We would immediately go to the shop from the clinic and buy the medicines.
Interviewer: The price is less or high there?
Kavitha: No, (they are) all the same price.
Interviewer: Would you buy any medicines without consulting the doctor, for the problem like any headache, etc.?
Kavitha: Yes, we crush the ginger, pepper, and boiled with water and prepare a kind of thick juice/sap at home; it would arrest the cough and fever if we had a glass.
Interviewer: Would you buy any medicines from the shop without going to a doctor?
Kavitha: We have bought (in this manner). If we tell them that we have headache or cold with cough and ask them to give medicines, they would give it to us.

Several issues pertaining to medical attention are relevant here. Sometimes, the seller at the pharmacy administers medicines after hearing symptoms. People usually visit doctors when they are severely affected by an ailment to the point of reducing earnings or when their children suffer from ailments. Otherwise, they may try some home remedy or ask the pharmacy for some medicine. When visiting the doctor, they develop a relationship, often considering whether a particular doctor is lucky for them. Perceptions of "lucky doctors" stemming from past experience play an important role in deciding on doctors. With medicines, individuals may buy a small, affordable fraction of the total prescribed. Sometimes, individuals may diagnose their own conditions and buy and use medicines prescribed for previous illnesses that appear to be similar.

1.6.4 *Clothing and Ornaments*

Clothing is often bought at sidewalks or at specific large stores, which cater to the low-income clientele with lower prices or through door-to-door resellers. Whereas sidewalk vendors provide cheaper prices, they usually do not sell matched sets of clothing and require more search when compared to stores.

With daily urgency relating to basic necessities, other possessions take a back seat or have symbolic value. For example, buying a silk sari (costing about Rs. 2,000 or more) or jewels symbolizes good times and individuals do treat themselves to these possessions for occasions, such as a festival or a wedding. But this is distinctly different from the desire to constantly accumulate possessions. Rather, the general frame of mind is one of fixation on the next meal and on food and basic necessities, coupled with the occasional, symbolic materialistic purchase to treat oneself to better things, to keep as a reminder of better times, and sometimes to use as an investment to pawn or sell in times of need.[12]

1.6.5 *Financial Products*

Financial products are, of course, central to day-to-day living in subsistence contexts. The literature has examined the complexities associated with financial services for the poor (cf., Rutherford, 2000). We report on a variety of financial services. This discussion is organized into savings and loan alternatives.

1.6.5.1 Savings

Different savings schemes abound, often motivated by fear of interacting with larger banks, anxiety about filling out forms due to problems with literacy, or anxiety about the perceived need to know English. In some communities, NGOs or self-help groups run savings schemes to encourage regular savings, with collection even occurring door-to-door. The neighborhood retailer may also be willing to safeguard money from neighbors, family members, and thieves for a fee. Stores may also offer "financial" schemes, for example, a savings requirement of Rs. 10 per day over 100

---

[12] Jewels are particularly useful in this regard. Consumers purchase jewelry in good economic times and pawn them in times of need. This is discussed in more detail below.

days, with a bulk amount of Rs. 900 returned. Accounts are maintained by such means as marking a card with a 100 squares – a pictorial representation equally meaningful to the literate and low-literate. Savings amounts vary and can be as low as Rs. 1 per day. Savings amounts can also vary between visits (e.g., a customer visits with Rs. 10, buys items for Rs. 8, and leaves the balance toward the savings plan). The record keeping system varies based on the arrangement.

Some savings schemes are communal, as when a financial scheme organizer enrolls members into schemes that vary by maturity period, amount due, and net amount received based on saving capacity of members. If ten members joined in the scheme with a sum of Rs. 10,000, the scheme organizer would invite bids from the members on a specific date every month to receive the collection for the month. Members who are in need would bid if they are ready to receive something less than the monthly collection of Rs. 10,000, for example, Rs. 9,000. This discounted Rs. 1,000 would be shared by all members as a benefit of the scheme and the members can pay Rs. 900 instead of Rs. 1,000 as the due amount for that particular month. At the same time, the bid amount or discount is a form of interest charged on those receiving the money in advance or prior to the completion of the period for the financial scheme, i.e., 10 months. In this order, nine members would receive the money in advance and prior to the completion and pay the bid amount, akin to paying interest. The tenth person who receives the money at the end or the tenth month would receive the full amount, Rs. 10,000, but would have paid less than the monthly due for the 9 months.

Interviewer: Suppose this woman is a (financial) scheme organizer, would she visit door-to-door?

Kavitha: They won't visit; they would invite the neighbors and people known to them for the enrollment. They would tell us that she is going to start chits and would ask us whether we are interested in joining. We should be present there (at the scheme organizer's house/place) promptly on every tenth day (of the month). We should be ready with the chit amount when the bidding starts. Collected chit money would be available for bidding. Those interested can join in the bidding. Whether you join the bid and take the money or not, you should remit your monthly chit dues immediately to the organizer.

Here, the organizer is a de facto member of the team and fully responsible for collecting amounts from other members and providing funds to the bidder within a reasonable time frame. The benefit for the organizer is that he or she may be able to take the full amount of the second month's collection bidding. Another benefit may be that each month, bidders may pay 2% of the total amount (Rs. 10,000) to the organizer (Rs. 200). Chit schemes are examples of need-based savings services originating in the community. Peer pressure is an important element in these schemes.

1.6.5.2 Loan Alternatives

Loan alternatives include buying for credit at the neighborhood store.

Interviewer: You make purchases in wholesale shops for cash or any credit?
Velamma (female, 45 years, 5th grade education): No credit, only cash payment on hand.
Interviewer: Cash on hand purchase?

Velamma: Yes, cash on hand.
Interviewer: Have you bought anything on credit recently?
Velamma: I won't buy on credit. I have to pay back the credit. They may raise the due from Rs. 5 to Rs. 6. I am saying as an example, it is just for the sake of argument. Again, they may record it as Rs. 8 instead of Rs. 6. I don't want these things and decided so.

This woman avoids credit due to loss of control over the accuracy of transactions and the possibility of being charged more than she owes. Another person related the loss of respect that came with credit purchases. Avoiding credit protects the individual from such loss of public face.

Interviewer: Do you feel that when you are going there, making purchases, the people at the shop respect you using kind words and enquiring about your needs?
Rani (female, 30 years, no formal education): How can he? If we have money, every one would respect us…when my husband, he used to go for jobs. Once, he had a problem, I approached the (local shopkeeper). He told me that he was ready to give more credit. I won't buy on credit usually. I fear whether we could repay it or not. However, what could I do? He (husband) never went for a job for 10 days once. During that time, I got credit for Rs. 100. He (local shopkeeper) harassed me a lot, while my husband was there. I felt so sad. Then I got money unexpectedly, and the first thing I did was to settle the credit. From that incident, I feared about credit. I won't buy on credit from anybody.
Interviewer: So, the local shopkeeper shouted because you bought on credit.
Rani: He shouted loudly. Why do we need this? We don't want credit.
Interviewer: Will he respect and speak politely if you don't buy on credit?
Rani: Yes, people would respect, whoever.

Here, the local shopkeeper disrespects the buyer who purchases on credit, who is dependent on him for credit purchases. Such disrespect stems from the lower means of the buyer. We also found situations, however, where the relationship is amicable and respectful. The neighborhood retailer is likely to exert influence if the buyer who owes money purchases from a different store, such as a large reseller. In some instances, the neighborhood retailer may ask that some items be bought at his or her store and others at the large reseller.

There are many forms of loans available. Here is an example of a loan without collateral.

Mythili: (female, 40 years, 4th grade education): It is borrowed money. I won't borrow for interest. I would borrow for temporary receipt. If no one is there to help me, I would go for (high-interest non-collateral loan)....
It is with daily repayment arrangement.
Interviewer: How much have you borrowed?
Mythili: I would borrow Rs. 1,000 from (high-interest non-collateral loan) sir. … I would agree to pay Rs. 10 daily.
Interviewer: How many days do you have to repay?
Mythili: I have to pay for 90 days.
Interviewer: OK, it is for Rs. 1,000.
Mythili: 90 … 100 days.
Interviewer: How much would they deduct when paying you?
Mythili: They would deduct Rs. 150.
Interviewer: They deducted?

Mythili: They would give me Rs. 850 after deducting Rs. 150. I should repay it correctly in 100 days. Rs. 1,000 in 100 days.

This is similar to a Rs. 850 loan at an average balance of Rs. 425 over 50 days with a Rs. 150 interest, which works out to an interest rate of 258% [(150/425) × 365/50], with higher rates being common. Loans without collateral can be obtained at extremely high-interest rates. Non-collateral lenders enforce payment through public humiliation, such as through using offensive language and expletives outside a person's house when he or she fails to make a payment. Collection schedules vary from daily to weekly or monthly. Avoidance of non-collateral loans or repayment of such loans is motivated by public humiliation suffered when not making payments. Traumatic events often lead to such attitudes, self-respect, and respect in the eyes of others being central to individuals. Avoiding loans in neighborhoods where they reside is one strategy adopted by individuals.

Interviewer: Have you borrowed on any occasion and anyone questioned you like that?
Sumitra (female, 46 years, no formal education): We had borrowed Rs. 30,000 when my husband was ill. The moneylender came once and shouted with filthy words. We felt sad and worried much. My husband felt that the person who came up well (in life) with his support shouted at him because of the credit. So, he instructed that I should not go to him (moneylender), whatever the family situation is in the future.

This woman was deeply pained about the public humiliation many years later, recounting how her husband was anguished by the event and how the lender had been someone the husband had helped before. There is genuine fear of such humiliation and it appears to be an effective mechanism in a one-to-one world, where, sometimes, the only thing that people possess is their dignity. Some avoid taking loans solely because of this fear while others have learned through experience.

Pledging jewelry is a preferred option for those with the means to make the initial purchase. Possessions can be used as savings, such as by pawning jewels in times of need with typically a 1-year time frame to redeem them and a relatively lower interest rate than cash loans without collateral. Also, pawning possessions comes without the threat of public humiliation by lenders when there are lapses in repayment. Seasonal or uncertain income or very low income can lead to savings through pawning and repossessing jewelry. Such a scheme minimizes interest (for example, to 3% a month!) and allows for enjoyment of possessions, without the threat of public humiliation due to nonrepayment.

When financial situations are relatively good, individuals will often purchase some pieces of jewelry (e.g., gold bracelets, pendants), which serve both as an adornment and a "rainy day" savings account. They will pledge their jewelry in bad times for a loan with a year to redeem. Whether they actually redeem the jewelry or not, the choice of redemption is one that individuals like to have. Individuals often prefer buying jewelry to regular savings. There is symbolic value in owning and using it, a remembrance of good times. Moreover, pledging does not require individuals to commit to regular payments with uncertain future income, when compared to other loan arrangements.

Interviewer: So, you would pledge the jewels, when you have money problems and then you would redeem it? You talked about the redemption. What would be the amount when you pledge and what would be the redemption amount?

Murali (male, 40 years, 8th grade education): Yes sir, it would be less. We buy material for Rs. 1,000 or Rs. 800. We may have to pledge it for Rs. 400. If we don't have a regular job in the subsequent months, we have to lose that article (without redeeming it). It becomes a big loss to us. We have only those items to manage our crisis situations on time. We have nothing else.

Interviewer: Rainy seasons are difficult times in your profession?

Murali: Yes, we have to suffer on those days.

Interviewer: So, this is an option you have and you adjust?

Murali: Yes sir.

Interviewer: I mean you buy jewels or articles and pledge it when you are in need?

Murali: Yes, we used to pledge. If we join in the chit, we may not be in a position to pay it regularly, especially when we don't have a regular job. It would be a problem when we could not pay on time. Hence, we prefer to have articles or jewels (to pledge) and we would adjust.

Chandra (female, 28 years, no formal education,): Yes, I have done so even very recently. We have pledged the jewels. Still, we are not in a position to redeem it.

*Interv*iewer: You are unable to redeem it and it is still there. So, sometimes you pledge the jewels and get the money to manage ...

Chandra: Yes ...

Interviewer: Why do you pledge like that? Some people take loans without pledging any items and some get money after pledging their jewels as capital. Why do you borrow like this?

Chandra: They would come to my house and shout if I get a loan. If I pledge my articles and get money, I can be fearless. I can redeem it whenever I wish. They won't come and shout in front of my house. So, we decided that we should borrow after pledging our articles.

Interviewer 2: How much interest for this? How much do they charge from you as interest, if you pledge the jewels and get money?

Chandra: They fix and charge Rs. 2.50 or Rs. 3.

Interviewer 2: How much would you be charged with interest, if you take a loan from someone without pledging any articles?

Chandra: I don't borrow for interest like that. ... May be for temporary cash rotation of about Rs. 500.

Here, the rate of interest is Rs. 2.50 or Rs. 3 per month on Rs. 100. In addition, Rs. 10 may be levied for document charges and a month's interest may be deducted in advance from the loan amount. Loans through pledging valuable items versus loans without collateral, which come with the potential for public humiliation, are often the set of alternatives that individuals consider.

1.6.6 Entertainment Options

Movies, either on television or in theaters, and soap operas on television, are among the primary means for entertainment, along with fairs during religious festivals. With severe income constraints, individuals may avoid going to movies or even avoid going out of the home except for work. They may avoid going to a nearby food vendor even to buy and drink tea due to lack of money, either making items at home or foregoing them altogether. Even under these circumstances, festivals are often celebrated. For certain festivals, individuals may take a trip to their home village or town or spend some money at a fair. Television ownership is increasing, with this medium representing the entire set of entertainment alternatives for many subsistence families. Through installment plans, individuals may buy a black-and-white television for about Rs. 2,400 (say, in installments of Rs. 100 a month for 24 months), with cable costing around Rs. 100 per month. Some may prefer to buy a newspaper or go to a movie rather than consider buying a television because it involves a longer-term financial commitment.

1.7 Market Interactions

The discussion to this point has centered on the set of products purchased by the subsistence customer. Embedded in this discussion were interactions with sellers and the marketplace, which are difficult, if not impossible, to separate from the set of products. This section focuses on interactions of subsistence customers with the marketplace and the primary economic relationships they form.

1.7.1 Neighborhood Retail Stores and Large Resellers

The typical individual in these communities has a primary economic relationship with one store. Usually, in urban areas, this is likely to be a small neighborhood retail store that buys generic products at wholesale rates and sells to the local community. Geographic proximity in terms of neighborhoods and lack of mobility are key considerations, due to the cost of travel to distant locations, time constraints due to restrictive work schedules, and just-in-time daily wages (say, wages earned by evening and the need to prepare one meal soon after). The primary relationship may also be with a larger reseller located farther away that sells to retailers as well as to individuals.

Both retailers and large resellers are characterized by being responsive to customer needs and having very detailed knowledge of individual customers, akin to, and in some ways better than, sophisticated databases. They accept product returns, allow exchanges for bad products, adjust supply based on customer complaints, sometimes deliver products to homes, and generally strive to satisfy customers. Customers may resort to trial and error to try out products, and often provide feedback to sellers about products.

Due to income constraints, people often buy from neighborhood retailers at higher prices. The retailer is also used for last-minute convenience purchases, such as for a final ingredient during cooking, a common occurrence with daily wages. The large reseller sells to retailers as well and may reserve credit only for customers with large monthly expenditures, beyond what is typical for low-income households. The neighborhood retailer is more likely to offer credit for low-income residents of the neighborhood. For those with sufficient money at the beginning of the month, the large reseller provides practically all the necessities, responsive service, and refunds/returns. However, with weekly or daily incomes, or later in a month with monthly income, the large reseller is often not a viable alternative. Individuals buy from a retailer, who usually charges higher prices and offers credit. Thus, the customer is tied to the retailer who may likely ask for full repayment if patronage stops or decreases. The retailer is usually responsive to customer needs. Regular customers often receive better treatment in terms of weighings, extras, and discounts.

The neighborhood retailer may price higher for credit purchases, usually without explicitly communicating with customers and usually on generic products (e.g., charging Rs. 16 for a kg of rice instead of Rs. 14). By helping in times of need, being responsive, and providing credit, the neighborhood retailer often cements relationships with customers and elicits loyalty. One customer, when asked whether she enquires about the price of a product she is buying from the neighborhood retailer, wondered aloud how he would feel because he helps by providing credit in times of need. In fact, when customers begin to purchase regularly at an outlet, they may tend to stop checking prices even when they are capable of doing so.

A number of factors lead to loyalty to specific outlets, primary among them being credit received in times of need. In a world of geographic proximity, patronage of a different store when owing money to a specific store may not be viable. The fear of needing credit in times of need in the future is a strong motivator. As discussed, the balance between purchases at large resellers versus neighborhood retailers, while triggered by income, involves other complexities. Purchase patterns are not solely due to income management but also due to consumption management, wherein buying things in larger quantities may not be preferable when consumption may have to be restricted to a minimum down the road. The retail shopkeeper also provides more customized service than the large reseller in some respects.

Interviewer: Now, you buy from a shop in bulk. Suppose you wish to return anything, would that shop accept it? Do they know who you are?

Kavitha (female, 38 years, 5th grade education): Yes, they know. This is the shop where we buy always. Suppose we don't want an item or an item is missed in the supplied provision, we go and ask, and they would give (the item) though we don't show the bill. It is a trusted shop.

Interviewer 2: So, you say that every month, first you used to buy from the large reseller. Instead, if you buy the same from the local shopkeeper (neighborhood retailer), he will get some income. Now, he loses that income (because you visit the large reseller). Would he not be concerned about this?

Kavitha: He would ask. I would tell him that I bought the items that were not available with him from the large reseller. He would tell us: "Okay you buy few there and few here."

Interviewer 2: OK, you are aware that Rs. 1 is the difference in the price between the two shops and you are the ultimate loser ... suppose you buy from the wholesale shop, you can save Rs. 100 or Rs. 150 in a month, perhaps. ... Why don't you go and buy there?

Kavitha: Sir, we don't have money, money won't be available. He (husband) gives me the money daily. I save from this and buy ... from the nearest shop.

Here, the buyer balances purchases between the large reseller and the neighborhood retailer, essentially providing some business for each. Daily income is a major constraint in buying at the large reseller, which requires having sufficient money but can also lead to savings. Because of an established relationship, the seller is responsive to needs, returns, and refunds, adjusting his supplies based on feedback from customers.

Whereas urban areas are characterized by a plethora of stores, lack of mobility makes the neighborhood store a central part of individuals' economic relationships. In a rural setting, access is severely restricted and a larger town nearby may be miles away with few modes of transportation. Retailers or mobile vendors may charge sizably higher prices due to transportation costs to buy from larger towns.

1.7.2 Installment Plans for Bigger-Ticket Items

Occasional purchases of somewhat big-ticket items are made through installment plans. Individual sellers buy clothing and small appliances (big-ticket items in this context) from retail or wholesale outlets and sell on an installment plan, thus enabling customers to procure products beyond their immediate means, although at very high interest rates. Companies offer lower interest rates, but usually for much bigger purchases, such as televisions. Thus, the installment seller, often a member of the same community, offers a product and service that caters to the needs of the community. As discussed, the low-income, low-literate marketplace studied here in some ways reflects a truly free marketplace with seller and buyer exerting balancing influences.

A number of community-based services include installment plans for relatively more expensive items. Individuals offer schemes to buy relatively expensive products, such as large vessels, through installments with monthly payments over many months. What constitutes bigger ticket items is, of course, relative. Products like clothing could be bought through installments. Mixies (blenders), cookers, and chairs may also be bought through installments.

Interviewer: What are the items you have purchased in installments?
Badri (husband, 37 years, 5th grade education): Clothing for women.

Sivakami (wife, 30 years, no formal education): We have bought articles and simple (clothing for men) and saris.

Interviewer: Have you bought (clothing) in installment and are these items up to the standard?

Sivakami: We don't know that it is of good standard but we buy it.

Badri: But due to the circumstances we buy. We cannot pay in full since we have to meet daily expenditure and hence, we will pay Rs. 5 or Rs. 10 daily and clear the account.

Interviewer: But the quality is not so good?

Sivakami: No.

Badri: These clothes have been bought through this way. We cannot pay the price in full. In a shop, a good (men's clothing) costs Rs. 70 but we cannot pay the price in full. We cannot save that amount, and if we do, there will be some (other) expenditure to be met.

Interviewer: Do you return the (clothing for men) bought in installment if the color goes away?

Badri: They will not take it back sir.

Interviewer: What will you do?

Sivakami: We will reduce Rs. 10

Interviewer: So you will say that the color is fading and reduce the amount of payment?

Interviewer 2: Have you ever said that you will not wear such clothes bought in installment?

Sivakami: No sir we will not say like that. Even if we say so, the seller will not agree. So we will reduce Rs. 5 or Rs. 10, stating that the color is fading and the clothes are not of good standard and not good clothes. But they will not reduce in full.

Even though products are of lower quality, the installment plan enables low-income individuals to buy them. Installment plans, even for relatively inexpensive products, such as clothing or small appliances, are common and make purchases affordable, while also forcing individuals to save appropriately to make payments. With defective products, adjustment is made in the price. In some cases, the buyers may just stop paying. Buying on installment may often lead to poor-quality products. Using a fictitious example, "Malathi" stove may be a reputed product. However, "Mala*n*thi" (emphasis added) stove is not as good but may be sold as the former. Low-literate customers who match patterns rather than read, are susceptible to such tactics.

Interviewer: Where do you buy this and how do you buy?

Kala (female, 44 years, 8th grade education): Mostly I buy in installments. To buy in the shop is very difficult. Rarely, I buy from the shop. Even saris, the sari merchant brings it to my house and sells. ... Hence I will buy a sari once or twice in a year. For children I will buy a sari once or twice in a year. For children, I will buy new clothes. My elder son will buy me once and another time I will buy once. He is also doing business, so he will also buy on installment in the shop itself where the merchant sells. He buys it from them and pays it on daily collection. He will bring and give it once. Another time, I will buy once.

Interviewer: How do you buy in installment?

Kala: I know that the price is high. But if I go and buy a sari directly, it will be Rs. 100. I know that price. But they will sell it for Rs. 150. If they sell it at this price, they charge only Rs. 25 per month from me.

Interviewer: Is it the shop which sells for Rs. 100?

Kala: No.

Interviewer: Is it a separate shop?

Kala: They buy it from the shop and sell it in our house itself. They bring it in a heap to our house. They can bring about 50 saris. We will select whatever we need and take it. They will give a card and every month on a fixed date when they come, we should pay the cash on this stipulated date to them. They will mark on the card given to us as paid for that month.

This is another example of an installment scheme. Community-based services may have mutual advantages, reducing cheating by buyers and sellers.

1.8 Characteristics of Product and Market Interactions

Some important characteristics of this context stemming from the product and market interactions of individuals as customers described earlier are discussed here.

1.8.1 Uncertainty, Complexity, and Lack of Control

Among the most important factors to understand in gaining insight into the subsistence marketplace are uncertainty and lack of control over many aspects of day-to-day life, whether it is the quality or quantity of water or the availability of electricity. This, of course, follows directly from being resource-poor; with very little resources, the poor have little control over the basic amenities that may be taken for granted by people in higher strata of society. Overlaying these issues is the level of complexity in a variety of realms of day-to-day life that distinguishes a transitional context such as India from Western societies. Basic services, such as transportation, are subject to greater variation in India when compared to the West. The level of complexity in a number of domains is very high due to the number of variables involved, the interactions among these variables, and the considerable uncertainty and variation experienced on these variables. Complexity is inherent in meeting basic necessities, such as food cooked from generic ingredients, which in turn, is dependent on uncontrollable factors, such as quantity and quality of water and quality of generic ingredients. For example, as discussed, the quality of boiled rice is subject to variations in the quality of rice, the water used, and the method of boiling employed.

1.8.2 One-to-One Interactions

Perhaps the most striking characteristic of the marketplace in subsistence contexts is the network-rich, one-to-one interactional nature, such as the one-to-one relationship between and among buyers and sellers. This leads to accountability and service considerations on the part of the seller. The environment is characterized by continuous interaction between buyer and seller. The seller knows buyer preferences and there is continuous communication. Price and quantity are negotiated, installments are not paid for defective products, and prices are adjusted for personal circumstances, both to buyer and seller advantages. Community-based service providers balance buyer and seller needs, enforce contracts, and are aware of specific needs and purchasing power.

Credit and help in times of need lead to strong relationships between buyer and seller. Creditworthiness is determined by the retailer (or by the individual seller on installment purchases or the moneylender for loans). This system is, in some ways, more sophisticated than complex customer databases. Retailers offer additional "services", such as credit purchases, to people in need. In turn, retailers keep accounts and may overcharge for credit purchases without explicitly informing the customer, although this practice is implicitly known. Retailers also provide the service of ensuring that customers' savings are secure in return for a charge (e.g., a 10% negative interest). Customized service and product returns are often the norm, sometimes an almost customer-level democracy in action where accountability is expected or demanded at the grass-roots level. Shopkeepers may respond to feisty behavior from customers with better treatment. Small numbers in terms of customers and local ownership, direct interaction, and powerful word of mouth, are all pertinent factors. Direct feedback on products leads to appropriate stocking decisions by sellers. Large resellers may also deliver products, and accept product returns from some regular customers. Savings schemes reflect the one-to-one interactional marketplace and are characterized by a sense of community.

As discussed, several services are offered that address community needs, such as resellers going door-to-door to sell products on affordable installment plans, although at extremely high interest rates. Buying on installment may sometimes lead to poorer-quality products. Customers may also be able to stop payments for poor products. Refusal to pay subsequent installments for a defective product is one form of redress. Word of mouth is very strong, whether between customers or between customers and sellers.

Irrespective of financial constraints, certain traditions during death, marriage, or religious ceremonies are usually maintained, often even by borrowing money. A salient motive here is to avoid being spoken ill off. Maintenance of tradition, even in dire financial circumstances, follows from the centrality of one-to-one interactions. One-to-one interactions in the realm of health include patients asking their doctors to check filled prescriptions from pharmacies for accuracy. Medical doctors are identified and assessed for effectiveness, with loyalty usually following.

1.8.3 Make or Buy Decisions

A key aspect of customer interactions is the make or buy decision or the make or buy or forego decision. The make or buy decision applies in several realms, such as visiting a restaurant, or making ingredients, such as powders for cooking. The make option may be cheaper, while allowing customization even across family members (e.g., making cooking powders with different ingredients depending on the age of the customer).

Interviewer: So you grind these items. What is the difference in going to a shop for purchasing these items and grinding these items?

Badri (37 years, 5th grade education): If we buy these items, it will not be good. It will not be hot and it will be different. These items are adulterated. I buy chili and (type of spice) powder from the shop and give it for grinding which is good for health and also very tasty.

Interviewer: What we make in the house is good for health?

Badri: It is good for health.

Interviewer: What is the price when we buy it outside versus when we prepare at home?

Badri: In the shop, the item will be less but when we prepare in the house it will be more and the quality will also be good.

Interviewer: When we make the item in the house it will be costly?

Badri: It will be clean.

This is another example of a make or buy decision. Here, the make decision is considered to be costlier, yet providing more benefits.

Interviewer: Is it OK? Do you prepare anything at home which is needed for cooking anything?

Mythili (female, 40 years, 4th grade education): I would make it (chili powder).

Interviewer: Would you grind it yourself?

Mythili: Yes, for chili.

Interviewer: You buy all ingredients and ...?

Mythili: We would grind at a machine (flour mill).

Interviewer: Why are you not buying at shops?

Mythili: We even get stomach pain because of it. We don't know what they are mixing in the shop with the chili powder. ... Last month, the chili powder was over. We all had stomach pain because we ate the food prepared with the powder bought at the shop.

Interviewer: It was not good?

*Myth*ili: It was not at all good. ... I don't know why. We don't know what they are mixing and doing. They are talking about (leading brand), it causes stomach pain. Stomach pain for everyone in our house. So, we always buy chilies and grind it first whether we have anything else or not. Last month, that was month end, I had no money. Since I bought it in the shop, it was happening like that.

Interviewer: OK. Is there any price difference between the chili powder bought in the shop and grinding powder in the machine yourselves?

Mythili: It would be little more (quantity) than buying the powder at the shop. The price would be less too. ... If you spend Rs. 100, now the price of chili is high. Suppose you spend Rs. 100 or Rs. 150, it could be used for 3 months freely. Money could be saved and the item too would be a quality one. We grind it with our supervision. It would be clean and good for everything.

The make or buy decision is also related to the idea of consuming natural foods rather than something in a packet, which may contain contaminants. In fact, hand-ground spices may be preferred over packaged foods, which may not be fresh. Small packages may also lead to wastage during transfer, another reason cited for the make option. The make option is more difficult when women work outside the house, leading to more of the buy option. The forego option is, of course, pervasive in many realms, such as in rationing or foregoing medicine and treatment for illnesses.

1.8.4 Transactional Fluidity

Another striking aspect in this context is the nature of transactions in terms of their fluidity. Pure exchange is not necessarily of the arm's-length variety. The transaction is often fluid, price and quantity is negotiated, installments are not paid, prices are adjusted for personal circumstances both to buyer and seller advantages, and community-based service providers balance buyer and seller needs, enforce contracts, and are aware of specific needs and purchasing power. Even weighing of products may differ depending on the negotiated prices, with deliberate variations in the way the weighing balance and the chain links are held (sometimes, weighing pans may be of different weight). If negotiated price is low, customers may be shortchanged in the weighing. As one seller said when a relatively low price was negotiated for three pounds of grapes but the amount seemed to be less by half a pound when weighed elsewhere: "That is the weighing you will get for that price!" Accurate weighing may occur when full price is given.

1.8.5 Summary

The set of products purchased by the subsistence customer can be organized into several categories (Figure 1). At the surface level, this list does not seem very different from the needs of individuals in other segments of society. But underlying this surface similarity is affordability, with a very narrow range of product options being accessible to subsistence customers, and trade-offs between what the more affluent customer would consider necessities to be made when crises arise. In terms of a hierarchy of needs (Maslow, 1970), "lower-level needs", i.e., physiological needs, of course, take precedence, along with safety needs, but social, esteem, and self-actualization needs are vitally important to individuals in subsistence contexts. Our categorization of needs is at a level appropriate for examining relationships with products and markets. However, needs can be categorized at a number of levels of abstraction to cover social and self-esteem needs. In the constant trade-off between various needs that is the daily reality for individuals living in subsistence, product and market interactions center around physiological and safety needs. Moreover, the tenuousness of life circumstances creates a complex web of interdependencies and interactions between buyers and sellers, and may lead to loyalty to the neighborhood retailers who are not the low-cost option. Several characteristics of these marketplace interactions are noteworthy, including the one-to-one nature of the environment and the fluidity of transactions. "Bigger ticket items" may include clothing, large utensils, jewelry, appliances, and financial services. Many of the services are offered through community-based service providers.

The broad context in which the product and market interactions occur is characterized by uncertainty in basic infrastructure, services and income, and lack of control over many aspects of daily life. As discussed, the complexity of life domains can be very high due to the number of variables involved, the interactions among these variables, and the considerable uncertainty and variation experienced on these variables. In this larger context, product and market interactions are characterized by a network-rich, one-to-one interactional environment, which, coupled with product complexity, may lead to experiential evaluation of products and stores. Decisions on retailers to patronize are closely intertwined with product decisions; often, the two are inseparable. Also important is the make or buy (or forego) decision. At a broader level, adaptive strategies in response to adverse conditions require extraordinary adjustments in daily life. Notions of rationality rooted in relatively resource-rich environments need to be revised for subsistence contexts.

1.8.6 Relevant Past Research

With the exception of specific disciplines such as anthropology, research in the social sciences has focused predominantly on relatively resource-rich and literate contexts, limiting their relevance to subsistence contexts. Nevertheless, there are many examples of relevant research, and a few such examples are presented here for illustrative purposes. One such stream of research relates to the nature of exchanges, which have been categorized into reciprocal exchanges that are based on "informally enforced agreements to give goods, services, information, or money in exchange for future compensation in kind" (Kranton, 1996, p. 830), versus market exchange which "takes place among anonymous agents who use money as a medium of exchange" (p. 833). Kranton notes that reciprocal exchanges are prevalent in developing contexts. In his analysis, he notes that reciprocal exchanges occur when anonymous markets are small or when goods are heterogeneous and when people do not expect to interact frequently. Our data suggest that reciprocal exchanges in a subsistence context seem to occur for a variety of reasons, such as the need to establish ongoing relationships to handle financial crises, and the interdependence among individuals living in subsistence.

The fundamental psychological impetus here stems from the extreme uncertainty and adverse conditions that warrant longer-term relationships to establish trust, to multiply purchase volume, and to tide through bad times. Molm (2001) distinguished between negotiated exchange involving a joint decision process about the terms of exchange and reciprocal exchange where each actor's contributions are separate and not negotiated. The long-term relationship between an individual in a subsistence context and the neighborhood retail store owner resembles such reciprocal exchange in a number of ways. In the context of social exchanges, the relationships between behaviors and outcomes have been categorized as being independent, dependent, or interdependent (Michaels and Wiggins, 1976). Our data also suggest that many relationships in subsistence contexts are defined by interdependence among individuals living in subsistence as reflected in financial alternatives, such as community based financial schemes. Temporally, transactions can be independent or serially dependent, with reciprocal transactions assuming the latter. Such continuing relationships have been argued to be characterized by the use of influence and the emergence of elements such as trust (Molm, 1994), which we found to be central among our informants.

The one-to-one interactional marketplace emphasizes the importance of social relationships and social capital in these settings. These contexts are, of course, resource-poor, but can be network-rich. They may be relatively rich in social capital, institutions, relationships, attitudes and values governing interactions amongst people, and contributing to economic and social development (Coleman, 1988; Iyer et al., 2005). A number of cultural and societal factors may give rise to a strongly networked society in subsistence marketplaces. The lack of resources and heightened sense of insecurity leads to dense interdependence between individuals in subsistence markets. The subsistence marketplace reflects a unique context where word of mouth and one-to-one relationships take a center stage. The network structure in which the individuals seek their identity in conjunction with their affiliation with others makes this context unique. The role of different types of social capital in enabling marketplace exchanges is crucial to understand in these settings.

1.9 Consumer and Entrepreneurial Skills in Subsistence Marketplaces

Using the research described earlier as a basis, this section presents a discussion of consumer and entrepreneurial skills in subsistence marketplaces. We cover the vulnerabilities and innovative practices of subsistence customers and entrepreneurs, and the development of consumer skills. We contrast skill development in these contexts with those of low-literate customers in the USA.

1.9.1 Vulnerabilities and Innovative Practices of Subsistence Consumers and Entrepreneurs[13]

Our research provided rich insights into the lives and marketplace interactions of low-literate, low-income buyers and sellers. There were many examples of innovative practices that our informants educated us about along with many pitfalls where individuals are vulnerable and suffer negative consequences as buyers and as sellers (Table 2). Vulnerabilities ranged from lack of awareness of rights to lack of confidence or lack of skills for day-to-day customer tasks. Tasks such as planning, creating shopping lists, checking prices, checking products, or requesting a bill were often not

[13] The material in Section 9.1 including Table 2 is reprinted with minor editing with permission from Elsevier from Viswanathan, Gajendiran, and Venkatesan (2007). This article was published in the International Journal of Educational Development (2007), doi:10.1016/j.ijedudev.2007.05.004, Viswanathan, M., S. Gajendiran, and R. Venkatesan, Understanding and enabling marketplace literacy in subsistence contexts: The development of a consumer and entrepreneurial literacy educational program in South India, Copyright Elsevier, 2007.

Table 2 Illustrative Customer and Entrepreneur Quotes

Customer-related Illustrative Quotes[a]	
Malini (female, 35 years old, no formal education): We don't know how to calculate and account. … We know a little based on our assumptions. Suppose I visit a shop regularly and buy the items every day … I try to change the shop I buy from when I feel that the rate is high in a particular shop. I try to change the shops and buy from different shops to gain one or two rupees. I search and see whether I could get items for lower price and visit shops that are nearby. If I have good education and knowledge I could visit shops anywhere or shops with high standards. I could go for any job. Since I have no education, I hesitate to approach others and shop wherever I go. I hesitate to approach others freely. This is why I feel sad. *Gauthami* (female, 28 years old, 3rd grade education): The neighbors used to tell me … that they (seller) would quote Rs. 5 (for a product) and scold us if we don't buy, compelling us to buy. … They would ask us "Won't you buy, if the price is little higher? Would you buy only when the price is less?" They (neighbors) say that they (the shopkeepers) scold in this manner. I would have all this in my mind and have a kind of fear that they may scold me like that as well.	Fear of shopping situations due to lack of literacy
Menaka (female, 32 years old, 3rd grade education): They (shopkeepers) would give the bill. They would calculate the amount and issue the bill for purchased items. I would bring it and show it to my daughter. If the bill was accurate, I would leave it. If she found any error in the calculation or bill, I would show it to the shopkeepers and discuss it. As I would visit the school the next day (to pick up my son), I would go to the shop on the way to the school and clarify the errors. The shopkeeper would recheck it and return the amount even if the difference or error was one or two rupees.	Seeking help, seeking corrections from shopkeepers
Interviewer: In fact, when we visit a provisional shop, we buy 15–20 items. Would you be able to check all the items and verify the prices and calculate the bill amount? *Kavitha* (female, 38 years old; 5th grade education): They issue the bill while they deliver the items. So, we can check the items in the bill one by one. *Interviewer*: Do you have any difficulties in this? *Kavitha*: I can't identify the moment I look at it. … I would think about it and verify the details after reaching my home. It would be in grams, and I would feel sad at that time.	Planning purchases, checking products, prices, and bills during shopping

[a] Fictitious names are used to maintain anonymity.

Bhuvanesh (male, 31 years old, no formal education): Whether the medicine written and given by the doctor is the same must be compared and seen, is it not? Mostly, his handwriting cannot be understood, and we don't know English. So we send our children to the medical store to buy it. They (shopkeepers) sometimes even change the medicine and give. But when we ask, they will say that the company is the same and that there is no difference. So I may buy the changed items.	Checking accuracy of product purchase, matching patterns
Interviewer: Will they give the correct medicine? *Bhuvanesh*: They will give the same medicine which he prescribes. *Interviewer*: How do you check that? *Bhuvanesh*: I will see the first letter sir. *Interviewer*: How will you find out that the items bought by you are of good quality? *Bhuvanesh*: How do I know? It is a good shop and the things that are there seem to be good and so I buy them. That is all I can say.	Trusting shops, checking quality of products
Kavitha (female, 38 years old, 5th grade education): If I have more money or a sufficient amount of it, I can buy in bulk and stock up. Because we don't have money, we have to buy a little in bulk purchases and use it for 10 or 15 days … again we have to buy one or two kilograms for urgent need from the nearby shops, as and when we get money. What do we do? The local shops too buy from there (wholesale shop) and sell it to us; they would get a profit of Rs. 1 or Rs. 2. When we buy, it is loss to us, is it not?	Choosing between neighborhood retailer and large reseller
Rani (female, 30 years old, no formal education, food shopkeeper): If it is a high price, we would bargain. Why is the rate this much here, while it is less there? He (shopkeeper) buys the vegetables in the market (and knows the market price). Suddenly, how could he raise the price in the nearby shop? We would visit the market, when there was no sufficient stock of items like green chilies at the nearby shop. When we buy those at the market, we would compare the prices in both places. The price would be higher here (at the local shop). We would ask the shopkeeper: "Why are you charging Rs. 2 per 50 g of green chili while the prices of a kilogram is Rs. 6 only at the market?" The shopkeeper would ask us: "Who is selling for such a low price?" We would say we visit daily and buy this product. "Don't we know even this." We would tell them that it is unfair and unjust. The (local shopkeeper) will get angry. Then I will come back quietly.	Bargaining, comparing products

(continued)

Table 2 (continued)

Kamala (female, 44 years old, 8th grade education): Yes, I will crush even chili powder. Crushed chili powder is sold in the market, but I will not buy it. I will crush chili and dhania (ingredients) in my house. I will crush and prepare even turmeric powder. *Interviewer*: So you gain from doing this? *Kamala*: Yes, I gain. It will also be clean. When we do this, we will be satisfied because they (shops) may also adulterate the product. We will watch the process when chili powder is crushed in the machine. When chili and dhania are crushed in the shop, they add rice powder. I have seen this. What we make ourselves is good for health. Seragam, pepper, and dhal (ingredients) are added to crush chili powder. They are not added in the (chili powder made at the) shop.	Making versus buying decisions
Kavitha (female, 38 years old, 5th grade education): First, I would buy a kilogram of rice as a sample to cook and test it. Suppose we find the cooked rice is good and tasty, then we would buy 5 kg or more and prepare the regular food. Our local shopkeeper also used to buy the rice (from wholesale) and sell. If we tell the local shopkeeper, "I bought this rice from this particular shop and it is good, so you buy the same and stock it for selling to us", he would comply with our request and would be prepared to supply whenever we need it.	Assessing quality of products
Interviewer: You say that every month, you first buy from the wholesale shop (large reseller). Instead, if you buy from the local shopkeeper, he will get some income. Now, he loses that income, won't he think anything like that? *Kavitha* (female, 38 years old, 5th grade education): He (neighborhood retailer who offers credit) would ask. I would tell him that I bought items that were not available with him there (at the large reseller). He would tell us: "Okay, you buy few there and few here."	Developing relationships with shops, credit purchases
Sumitra (female, 46 years old, no formal education): Yes, while weighing he shakes (the balance) and uses some technique to balance the needle of the scale and push down the plate. He would say that it is having excess and give extra to the buyer. If it is bought in the next shop, he would weigh it perfectly. He won't shake the hand that holds the scale. He would hold the scale at a perfect angle when you watch carefully.	Weighing

Kavitha (female, 38 years old, 5th grade education): We would check while they weigh it. Suppose we feel that there is shortage in the weight and ask them to weigh it again. They would weigh and show us, it would be correct. Suppose there is any shortage in the weight, they would say that this package has shortage and ask their staff to change it and give us the packet with correct weight. They would take back (the package with shortage).	
Interviewer: Now, you buy different items from the wholesale market like (store name), prepare pickles, and sell it. Do you know what MRP (maximum retail price) is? *Jamuna* (female, 34 years old, 10th grade education, pickle seller): MRP means the rate of the product. It is the production cost; that is why it is called as MRP. *Interviewer*: Do you buy soaps? *Jamuna*: Sir, it is in that packet. *Interviewer*: What is printed on it? *Jamuna*: The rate of the soap is printed followed by MRP. *Interviewer*: Do you know the meaning or expansion of MRP? *Jamuna*: I know that they have printed the rate as MRP, that's all.	(Mis)understanding price notation (MRP refers to the maximum price that a product can be sold for)
Interviewer: You make purchases in wholesale shops for cash or any credit? *Velamma* (female, 45 years old, 5th grade education, utensils reseller): No credit, only cash payment on hand. *Interviewer*: Cash on hand purchase? *Velamma*: Yes cash on hand. *Interviewer*: Have you bought anything on credit recently? *Velamma*: I won't buy on credit. I have to pay back the credit. They may raise what is owed from Rs. 5 to Rs. 6. I am using this as an example. It is just for the sake of argument. Again, they may record what is owed as Rs. 8 instead of Rs. 6. I don't want these things and decided (to avoid credit).	Avoiding credit and costs associated with it

(continued)

Table 2 (continued)

Seller-related Illustrative Quotes	
Interviewer: When you give products, has any one complained that you are not giving a product worth the Rs. 300 they paid for it? *Velamma* (female, 40 years old, 5th grade education, utensils reseller): Few people are like that. … I would ask them to check the products that were given to others. I would tell them that I gave them the same products that I gave to others. Some may accept what I said and leave quietly, some may shout. I may have to adjust to both situations. *Interviewer*: How are you managing such situations? *Velamma*: I would invite them to check the quality of products supplied to other customers. The other customers would say that the product given was good and useful. This feedback would cool down their temper and they would leave quietly. *Interviewer*: Suppose they say even after the explanation and feedback that the product is not good and that they don't want it? *Velamma*: If they don't want, they can choose any other product available with me. But I won't return the money. At any cost, I won't give the money back. *Interviewer*: Your principle is not to return the money. *Velamma*: I won't give (back money), only products.	Treating customers similarly, managing customer to customer communications
Rani (female, 30 years old, no formal education, food shopkeeper): After arranging the products that I bought, I would calculate. We used to buy kerosene. I would buy it in bulk purchase. I would have bought LPG (gas) cylinder. I would add the cost of the kerosene and the LPG (gas) cylinder. Rs. 20 is the cost of this. By adding everything, it would have come to Rs. 100 or Rs. 120. *Interviewer*: Do you write it down? *Rani*: I couldn't write down all, sir. *Interviewer*: All oral calculation? *Rani*: Oral calculation.	Verbal counting, accounting

Velamma (female, 45 years old, 5th grade education, utensils reseller): I won't ask anyone (about creditworthiness of specific customers) any neighbors. … I won't ask anyone. I would give (products) based on my assessment and confidence. They may tell me (if asked) but they may have quarreled (with the potential customers). So they would tell me not to give products to their neighbors and say that they would move out of the area. Even the people paying me now would say that they don't know, when I am asking about their neighbors. They would respond without any seriousness.	Judging customers
Rani (female, 30 years old, no formal education, food shop owner): I won't talk much to them. It is our business. They should come again. I won't talk. This is because I want to run my business. I would get angry if they speak with anger. I would respond politely if they ask why something is like this. I would say that many people bought the same item earlier and never complained like this. "Only you complained."	Dealing with customers
Jamuna (female, 34 years old, 10th grade education, pickle seller): First, we would taste it. Neighbors are using it. They told us that we have added excess tamarind in the garlic pickles prepared this year.	Testing products through "research"

undertaken. Trade-offs between get and give components of an exchange were often not fully considered in terms of travel time and other non-monetary or indirect monetary costs. Similarly, as sellers, individuals did not analyze the marketplace or consider alternatives before starting enterprises. Lack of clear accounting was another issue as was lack of a full understanding of the costs of doing business. Individuals also had difficulty understanding return on investment.

As buyers, effective practices included bargaining, checking weights, checking prices, and checking product quality (Table 2). As sellers, effective practices included dealing with customers in difficult situations, responding to demands from customers, managing word of mouth among customers, and researching the marketplace. These innovative practices, which represent adaptation to the adverse conditions of subsistence marketplaces, informed the design of the educational program as much as the vulnerabilities. Our research enabled us to develop a detailed list of issues that individuals face as buyers and as sellers as well as a deeper understanding of life in the economic realm.

1.9.2 Development of Consumer Skills

Several factors appear to affect the development of consumer skills, primarily formal education level, experience, and income, through its effect on experience, with our hypotheses in this regard summarized in Figure 2. With any one of these three factors to lean on and use as a stepping-stone, individuals appear to be able to develop their

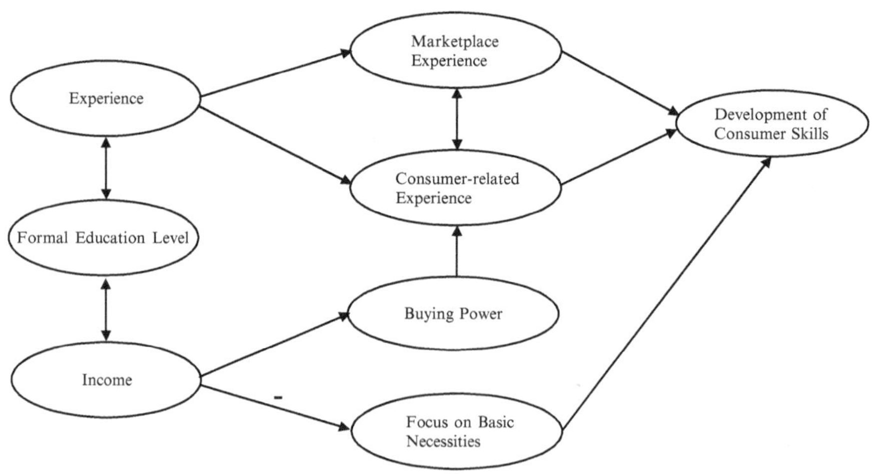

Figure 2 Development of Consumer Skills[14]

[14]Positive relationships between variables are hypothesized unless otherwise specified.

consumer skills by tapping into a rich, one-to-one interactional experience base. However, when all three are low, individuals usually have very poor skills.

1.9.2.1 Number Skills

Verbal counting skills develop through buying or selling experience; thus, people can usually compute totals and change received from transactions. However, more complex computation of interest rate is difficult. In turn, lenders and borrowers speak the simplified terminology of payments per month. Fixation on certain numbers such as MRP[15] is another characteristic, facilitated by ease of concrete use of numbers. Similarly, low-literate customers may fixate on stores without much price search. Even on rare occasions when prices are lowered, low-literate customers may not check prices.

1.9.2.2 Adaptivity in Adversity

Adaptivity has been a central theme of the decision-making literature in psychology, economics, and related disciplines. Adaptivity in consumer behavior and elsewhere has been conceptualized in terms of using appropriate decision strategies in light of limited cognitive resources. However, in the context studied here, adaptivity is much more than finding the right decision strategy to fit a situation. Adaptivity involves making ends meet, such as by using homemade medicine, rationing medicine to save money or to trade off lost income due to illness, adjusting and reducing meal items, substituting lower-priced ingredients for some "less-important" meals,[16] and making rather than buying some food ingredients. Customers often make rather than buy products or ingredients to save money, to customize to their tastes and even to the individual tastes of members of their family, and to consume fresh products.

1.9.2.3 Income and Consumer Skills

Severe income constraints can lead to skill development by necessity, planned purchases, and rationality about the next meal. Income is a double-edged sword, where extreme constraints and necessity can lead to planning and careful purchases. Whereas some income may lead to buying in installments and other forms of

---

[15] MRP is stipulated by the government and refers to the maximum retail price that can be charged. However, it is commonly misunderstood to mean the actual price of a product. Faced with the inability to read most package information except concrete numbers, such as price, low-literate consumers fixate on MRP.

[16] Noteworthy here is that having a reasonable meal at least once a day is top priority; hence, considerable effort is expended toward making this possible.

borrowing, very low income coupled with the fear of humiliation in not being able to repay loans can lead to full cash purchases at affordable prices. With very low income, there may be a tendency to avoid high-interest loans, or avoid buying gifts due to peer and familial pressures or the demands of tradition. Thus, in a sense, extreme income constraints appear to lead to effective decision-making. Severe income constraints can engender an attitude of living within means and blocking out unnecessary expenses. In fact, some customers report that they do not have any unnecessary expenses. Television advertisements and the like are not given much serious attention but viewed for entertainment value. A type of next-meal rationality leads to necessity-based skill development. Some may stop borrowing, buying, or maintaining traditions. In fact, the centrality of one-to-one interactions and people-orientedness may break down when income constraints are too severe and families have to isolate themselves from participating in any social activity that costs money. Some families reported being isolated from other relatives because they are unable to participate in traditional activities that involve monetary expenses (e.g., attending a wedding or a funeral).

Whereas very low incomes can engender the development of certain kinds of skills through the need for planning and careful purchase, very low income combined with laborious work schedules can lead to lack of product evaluation. When income constraints are severe, "filling one's stomach" is the black-and-white priority. With very low income and laborious work schedules, eating per se is what matters, the quality or taste is not important. Thus, consumption is black and white, either/or, with no gray gradations of taste or quality. There is rarely time for planned purchases and price discrimination. Thus, quality judgments and price comparisons are hampered.

1.9.2.4 Formal Literacy and Consumer Skills

We report many examples of ingenuity and resourcefulness that individuals display in the face of low literacy. However, we also found that low literacy can lead to fear of exploring the marketplace, particularly with respect to banks and other institutions. Experience is often at local retail stores; sometimes even buying wholesale is challenging. Over time, low literacy, lack of experience, and extreme income constraints combine to exasperate the situation and thwart learning. Low literacy can lead to fear of conversation, inability to ask a question or answer a question in a conversation, fear of unknown prices, and hence avoidance of many products, fear of enquiry, and feelings of futility in making enquiries or demands. An interesting parallel with low-literate consumers in the USA (Viswanathan et al., 2005) is avoidance of confusing price displays or of "% off" signs due to computational problems.

With low literacy, there is a tendency to accept conditions as they are, without questioning. It also appears to lead to acceptance of products and their quality as is. "Quality is fine, that's all one can get", "Arguing is futile", "That's what you get for what you paid," or "Alternatives are few", are some of the refrains we heard from low-literate individuals. Low literacy leads to the assumption that available products are of the right price and the right quality for that price. Information search can be rare and low literacy can lead to lack of quality evaluations. Products may be evaluated through trial and error due to low literacy, with this outcome accentuated for generic products. Low literacy leads to intuitive, rather than explicit, listing, planning, or budgeting, and concrete methods of accounting, such as placing money (say, investments versus profit for an entrepreneur) in different locations. Defensive rules employed include not carrying money to avoid unnecessary purchases and pattern-matching when unable to read the name of a medicine or a bus number.

Low literacy can lead to lack of awareness when cheating occurs. In fact, loyalty, a sense of obligation, and the lack of price and shop comparisons may compound these issues and lead to a conviction that cheating does not occur. With low literacy, low income, reliance on credit from one store, and inability to plan and buy wholesale, customer-related experiences may not develop. Relationships with stores build loyalty, but can inhibit development of skills to evaluate alternative shops and perform price and product comparisons. Such experiences as computing totals, evaluating products, or interacting with sellers lead to the development of consumer skills. Moreover, even if cheating is thought to occur, there is a sense of futility about argument or action as well as a lack of awareness of rights, the net result often being no change in behavior.

Low literacy per se affects confidence in dealing with some large organizations, such as banks or English-oriented large stores.[17] Low-literate customers may depend on literate children to read or compute or on a mother or mother-in-law to teach them some basic shopping skills. Dependence and word of mouth are both significant. Dependence occurs when dealing with institutions, such as completing forms at banks, for informational issues such as dates on products, or for computations, such as totaling up a bill or preparing lists. Dependence is also inherent in some community-based services, such as savings plans. In a broader sense, a one-to-one interactional marketplace is really a dependence on everyone, reducing somewhat, the need for dependence on specific individuals.

Literacy engenders confidence in dealing with shops and institutions. Here, the difference between no formal education and even a 5th grade education can be stark. Literacy or experience can provide a foundation to build on, and combined with income, lead to experiences, skills, quality judgments, and the like. As discussed earlier, adult education leads to exchange of information among customers and can be transformational for low-literate individuals with regard to their marketplace behaviors. Adult education can convey awareness of issues and rights and lead to concrete redressive actions, such as switching store loyalties and shopping elsewhere.

---

[17] English language skills are an issue in India because of the use of English in many large organizations. India is characterized by having many different languages and numerous dialects. People speak Tamil in the state in which this research was conducted, i.e., Tamil Nadu. In poorer segments, parents often strive to educate their children in English, a way out economically and a source of pride.

1.9.2.5 Experience and Consumer Skills

In the rich context of one-to-one interactions and the need to evaluate generic products, experience can be a very effective teacher. The key in the Indian environment is to have a trigger that leads to experience, which in turn is very effective in teaching skills. Experience leads to knowledge about what works and what does not, whether with products or in money management. However this trial-and-error learning by itself does not safeguard against making errors on single purchases that are information-oriented, for example, purchases based on price or weight.

Low literacy is often associated with perceptions of lack of ability in specific domains. Experience in a trade or through selling can provide a sense of dignity and confidence. In a sense, experience provides a specific form of functional literacy in the here and now, literacy in a trade or in a certain domain, which, in turn, broadens functional literacy. Experience can lead to functional literacy in a specific domain. It enables individuals to overcome fears and, thus, triggers the process of learning. Proxy buying experiences can be gained through work experiences. Work as housemaids can involve purchases and consequent learning. Work-related experiences can lead to skills in counting and buying. Experience can accumulate through selling and buying. Whereas low literacy can lead to fear of exploring the marketplace and low income can inhibit experience, some form of experience can, in turn, alleviate the negative consequences of low literacy and low income and trigger learning. The interaction between education level, income level, and experience is central to the development of consumer skills, with learning perhaps being accelerated when certain threshold levels of these variables are reached.

1.9.2.6 Comparing Low-Literate Customers in India Versus the USA

Research to date in the USA versus India suggests some interesting differences. This discussion of differences between India and the USA, although based on many years of field research, is speculative in nature. In the USA, perhaps most striking is the difficulty experienced by functionally low-literate customers when faced with abstractions, labeled concrete thinking (Viswanathan et al., 2005). A related predilection is pictographic thinking – the tendency to view brand names and prices as images in a scene rather than symbols, and think about product quantities by picturing them rather than using available symbolic information. Low-literate customers in the USA develop several coping mechanisms to deal with these limitations, including depending on others, or buying one item at a time from a menu. Moreover, central to their marketplace interactions is a need to maintain self-esteem in public settings that could potentially "expose" their low literacy. Our research in India suggests that concrete thinking and pictographic thinking are also common in subsistence marketplaces, as are coping mechanisms to compensate for individual shortcomings in marketplace proficiency. Self-esteem issues are also widespread, as documented earlier in this chapter, with low literacy leading to fear of interaction, inability to ask or answer questions in conversation, avoidance of unknown products and unfamiliar pricing schemes, and feelings of futility in making enquiries or demands.

Although subsistence customers in India struggle with many of the same challenges faced by low-literate customers in the USA, the one-to-one interactional marketplace appears to afford some unique advantages that can enhance coping ability. Opportunities to develop consumer skills appear to be generally higher for an individual with a low level of formal education in India when compared to the USA. A key factor here is the rich, one-to-one interactional experience base from which customers can learn. Dealing with vendors requires developing the ability to judge products and mentally count money. Frequent one-to-one interactions with sellers and other customers lead to the development of such skills as what to buy, where to buy it, and how to get a bargain. Customers commonly seek advice from neighbors and people on the street, a sort of perceptual, off-line community. Because many generic products are not packaged or presented with nutritional information, customers have to learn to judge the product for themselves. This should be contrasted with the typical context in the USA where customers deal with large chain stores, products with package information about nutrition, and registers to compute transaction totals. Ironically, the US environment rich in symbolic information and technology is not necessarily conducive to the development of skills for low-literate customers.

Consumer skills also develop from learning skills as sellers, often the way out economically for many individuals in India. This is in contrast to working for a larger organization in a certain clearly defined capacity. Experience in India can be twofold, buying and selling; in the USA, employment is often for a larger organization. Being a vendor in India requires the development of a variety of skills, such as bargaining, counting, and completing transactions, that then transfer to the customer realm.

Another factor that may lead to higher consumer skills in India is the more severe income constraints which lead to careful planning out of necessity. Often, when the decision involves the next meal, careful purchase and consumption habits develop. Discounts and "free" promotions are carefully pursued, income constraints being severe, and possessions few.

Striking differences between the USA and India among low-literate customers include the ability of customers in India to plan carefully, their level of numerical skills, and the lack of impulse purchases. Some factors, such as lack of impulse purchases and planning, may well be the result of extreme income constraints. Numerical skills may necessarily develop from dealing with small vendors in small transactions. Compared to the USA, experiences in a one-to-one interactional world may be richer and lead to faster development, in subsistence contexts in India, with formal education enabling absorption of richer experience and exploration of the marketplace environment and leading to more advanced skills. In the USA, experiences may not be as effective in developing skills; product information is symbolic, computations are mechanized, and one-to-one interactions may be lower in frequency and nature. Work experience and shopping experience may both be narrower in the USA from the perspective of consumer skill development.

Low-literate customers in India may also be less dependent on others when compared to customers with similar formal educational levels in the USA; they depend on word of mouth for some purchases such as appliances. Generally speaking, Indian customers appear to be less passive, willing to exercise their rights and redress grievances. However, low literacy is certainly a significant factor in many situations, such as in making habitual purchases, with little search unless told by someone, or in evaluating weight, price, date, and other symbolic information. In fact, when having no formal education, little experience, and low income, the low-literate Indian customer resembles the low-literate US customer at the lowest level of literacy. There may also be less stigma attached with being low-literate or poor in India when compared to the USA. As mentioned, this discussion of differences between India and the USA, although based on many years of field research, is speculative in nature.

1.10 Implications for Marketplace Literacy Education[18]

The research was invaluable in educating us on a wide range of issues. A striking issue is the complex social environment in which marketplace exchanges occur, with myriad one-to-one interactions. Individuals seek help from people on the street, develop relationships with shops, and engage in constant conversations with other buyers and sellers. Skills, such as communication through spoken language, verbal counting, or bargaining, develop through these interactions as well as through experience as vendors, despite low levels of literacy. Central to the development of any educational program is the need to leverage these existing skill sets in the social domain.

Another issue relates to buyers and sellers in the environment of one-to-one interactions being two sides of the same coin. This is in contrast to the customer to large corporation contexts in western countries. Skills associated with being a buyer versus a seller are mutually reinforcing. Although we found some sellers with little experience as buyers and buyers with no experience as sellers, learning how to assess the value of an exchange as a buyer can lead to learning how to provide value as a seller. Many individuals make a living by being sellers. Moreover, buyers and small sellers share similar life circumstances and learn from each other's roles about the marketplace at large through one-to-one interactions. Marketplace literacy education that addresses both sides of the exchange can capitalize on their mutually reinforcing nature.

[18] The material in Section 10 is reprinted with minor editing with permission from Elsevier from Viswanathan, Gajendiran, and Venkatesan (2007). This article was published in the International Journal of Educational Development (2007), doi:10.1016/j.ijedudev.2007.05.004, Viswanathan, M., S. Gajendiran, and R. Venkatesan, Understanding and enabling marketplace literacy in subsistence contexts: The development of a consumer and entrepreneurial literacy educational program in South India, Copyright Elsevier, 2007.

Another issue that was apparent from our research was the transformational effect that practical adult education in the marketplace realm could have on people. Some of the individuals we interviewed had practically no marketplace skills for much of their adult lives. Yet, the effect of enrolling in an adult literacy program that addressed the customer realm was extraordinary, in enabling self-confidence, leading to bargaining, switching, questioning shopkeepers, and so on. The low-literate buyer described at the beginning of the chapter provides an excellent example of the transformational effect of adult literacy programs.

1.11 Conclusion

Our research provided insights into the individual and larger marketplace context, product and market interactions, and the development of consumer skills in the subsistence marketplaces we studied. Our research provided a basis for the development of a consumer and entrepreneurial literacy program in a number of ways. It provided a window into the strengths and vulnerabilities of subsistence customers and entrepreneurs, thus enabling us to design the program in terms of content and instructional methods. Perhaps most importantly, the research served to educate us on a variety of issues. Our approach of beginning with and constantly conducting research was motivated by the need to co-create the program with the participants rather than assume and impose a predetermined program based on our preconceptions. Chapter 2 describes how we developed the educational program.

Appendix: Overview of Issues Covered in Interviews

This listing is intended to illustrate the nature of issues covered. Rather than use the list in a structured form, the interview was a conversation where interviewers made an effort to cover the issues listed but were not constrained by them in terms of content or sequencing.

Sample of Questions and Sequencing for Buyer Interviews

Shopping

Describe your last trip to the grocery store:

- Why do you go to that store?
- What did you buy?
- What do you buy often?

What other stores do you go to?
How do you choose between buying from a large reseller versus a neighborhood retailer?
How do you shop for products? Describe how you decided to buy a specific product/ brand:
(Specific follow-up questions)

- Do you look for price?
- Do you look for other attributes?
- How do you abstract across price and size?
- How do you assess value?
- How do you assess quality?
- How do you assess customer service?
- How do you use numerical information on packages?
- What does MRP (maximum retail price) mean?

(Repeat process for packaged goods, cover multiple brands)
(Repeat process for various categories)

- Rice
- Cooking powders
- Soap
- Clothes
- Meat
- Vegetables
- Medicine/doctor
- Leisure – restaurant/theaters/television/festivals

How do you decide on making versus buying some of the products discussed?
How do you prepare a shopping list?
Describe a good bargain?
Describe the most expensive thing you bought?
Describe advertisements that you know of:
(Specific follow-up questions)

- Describe ones you like?
- Describe ones you dislike?
- Describe an advertisement that made you buy?
- What do you think of this ad (ad shown)?

Do you seek people's advice?:
(Specific follow-up questions)

- Do you seek the advice of your children?
- Do you seek the advice of your spouse?
- Do you seek the advice of others?

Budgeting

Provide details of monthly expenses.
Provide examples of situations without money.
Describe what you do when you run out of money.
Describe buying in installment. What is the quality of the product?
What is the interest you pay on loans?
Have you reneged on payments?
What are your unnecessary expenses?
What are your unanticipated expenses?
What are your ways of saving?

Attitude toward businesses

Are you treated differently?
Are you treated rudely? Please describe situations when you were treated badly.
Have you been cheated?
What are some things you do to protect yourself?
Describe others you know and problems they have faced (e.g., rudeness, cheating).
Describe any other experiences in shops that you can remember that you found interesting.
What could shops and advertisers do to make things easier for you?
What is your attitude toward foreign companies?
What is your attitude toward high technology?

Adapting

Name a product you are very knowledgeable about. How do you buy that product?
Name a product you are less knowledgeable about. How do you buy that product?
How do you decide to buy products?
Do you change how you decide depending on what you buy? How?
How did you learn to decide?
Give examples of bad decisions and how they helped you learn.

Literacy

What are some things about your own skills that frustrate you when shopping?
Have you taken an adult education class? How has it helped?
How has your shopping improved?
Provide an example of a bad decision. What did you learn?

Local NGO

Compare the NGO to a bank in terms of financial services.
What does it do well?
What can it do better?
Why do some people not participate and benefit from its services?

References

Coleman, J. S. (1988). Social capital in the creation of human capital. *American Journal of Sociology*, 94, Suppl., S95–S120.

Iyer, S., Kiston, M., and Toh, B. (2005). Social capital, economic growth and regional development. *Regional Studies*, 39, 1015–1040.

Kranton, R. E. (1996). Reciprocal exchange: A self-sustaining system. *The American Economic Review*, 86, 830–851.

Maslow, A. (1970). *Motivation and Personality*. New York: Harper & Row.

Michaels, J. W. and Wiggins, J. A. (1976). Effects of mutual dependency asymmetry on social exchange. *Sociometry*, 39, 368–376.

Molm, L. D. (1994). Dependence and risk: Transforming the structure of social exchange in the eye of the beholder. *Social Psychology Quarterly*, 57(3), 163–176.

Molm, L. D. (2001). Theories of social exchange and exchange networks. In: G. Ritzer and B. Smart (eds.), *The Handbook of Social Theory*. London: Sage.

Rutherford, S. (2000). *The Poor and Their Money*. New Delhi: OUP.

Strauss, A. and Cobin, J. (1998). Basics of qualitative research: Techniques and procedures for developing grounded theory, Beverly Hills, CA: Sage.

Viswanathan, M., Rosa, J. and Harris, J. (2005). Decision making and coping of functionally illiterate consumers and some implications for marketing management. *Journal of Marketing*, 69(1), 15–31.

Chapter 2
Developing a Consumer and Entrepreneurial Literacy Educational Program

This chapter outlines the development of a consumer and entrepreneurial literacy education program based on the research described in Chapter 1. We describe the need for such a program, and the philosophical orientation, content, and instructional methods, relevant to the development of the program. The details of the 5-day educational program are presented. Piloting, implementation and assessment of the program to date are discussed.

2.1 Overview

Business education offers low-literate, low-income individuals a way up economically and can enhance the economic well-being of poor communities. Whereas microfinancing and vocational literacy have been emphasized in recent decades, our emphasis on generic consumer and entrepreneurial literacy supplements these very important efforts in the economic realm and addresses a central need. Some organizations provide adult education that helps individuals to develop consumer skills. Such adult education focuses on basic reading and counting skills as well as day-to-day functional skills that individuals need in their roles as customers. Through techniques such as role-playing, adult education tends to be very functional and of immediate use to participants. Our research suggests that such classes can be transformational experiences that open the door to an altogether different existence where individuals are aware of their rights as customers, willing to bargain and argue, and willing to take action against unfair practices. Some organizations also provide training to individuals to start very small businesses. Topics covered include understanding costs, understanding product design, making safe and clean products, packaging, delivering customer service, and determining fair pricing. Such training empowers individuals to explore options for starting a business and gives them the confidence and basic skill sets to be successful.

Individuals are faced with at least three barriers to starting a business: (1) intellectual, relating to the skills needed to run a business successfully; (2) psychological, which prevents them from contemplating the possibility of starting a business or having the confidence to pursue such a venture; and (3) financial. Our research on low-literate, low-income buyers and sellers provided a basis for developing an educational program that will help individuals overcome the first two barriers. By providing insight into the unique issues that customers and sellers face in a developing context, the research provided a basis to translate generic business principles into educational materials and guidelines for an educational program.

2.2 Development of the Consumer and Entrepreneurial Literacy Educational Program[1]

In 2003, using the research as a basis, our team which combined over three decades of experiences in social service organizations and two decades of experience with business research and education, developed a curriculum for an educational program in entrepreneurial and consumer literacy for low-literate, low-income individuals. The curriculum grew out of extensive discussions of learning goals, content to be covered, and methods for conveying the content. We drew from experience in business education, vast experience in developmental work in low-income communities, and our extensive research.

2.2.1 Overview of Program Development

The method employed here in the development of an educational program involved several phases. In the first phase, an analysis of a small sample of existing educational materials and educational programs for both customers and sellers was undertaken.[2] The aim here was to assess existing programs and identify key issues. In the second phase, the educational program and materials were developed, essentially by customizing generic business principles from contemporary education and generating new educational material that fit the unique context using our research as a basis. This phase involved the translation of generic business principles into a form that can be employed in educational programs. Rather than a one size (of business education) fits all (contexts) approach, the aim here was to combine business principles with localized research, an approach very much in tune with reality. Such an approach allows for modifications and extensions of existing business principles as well as the development of new business principles. The third phase involves assessing these educational materials and guidelines by running educational programs, and making

[1] The material in Sections 2, 3, 4.1, and 4.2 is reprinted with minor editing with permission from Elsevier from Viswanathan, Gajendiran, and Venkatesan (2007). This article was published in the International Journal of Educational Development (2007), doi:10.1016/j.ijedudev.2007.05.004, Viswanathan, M., S. Gajendiran, and R. Venkatesan, Understanding and enabling marketplace literacy in subsistence contexts: The development of a consumer and entrepreneurial literacy educational program in South India, Copyright Elsevier, 2007.

[2] Although our focus is on entrepreneurial education for low-literate, low-income individuals, the literature on entrepreneurial education aimed toward somewhat higher levels of literacy in developing contexts is noteworthy (e.g., Nelson and Johnson, 1997).

further modifications as needed. In this phase, observations and discussions were used to gauge responses to aspects of educational materials and guidelines that were developed. Follow-up sessions a few months later were used to evaluate the impact of the educational program on people's experiences as buyers and sellers.

The process of developing the educational curriculum and materials began with a year of interviews of buyers and sellers. This data provided a rich basis, in terms of concepts as well as concrete examples. In terms of curriculum development, four levels were considered ranging from learning goals, topics, methods of teaching, and instructional material. Learning goals referred to very broad educational objectives of professionalism and ethics, marketplace literacy, consumer literacy, and entrepreneurial literacy. Topics within these learning goals were listed in details. For example, entrepreneurial literacy covered broad areas such as the basics of exchanges, philosophies for conducting a business, specific functions within business (such as marketing and finance), and sub-functions (such as product design, pricing, promotion, and distribution within marketing). Through top-down listing of topics and concepts and bottom-up considerations from data and experience, these levels were each explicated.

2.2.2 Issues in Program Development

Several issues needed to be taken into consideration, given our target audience. Discussion of specific concepts and their communication led to several insights, including issues of content and form. Concepts, such as segmentation, need to be modified and conveyed at a concrete level to enable the audience to relate to them. The aim was not to convey a concept for its own sake as much as to convey useful, understandable concepts. Pedagogical methods need to be innovative, combining songs and games and transferring home management skills to management elsewhere. Personal/family situations have to be taken into consideration. Individuals who typically live in the same neighborhood and go through the educational program together may be members of a self-help group or could potentially form a group that provides a sample set of customers, word-of-mouth, and a source of ideas. The self-help group formed from individuals could also be used as a financial resource or as a source for potential business partners.

Concepts and their presentation have to be tempered by the practical constraints faced by individuals. For instance, individuals may live in the here and now and focus on a skill they possess that they may have acquired growing up. However, the key to our educational program was to broaden their approach to consider other possibilities, such as variations in product offerings or location. Shifting thinking from the very specific and immediate to the somewhat less specific, more general, through the iterative process of covering business concepts and examples is the educational goal. Low literacy leads to living in the here and now, the immediate, and thinking in situational, concrete, graphic terms. Notions and abstractions have to be introduced carefully to broaden situational thinking incrementally.

This exercise in curriculum development also required filtering business education to its very essence to convey the core topics, and perhaps, more importantly, the approaches to thinking in the domain of the marketplace in general.

Communication among team members, each with their unique experiences, in itself was a microcosm of the educational program and an important source of learning. We developed a thorough list of topics from the data, representing a bottom-up approach. We took a sequential approach to covering topics, beginning with Day 1 of a possible educational program. Whereas our 4-tiered model of learning goals, topics, methods of teaching, and instructional material applied to our thinking, the educational program itself was developed in chronological sequence. The iterative process of matching bottom-up and top-down approaches was followed.

2.2.3 Content of the Educational Program

We developed a 5-day educational program that covered entrepreneurial and consumer literacy. Our philosophical orientation was to enable participants to learn how to learn and create their own opportunities. Our 5-day educational program uses teaching methods, such as picture sorting, group discussion, and role-playing, and assumes that the typical participant cannot read or write. Day 1 focuses on marketplace exchanges. We cover the process of exchange and its evolution over time and how value is added in multiple exchanges along a value chain from production of products to consumption. The importance of serving customer needs in order to succeed in a business as well as notions of goods, services, and segments are covered in the first day. On Day 2, participants assume the role of customers. We focus on consumer literacy by using simulated shopping environments with common "traps" identified in our research as being issues that low literate customers are vulnerable to. We use the notion of value for a product as the guiding concept to communicate the importance of informed consumer behavior. On Days 3–5, participants assume the role of sellers. We emphasize a customer-oriented philosophy of doing business that makes a profit on the basis of satisfying customer needs and providing a valuable product. This orientation flows from the customer orientation of Day 2 and the importance of value in a product. Starting with a discussion of business philosophies, the material moves to a customer focus. Following through on a customer-oriented business philosophy, the next step is to begin to understand the customer need to be served. The notion of a segment represents some summary description of a group of customers to focus on. A situational definition, such as people who live nearby, has to be expanded to an improved understanding of who the customers are, what describes them, and what their needs are. Such expansion of individual instances can lead to broader understanding of segments and more specific descriptions of customers, thus enabling appropriate actions.

We start out with a discussion of how business opportunities can be evaluated based on customer needs served, competitors, and strengths and weaknesses of individual entrepreneurs. We cover several specific areas of business such as production and product design, distribution and management of the supply chain, pricing and related financial issues, and promotion. We end the program with a discussion of ethics and the need to balance societal concerns with profit making and customer needs.

2.3 The 5-Day Educational Program

Day 1 was planned to first facilitate participants being comfortable and then discuss and clarify expectations. Key issues addressed here include the nature of the program, to provide generic consumer and entrepreneurial literacy rather than specific trade skills. This was followed by covering the basics of marketplace exchanges. Various concepts were conveyed through discussion, exercises and games, rather than lectures. The evolution of technologies, products, and transactions over time was an important topic for the first day, such as transactions evolving from barter to currency to various forms of credit. This discussion highlighted the centrality of finding a demand and serving it better than the competition. Also, the notion of a value chain as comprising of multiple exchanges was introduced. One task in particular is illustrative, involving a number of pictures relevant to a specific value chain (say, a farmer growing fruits, through wholesalers, retailers and customers) along with a picture of money. Participants were asked to place the pictures on a chart with concentric circles, placing the most important picture in the middle and so on. Often, participants placed money at the center. When this task is repeated on the third day, most participants place the customer at the center, emphasizing the importance of satisfying customer needs to run a business.

On Day 2, participants take on the role of customers. The overriding concept on day 2 is that of the value of an exchange in terms of what is given versus got and the need to make informed choices. Simulated shops and role-playing by instructors were used to "cheat" participants or to recreate consumer-related activities where they may commit mistakes. The tasks were carefully designed to reflect pitfalls for customers. Our previous research identified a host of issues, which we cover here. A quiz in which stimuli are recorded statements covering different situations faced by customers was used to cover various issues. These issues include bargaining, weighing, buying wholesale versus retail, making versus buying, saving, understanding interest rates, switching stores and questioning sellers, being aware of rights, understanding discounts, paying in installment versus cash, checking prices and totals, planning purchases and preparing shopping lists, checking expiry on packages, and understanding MRP (maximum retail price).

From Day 3 onward, participants take on the role of a seller. An issue covered is identifying and evaluating a business opportunity through a relative assessment of one's own strengths and weaknesses, and competitors' strengths and weaknesses, in light of the customer needs to be addressed. Emphasized here is the need to carefully evaluate a business opportunity and work through it before committing to it. Another central issue covered is the basic business philosophy of being customer-oriented and engaging in mutually beneficial exchanges as a means of making a profit. Different philosophies are covered here to highlight distinctions, such as a focus purely on selling or on production without attention to customer needs. These two broader issues set the stage for a discussion of more specific issues. The notion of customer segments is an issue covered followed by a general introduction to consumer behavior in terms of steps in decision-making, such as need recognition, search for alternatives, and evaluation of alternatives, and the various influences on customer decision-making.

The next topic covered is information gathering and research. The importance of carefully collecting and evaluating information is emphasized. Included here are ways of gathering information, such as through talking to people, observing the competition, conducting an analysis of costs, getting feedback on specific ideas, and so on. Also covered here are some basic issues in asking questions when gathering information, such as planning questions to ask beforehand, avoiding leading questions and attempting to obtain an accurate picture. A role-play is used to bring out these issues. The importance of asking oneself tough questions and looking for accurate information is emphasized.

The next major topic covered is product design. Here, some basics such as what a product is and what customers look for in specific products is covered. A purpose here is to understand how physical product characteristics and ingredients translate to psychological benefits to customers. Also important here is the abstract benefit being served rather than the physical product itself. The distinction between goods and services is also brought out here. The importance of packaging to preserve the product and provide an attractive exterior is also covered. Exercises are used where participant-groups choose a product and decide on its design.

Distribution is covered by using the concept of a value-chain introduced on Day 1. Again, participant groups are asked to work with a particular product and work out various steps in the value chain from purchase of ingredients to distribution to wholesalers, retailers, and the end user. Exercises ask participants to choose from distribution alternatives. Factors to consider when setting price, the notion of value from the customer's perspective, the relationship between price and quality, and the relationship between price and volume are covered under pricing. Different types of promotions ranging from banner advertisements to fliers are discussed and related to different objectives, such as gaining awareness, generating interest, and encouraging purchase.

A number of miscellaneous issues are covered on the final day including the importance of sustainable consumption and production and the basics of accounting and finance. Ethical issues in business are discussed within the broader philosophy of balancing seller and buyer needs with societal good.

2.4 Implementation and Assessment of the Educational Program

2.4.1 *Piloting*

This program was piloted in June, 2003, and was an outstanding success, judging from feedback from participants. One task mentioned earlier reflects the learning that occured. On the first day, we gave participants a picture-sorting task with pictures representing several stages in a specific value chain by depicting farmers, retail outlets for food, and customers, and a picture of money. When asked to place the most important element at the center, most chose to place money. By the third day, the same groups placed the customer at the center, fully realizing the importance of customer needs and a customer orientation. This is a central aspect of the program, with much of the content being organized around the need to be customer oriented. We conducted a second program in January 2004 after modifying our pilot effort from summer of 2003. This educational program was also very effective, judging from the feedback from participants.

2.4.2 *Qualitative Assessment and Customization*

We conducted a follow-up session with participants we had trained in the summer of 2003, in our pilot effort. The feedback was overwhelmingly positive. All participants reported making considerable savings as customers and grouping their resources to buy staples, such as rice, wholesale. For instance, they reported collective savings of thousands of rupees by buying rice in this manner. About five participants of the group reported having started small businesses. Participants reported conveying the essence of the program to many others in their neighborhoods.

We also conducted a 5-day program in a rural setting in March, 2004, enabling us to customize our program to such a context. In July, 2004, we conducted follow-up sessions for groups trained in January, 2004, and in March, 2004, and once again found overwhelmingly positive results. For instance, the group of 20 women trained in a village in March reported being identified as women who have participated in the educational program by shopkeepers and receiving better treatment as customers. They reported savings of Rs. 100–200 per month, with several women reporting that they took over primary shopping responsibilities from their husbands. About 4–5 individuals in each group who attend the program report either starting a new business or expanding an existing business, while many others were open to considering this option subsequent to participation in the educational program. In August, 2004, we successfully conducted a 5-day program in an urban area specifically chosen because it was considered a challenge and a problem area in a variety of ways.

In parallel, documenting the details in drafts of a manual provided another way of evaluating the program. The process of articulating the details and the rationale led to revisions in the educational program, as did ongoing basic research, which continued in 2004 through additional qualitative interviews. Our record of attendance has been near perfect in all the programs conducted to date, reflecting the interest level of the participants. For example, through all the problems that participants in our 5-day programs faced including water shortage and illnesses in the family, they spent a total of 40 hours or more over a 5-day period dedicated to learning.

Our efforts to improve the educational program and its documentation will be ongoing. We offer the program at regular intervals to enable such assessment and improvement. We provide a different configuration of a 1-day marketplace and consumer literacy program and a 2-day entrepreneurial literacy program, as well as a combined 2-day marketplace, consumer and entrepreneurial literacy program, reflecting the flexibility of content developed here. Additionally, our experiences have ranged from demonstrating the program to nonprofit organizations to working with a large organization in India to scale the program to reach many participants as outlined in Chapter 8, providing a customized program to train entrepreneurs who run computer kiosks in semi-rural areas as sustainable businesses, and exploring ways to customize our program to other countries and contexts.

2.4.3 Quantitative Assessment

We are currently implementing quantitative assessments of the consumer and entrepreneurial literacy program. Our approach has been to personally administer pre-program surveys to participants a few days before the program, and repeat the survey some time (one or more months) after delivering the program. For these purposes, we offer a 1-day marketplace/consumer literacy program (combining the first two days of the program described earlier) or a 2-day entrepreneurial literacy program (combining the last three days of the program described earlier). Our data collection is ongoing, involving the marketplace and consumer literacy program and the entrepreneurial literacy program.

One version of our survey presented in the Appendix consists of questions about shopping behavior, such as outlets from which purchases are made and prices paid for categories of products, and self-reports of skill and confidence in a variety of arenas as buyers (Part III) and sellers (Part VI), administered before (pre-survey) and after (post-survey) the program. An additional set of self-reports in the post-survey assesses how much individual skills or confidence improved over time (Part IV for marketplace/consumer literacy and Part VII for entrepreneurial literacy).

We report the results of two phases of data collection with 66 and 95 participants who completed a survey one day to five weeks before participating in a 1-day marketplace/consumer literacy program and then completed a survey 1–6 months later. We specifically focus on responses to skills and confidence (Part III). For the phase of data collection involving 66 participants, we used a different version of the survey than the one shown in the Appendix, wherein responses were collected on the same aspects of buyer interactions with the marketplace shown in the survey but combined across skills and confidence. Significantly or marginally significantly higher ratings were found for skills and confidence on almost all aspects of buyer interactions with the marketplace.

For the phase of data collection involving 95 participants, we used a version of the survey shown in the Appendix wherein responses were collected on the same aspects of buyer interactions with the marketplace (Part III) along with self-reports of improvement because of the program (Part IV). Our results suggest that self-reports of improvement (Part IV) are very high for all aspects of skill and confidence – 6 or above on a scale of 1 (no change) to 7 (very big improvement). Moreover, mean ratings of skill and confidence on almost all aspects of buyer interactions with the marketplace were directionally higher and ratings on a number of aspects were significantly higher after when compared to before the program. Significantly or marginally significantly higher ratings were found for skills in planning purchases, bargaining, checking prices on packages, understanding MRP, buying without wasting time, demanding promotions, returning defective products, checking for fake brands, checking guarantees and warranties, being aware of consumer rights, evaluating marketing communications, understanding price–quality relationships, understanding instructions for products, understanding interest rates, totaling bills, and switching shops. Significantly or marginally significantly higher ratings were found for confidence in understanding MRP, buying without wasting time, checking for fake brands, being aware of consumer rights, evaluating marketing communications, understanding price–quality relationships, understanding instructions for products, and understanding interest rates. Our quantitative assessments are in progress and detailed results will be available at www.marketplaceliteracy.org and through research articles.

2.5 Conclusion

The development of our educational program was based on several sources including basic research, experience with generic business education, and grassroots experience in development work. Curriculum development led to the actual design of the content and instructional approaches for the program. Pilot testing and qualitative assessment was followed by customization in urban and rural contexts. Quantitative assessment is currently in progress. Over the past few years, we have constantly learned by offering the program and adjusting it. In the next few chapters, the actual details of the program are presented. The organization assumes a 5-day configuration for ease of presentation, although we have experimented with a variety of shorter programs.

Appendix: Sample Preliminary Version of Pre- and Post-Program Interviews Used after Translation into Tamil

I Personal Details

1. Date ....
2. Respondent's name ....
3. Occupation

   (a) Housewife
   (b) Housemaid
   (c) Street vending
   (d) Petty shop
   (e) Employment in private establishment
   (f) Employment in government

(g) Farming
(h) Other goods
(i) Other services
(j) Unemployed
(k) Other (specify) . . . .

4. Your individual income Rs. . . . .
5. Your total household income Rs. . . . .
6. Family size . . . .

II Buyer Details

1. Where do you buy rice?

(a) Supplier to house
(b) Ration shop
(c) Retail shop
(d) Wholesale shop
(e) Other (specify). . . . .

2. What is the frequency with which you buy rice?

(a) Daily
(b) Weekly
(c) Fortnightly
(d) Monthly
(e) Other (specify) . . . .
(f) No pattern

3. What is the price you pay for rice?

Rs. . . . . for quantity . . . .

4. Where do you buy vegetables?

(a) Street vendor
(b) Corner retail shop
(c) Large reseller
(d) Wholesale market
(e) Other (specify) . . . .

5. What is the frequency with which you buy vegetables?

(a) Daily
(b) Once in 2 days
(c) Weekly
(d) Fortnightly
(e) Monthly
(f) Other (specify) . . . .
(g) No pattern

6. Indicate three vegetables you buy the most

   (a) Onion
   (b) Tomato
   (c) Brinjal
   (d) Potato
   (e) Carrot
   (f) Banana
   (g) Drumstick
   (h) Ladies finger (Okra)
   (i) Beetroot
   (j) Bitter gourd
   (k) Cluster beans

7. What is the price you pay for vegetables?
   (Choose a suitable time frame and amount of vegetables to provide your answer)

Name of vegetable	**Daily**	**Weekly**	**Amount**
1.	Rs.	Rs.	. . . . . .
2.	Rs.	Rs.	. . . . . .
3.	Rs.	Rs.	. . . . . .

8. Where do you buy hygiene and cosmetic products?

[(1) Corner retail shop; (2) Large reseller; (3) Street vendor; (4) Other (specify)]

   (a) Soap . . . .
   (b) Detergent . . . .
   (c) Toothpaste . . . .
   (d) Powder (face) . . . .
   (e) Hair oil . . . .
   (f) Shampoo . . . .

9. What is the frequency with which you buy hygiene and cosmetic products?

[1 Daily; 2 Weekly; 3 Fortnightly; 4 Monthly'; 5 Other (specify); 6 No pattern]

   (a) Soap . . . .
   (b) Detergent . . . .
   (c) Toothpaste . . . .
   (d) Powder . . . .
   (e) Hair oil . . . .
   (f) Shampoo . . . .

10. What is the price you pay for hygiene and cosmetic products in a month (specify amount)

    (a) Soap Rs. . . . .
    (b) Detergent Rs. . . . .
    (c) Toothpaste Rs. . . . .

(d) Powder Rs. . . . .
(e) Hair oil Rs. . . . .
(f) Shampoo Rs. . . . .

11. What brand name of hygiene and cosmetic products do you buy most often?

(a) Soap . . . .
(b) Detergent . . . .
(c) Toothpaste . . . .
(d) Powder . . . .
(e) Hair oil . . . .
(f) Shampoo . . . .

12. Where do you buy each of the following provisions (groceries)?

[(1) Corner retail shop; (2) Large reseller; (3) Street vendor; (4) Other (specify)]

(a) Dhal (lentils) . . . .
(b) Chili . . . .
(c) Coriander . . . .
(d) Oil . . . .
(e) Mustard seeds, garlic, etc. . . . .

13. How often do you buy each of the provisions?

[(1) Daily; (2) Weekly; (3) Fortnightly; (4) Monthly; (5) Other (specify); (6) No pattern]

(a) Dhal (lentils) . . . .
(b) Chili . . . .
(c) Coriander . . . .
(d) Oil . . . .
(e) Mustard seeds, garlic, etc. . . . .

14. What is the average price you paid for each of the following provisions in the last month?

(a) Dhal (lentils) . . . .
(b) Chili . . . .
(c) Coriander . . . .
(d) Oil . . . .
(e) Mustard seeds, garlic, etc. . . . .

15. What are the products in the list below that you make at home?

(a) Idli (steamed rice cake – a snack item) powder
(b) Chili powder
(c) Coriander powder
(d) Wheat powder
(e) Turmeric powder
(f) Pepper powder
(g) Idli batter

(h) Rice powder
(i) Curd (yogurt)

16. Where do you buy clothes?

(a) Installment seller
(b) Platform (sidewalk) shops
(c) Retail shops
(d) Large textile shops
(e) Wholesale mandis (bazaars)
(f) Other (specify) . . . .

17. What do you use for cooking?

(a) Firewood
(b) Kerosene stove
(c) LPG stove
(d) Electric stove
(e) Other (specify). . . . .

18. What is the monthly average price you pay for cooking material (specify time frame)?
Rs. . . . .

19. Do you take loans? If yes, from where?
(a) Yes
(b) No

Source	**Amount of loan**	**Time frame**	**Interest**
Relatives	. . . .	. . . .	. . . .
Local moneylender	. . . .	. . . .	. . . .
Self-help groups	. . . .	. . . .	. . . .
Private banks	. . . .	. . . .	. . . .
National banks	. . . .	. . . .	. . . .
Other (specify)	. . . .	. . . .	. . . .

20. What is your monthly savings?

Source	**Mode**	**Amount**
No savings		
Relatives	. . . .	. . . .
Local shops	. . . .	. . . .
Self-help groups	. . . .	. . . .
Private chits	. . . .	. . . .
Banks	. . . .	. . . .
Other (specify)	. . . .	. . . .

21. What is your monthly budget for each of the following items?

    (a) Rice Rs. . . . .
    (b) Vegetables Rs. . . . .
    (c) Cosmetics Rs. . . . .
    (d) Provisions Rs. . . . .
    (e) Clothes Rs. . . . .
    (f) Fuels Rs. . . . .
    (g) Medical treatment Rs. . . . .
    (h) Principal and interest on loans Rs. . . . .

III (a) Skills as a Buyer – Marketplace and Consumer Literacy Program Only

Please use the 7-point scale and rate your level of skill on the following attributes:

Poor 1 2 3 4 5 6 7 Excellent

←——————————→

Rate your skill
[Scale 1–7]

S.No.	Attributes	Rating
1	Planning purchases	
2	Making lists	
3	Bargaining	
4	Checking price in several stores	
5	Checking product before purchase	
6	Checking price on package	
7	Checking quality	
8	Judging price and size	
9	Buying correct amounts	
10	Checking weight	
11	Understanding MRP	
12	Buying without wasting time	
13	Demanding promotions (free gift, etc.)	
14	Returning defective products	
15	Verifying expiry date	
16	Checking for fake brands	
17	Seeking advice on products	
18	Checking guarantees and warranties	
19	Being aware of consumer rights	
20	Taking care of health needs	
21	Evaluating marketing communications	
22	Weighing "get" versus "give"	
23	Understanding price–quality relationships	
24	Understanding instructions for products	
25	Asking for a bill	
26	Understanding interest rates	

S.No.	Attributes	Rating
27	Totaling bills	
28	Switching shops	
29	Buying wholesale versus retail	

III (b) Confidence as a Buyer – Marketplace and Consumer Literacy Program Only

Please use the 7-point scale and rate your level of confidence on the following attributes:

Poor 1 2 3 4 5 6 7 Excellent

Rate your confidence
[Scale 1–7]

Repeat of same attributes as in III a.

IV (a) Improvement in Skills as a Buyer – Marketplace and Consumer Literacy Program and Post-Survey Only

Please use the 7-point scale and rate the level of improvement in your skills in each of the following attributes after attending the educational program:

No change 1 2 3 4 5 6 7 Very big improvement

Rate your skill
[Scale 1–7]

Repeat of same attributes as in III a.

IV (b) Improvement in Confidence as a Buyer – Marketplace and Consumer Literacy Program and Post-Survey Only

Please use the 7-point scale and rate the level of improvement in your confidence in each of the following attributes after attending the educational program:

No change 1 2 3 4 5 6 7 Very big improvement

Rate your confidence

[Scale 1–7]

Repeat of same attributes as in III a.

V Seller Details – Entrepreneurial Literacy Program Only

1. Type of business . . . .
2. Where do you buy raw materials/goods?

   (a) From producers
   (b) Local/Retail shop
   (c) Wholesale shop
   (d) Other (specify) . . . .

3. What is the frequency with which you buy raw materials/goods?

   (a) Daily
   (b) Weekly
   (c) Fortnightly
   (d) Monthly
   (e) Other (specify) . . . .
   (f) No pattern

4. What is the approximate cost of material per month (specify amount)? Rs. . . . .
5. Where do you sell your product?

   (a) Mobile vending
   (b) Mobile and shop
   (c) Shop
   (d) House
   (e) Other (specify) . . . .

6. What is the approximate number of customers you serve in a week (choose a different time frame if necessary)?
   . . . .
7. What is your investment? (Choose a suitable time frame) Rs. . . . .
8. What is your revenue? (Choose a suitable time frame) Rs. . . . .
9. What is your profit? (Choose a suitable time frame)

   (a) Daily Rs. . . . .
   (b) Weekly Rs. . . . .
   (c) Monthly Rs. . . . .

VI (a) Skills as a Seller – Entrepreneurial Literacy Program Only

Please use the 7-point scale and rate your level of skill on the following attributes:

Poor 1 2 3 4 5 6 7 Excellent

← →

Skill only

S. No.	Attributes	Rating
1	Choosing a business	
2	Orienting around the customer	
3	Serving customer needs	
4	Designing products	
5	Pricing products	
6	Distributing products	
7	Promoting products, e.g., advertising	
8	Competing with other businesses	
9	Providing valuable exchanges	
10	Providing quality products	
11	Assessing competition	
12	Assessing business opportunities	
13	Gathering information about the market (i.e., market research)	
14	Understanding how consumers make decisions	
15	Understanding customer behavior	
16	Understanding personal selling	
17	Understanding costs	
18	Understanding accounting	
19	Understanding finances	
20	Engaging in ethical practices	
21	Establishing trust with consumers	
22	Managing conflicts	
23	Using techniques to create awareness for product	
24	Using techniques to encourage product trial	
25	Using techniques to increase customer knowledge about product	
26	Understanding how markets work?	
27	Understanding how products move from production to consumption?	
28	Understanding different customer groups	
29	Understanding value	
30	Understanding how needs evolved over time?	
31	Understanding the role of exchange in an economy	

VI (b) Confidence as a Seller – Entrepreneurial Literacy Program Only

Please use the 7-point scale and rate your level of confidence on the following attributes:

Poor 1 2 3 4 5 6 7 Excellent

←——————————→

Confidence only

Repeat of same attributes as in VI a.

VII (a) Improvement in Skills as a Seller – Entrepreneurial Literacy Program and Post-Survey Only

Please use the 7-point scale and rate the level of improvement in your skill in each of the following attributes after attending the educational program:

No change 1 2 3 4 5 6 7 Very big improvement

←――――――――→

Skill only

Repeat of same attributes as in VI a.

VII (b) Improvement in Confidence as a Seller – Entrepreneurial Literacy Program and Post-Survey Only

Please use the 7-point scale and rate the level of improvement in your confidence in each of the following attributes after attending the educational program:

No change 1 2 3 4 5 6 7 Very big improvement

←――――――――→

Confidence only

Repeat of same attributes as in VI a.

VIII Open-Ended Questions

Sample open-ended questions

1. What is the meaning of MRP?
2. What is the price of rice at wholesale versus retail currently?
3. Did you make a shopping list before your most recent purchases?

Reference

Nelson, R. E. and Johnson, S. D. (1997). Entrepreneurship education as a strategic approach to economic growth in Kenya. *Journal of Industrial Teacher Education*, 35(1), 7–21.

Chapter 3
Consumer and Entrepreneurial Literacy Program – Marketplace Literacy

3.1 Introduction

Day 1 focuses on marketplace exchanges. We cover the concept of a value chain from production to consumption. Day 1 begins by facilitating participants to be comfortable in a new learning environment, and then discussing and clarifying expectations. Key issues addressed here include the nature of the program, providing generic consumer and entrepreneurial literacy rather than specific trade skills. This is followed by covering the basics of marketplace exchanges. Various concepts are conveyed through discussions, exercises, and games, rather than lectures. How exchanges have evolved over time is an important topic for the first day, such as transactions evolving from barter to currency to various forms of credit. This discussion highlights the centrality of finding a demand and serving it better than the competition. The notion of a value chain as comprising multiple exchanges is also introduced. As mentioned earlier, one task in particular is illustrative, and involves a number of pictures relevant to a value chain (say, a farmer growing fruits through wholesaler and retailer to a customer) along with a picture of money. Participants are asked to place the pictures on a chart with concentric circles, placing the most important picture in the middle. Often, participants place money at the center. When this task is repeated on the third day, most participants place the customer at the center, emphasizing the importance of satisfying customer needs to run a business.

3.2 Introductory Activities

3.2.1 Registration & Welcoming of Participants

Participants are asked to register for the program by providing their names and other details. A welcome address or any formal inaugural address depending on the local circumstances may precede registration. Stakeholders of the educational program, such as conductors, organizers, facilitators, and instructors, are introduced to the participants. Once the instructors assume charge, they should discuss the ground rules of the educational program in consultation with the participants for effective participation. The following are few suggestive but not exhaustive rules on the rights and responsibilities of the entire team, before beginning the educational program:

- Freedom to express views and opinions and seek clarifications
- Time management and adherence to schedules
- Need for participation through the day and through the program
- Mutual respect in all interactions

Issues such as timings and logistic arrangements should be finalized in consultation with participants.

3.2.2 Ice-Breaking Exercise

3.2.2.1 Objective

Relaxation and stress reduction to enable active participation in the educational program.

3.2.2.2 Rationale

Participating in educational programs may be new to many participants. Factors such as low income, literacy level, age of participants, educational method, and environment may inhibit participants from socialization or active participation. Identifying other participants and introducing them through a game rather than simple self-introduction appears to be an effective ice-breaking exercise.

3.2.2.3 Input or Materials Required

- A small plastic box
- Passport-size pictures of objects

The total number of pictures should be equal to the number of participants. A picture should reasonably link with another picture, such as a flower and a garland, a needle and thread, or a matchbox and a candle. Participants should be familiar with the pictures used. Pictures and their linkages could ideally be from the economic realm to cue the content and topic of the educational program that follows (Figure 1).

3.2.2.4 Process

Each picture is folded and placed in a box. The box is placed on a table in the center of the classroom or wherever it is comfortable for participants to select pictures. Participants are asked to form a circle and listen to the instructions carefully. Each

Sample pictures

KEY

LOCK

Listing of sample items

1.	Flower	&	Garland
2.	Book	&	Pen
3.	Lemon	&	Pickle
4.	Candle	&	Match Box
5.	Rainy Cloud	&	Umbrella
6.	Cow	&	Milk packet
7.	Weighing scale	&	Weights
8.	Egg	&	Hen
9.	Sewing machine	&	Scissors

Figure 1 Paired Pictures for Ice-breaking Exercise

participant should select one picture from the box. When all participants have selected a picture, they should pass the unfolded picture to another person and receive one from someone else without unfolding it. This should be repeated at least three times. Finally they should unfold and check the picture but not announce it to anyone. They should look for the person who is holding the related object (e.g., flower and garland). After finding the person holding the related object, they should find out about each other and prepare for their mutual introductions to the group.

3.2.2.5 Expected Outcomes

Participants have opportunities to move around the room and meet other participants when passing the picture. The task may also lead participants to start thinking about the picture-matching task. After beginning their search, they may find a related object that they may never have guessed. They may have to adjust or compromise with available alternatives. Using pictures with marketplace linkages may also lead participants to think about the content of the program. In the process of looking for the person with the matching picture, they may have the opportunity to meet with other participants. After finding the person with the matching picture, they may learn about their background. This exercise may enable the participants to prepare for active participation in the educational program and cope with its demands.

3.3 Discussion of Expectations

3.3.1 Objective

Aligning expectations of instructors and participants.

3.3.2 Process

The instructor should ask participants about their personal expectations from the educational program. The instructor should encourage participants to express themselves. Narrated expressions could be paraphrased and written on a chart. When issues are repeated, a continuous flow to the discussion can be maintained by refering to the list on the chart. The instructor should attempt to involve many participants in this exercise of sharing expectations. The issues raised could be grouped as being related to topics, such as entrepreneurial literacy, specific skill training, and resource identification. An aim here is also to help the instructor to learn about the types of participants and their priorities.

3.3.3 Expected Outcomes

The participants' expectations may include the following:

- How do marketplaces work?
- How should business be run profitably?
- How should competition be managed?
- How should business be run with profit or without loss?
- How can individuals be successful in business and earn profits?
- Can any technical skill be learned or acquired?
- How should the right business be selected?
- How should a business be run from one's home?
- How should products be sold?
- How should quality products be produced?
- How should capital be mobilized to run a business?

- How should the needs of customers be identified when running a business?
- What type of character and personality should a business person possess?
- How should suppliers of materials be identified?
- How should smooth relationships with customers be maintained?
- Which is preferable between a partnership and an individually owned business?
- How should the location of a business be selected?
- How can low-literate individuals manage a business?
- How should customer become well informed?
- How should customers bargain and buy products at good prices?
- How can customers avoid being cheated?

The instructor can group the list of these issues as suggested below:

Entrepreneurial literacy

- Example – How should business be run profitably?

Consumer literacy

- Example – How should customers become well-informed?

Marketplace literacy

- Example – How do marketplaces and markets work?

Specific skill training

- Example – Can any technical skill be learned or acquired?

Identifying resources

- How should sellers find informational resources for running a business?
- Which is preferable between a partnership and an individually owned business?

Personal(ity) development

- How should sellers learn to be professional?
- What is ethical behavior when running a business?
- How can low-literate individuals manage a business?
- How should customer relationships be developed and maintained?

The instructor should note that there are many things to learn from the participants and their experiences. The instructor should reiterate that the educational program is a forum for mutual learning by both the team of instructors and participants because it aims to discuss practices in the marketplace from the perspective of buyers and sellers. The participants should not, however, expect any skill training on specific trades or readymade solutions to address their individual problems.

The instructor should outline the proposed agenda/topics for discussion in the 5-day program and emphasize that participants utilize this opportunity. Further, the focus on

Day 1 should be clarified as being on the basics of marketplace exchanges, such as the process of exchange and the evolution of technologies, products and transactions over time, different types of products including goods and services, different customer segments, and value chains from production to consumption. On Day 2, participants assume the role of customers and the focus of the educational program is on consumer literacy. From Days 3 to 5, the participants assume the role of sellers and the focus is on a customer-oriented philosophy of doing business where sellers and buyers engage in mutually beneficial exchanges.

3.4 Prioritizing Elements of a Business

3.4.1 Exercise

Placing pictures within concentric circles based on their role and importance in the business.

3.4.2 Objective

Assessing how participants prioritize various elements of a business.

3.4.3 Input and Process

Materials to be used include four sets of pictures relating to fishing, flowers, rice, and clothing, and charts for display. Each set of pictures includes those of production, wholesale distribution, retail distribution, and consumer usage, as well as money/currency notes (Figure 2).

After forming groups consisting of 4–5 participants, each group can be provided with a set of pictures along with a chart that has the same number of concentric circles as pictures. Each set of pictures represents different elements of a specific value chain. Each group should be asked what the most important element is to start or sustain a successful business. Each group should be asked to discuss the pictures and place them in concentric circles on a chart, so that the most important object is placed in the innermost circle, and the remaining are in outer circles based on their order of importance to start or sustain a successful business. Finally, participants should be asked to present their conclusions to the class along with the rationale for the choices made during the task.

3.4.4 Outcomes

Each group should place pictures on the circles after discussion with their group members. Their presentation may reveal the understanding and rationale behind

Figure 2 Sample Pictures for Exercise on Prioritizing Elements of a Business

their decision to place those pictures. Usually, money, or in rarer instances, the product, is likely to be placed in the innermost circle. Other elements are generally given less importance and placed in outer circles.

These charts can be displayed and the antecedents and effects of each of the elements reviewed in subsequent sessions. Participants should be informed that the chart would be reviewed at the beginning of Day 3 as well as at the end of the educational program to reassess whether pictures could be replaced in a different order. In a 1-day version of a marketplace and consumer literacy program, this exercise should be explained after the subsequent exercise on evolution of needs.

3.5 Evolution of Technologies, Products, and Transactions

3.5.1 Exercise

Placing pictures in order, based on the evolution of technologies, products, and transactions (i.e., transactional methods).

3.5.2 Objective

Understanding the process of exchange and the evolution of technologies, products, and transactions over time.

3.5.3 Rationale

This exercise enables participants to understand basic business principles and the role of business in society. Sets of pictures related to goods and services can be used including one that shows the evolution of human life and another that shows the evolution of transactions. Here, participants are asked to compose their ideas about the pictures and provide a narrative based on their understanding.

3.5.4 Input and Process

The participants should be divided into 4–5-member groups and each group given a set of objects as listed below for illustrative purposes (Figure 3):

- A set of pictures of different transportation vehicles
- A set of pictures of different cooking devices
- A set of pictures that reflect different stages of human development over time
- A set of picture of different stages of evolution of transactions or transactional methods

Each group should be asked to arrange the pictures in order, according to their period or evolution, place them on a chart, and then present their narrative. As groups make their presentation, the instructor should encourage participants to identify the rationale for changes in technologies, products, or transactions through questions. Here, the instructor can facilitate understanding of needs and wants of individuals. The discussion could begin with the bullock cart, which was a basic form of transportation decades ago in India. But motorcars have become a necessity for transportation now. In fact, people are prevented by statute from using bullock carts in specific areas, such as cities. Today, bullock carts are not in regular use or have been abandoned.

Figure 3 Evolution of Technologies, Products, and Transactions

The discussion can move from bullock carts to cycles and then to automobiles, covering different stages of development. Goods or services that were previously wants may become needs. Innovation is inevitable in leading to the development of new goods or services that serve needs or wants. Finally, the

Figure 3 (continued)

discussion should conclude by noting that contemporary goods or services are subject to changes to suit the changing needs of users or customers. Even though progress in science and technology and financial resources are necessary for these changes to occur, specific products should satisfy customer needs to succeed in the marketplace. The potential for some confusion here is noteworthy. It should be emphasized that although technology and financial resources are important factors, goods and services that are developed with financial resources and technology succeed or fail based on the extent to which they serve customer needs in better ways. Technological changes that

Evolution of Transactional Methods

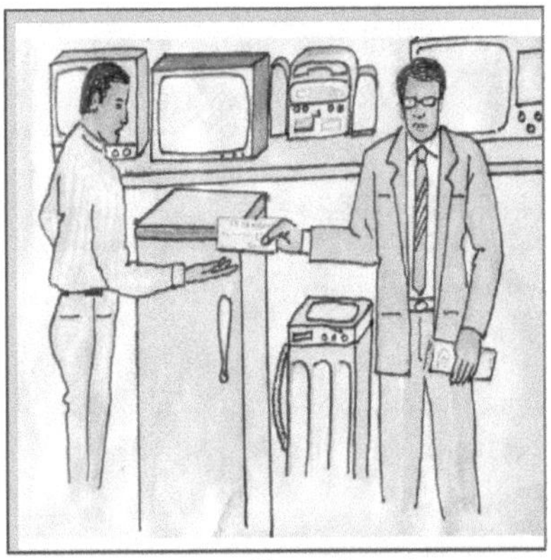

Using cheques or credit cards to buy products

Using coins to buy products

Using cash to buy products

Using products to buy products

Figure 3 (continued)

do not serve customer needs, such as additional, unnecessary features on a stove, can be used as examples to illustrate how changes need to serve customer needs better and be worth the additional costs if any.

The discussion can then turn to soliciting participants' responses about types of needs and how they are fulfilled. Examples, such as food and music, can be used to explore the issue further. This discussion should aim to enable the group to categorize needs in general into different types, such as physical needs and psychological needs.

The instructor should use questions, such as why people who used bullock carts shifted to motor vehicles, to lead the discussion. Typical responses from the participants may point to factors, such as technological improvement, wealth, and civilization.

The instructor should pose questions about innovations, such as the following:

- Was the innovation adopted solely to use modern equipment?
- Was the innovation adopted because it was new?
- Was the innovation adopted because customers had money and could afford to buy it?

Examples include switching to gas stoves from stone fire ovens. The aim is for participants to list out the rationale, such as the following, for switching over to new innovations:

- Convenience
- Safety and health
- Cost-effectiveness

The instructor should note than an innovation may not be adopted unless it provides benefits to the buyer when compared to competing products that serve the same need. Customers or users are not likely to adopt goods or service, just because of newness of innovation or technology. Goods and services in current use are not exempt from changes in the future. However, the nature of changes may be determined by a number of factors, such as technology.

A set of pictures about the "stages in the evolution of family life" of human beings placed in order on the chart can be used to elaborate about changes, covering the following questions:

- What goods and services were used by prehistoric human beings?
- How did the clan system evolve?
- How did governance originate?
- What were earlier family sizes?
- Why has the joint family system been replaced by the nuclear family system?
- How has specialization in production affected business?
- What is the relation between business and society?

For example, prehistoric humans:

- Hunted animals for survival
- Invented the wheel, which was the basis for many technological inventions
- Realized the need for group dwellings, learned to construct houses, and then established organized neighborhoods to live in safe and comfortable environments

Over time, individuals:

- Embarked on cultivation and produced specific farm products to meet demand
- Learned to exploit natural resources to benefit society which led to production of goods and increased interdependencies
- Engaged in exchange of goods through barter
- Specialized in specific occupations which led to specialists in fields and created more interdependencies, and new goods and services

Prehistoric humans used carcasses or the skin of dead animals as clothes. Over time, people identified and produced different materials, such as cotton, polyester, and wool, to meet the requirements of respective segments to suit climatic conditions, to be cost-effective, and to be long-lasting. Changes in the type of human dwellings and materials used to construct houses, evolution in lighting methods from fire and oil lamps to electricity, and changes in modes of transportation from walking to bicycles, motor vehicles, and aeroplanes can be used to provide other examples.

The discussion can then move to the set of pictures about the evolution of transactions. The focus should be on why transactions began, and how they are completed. For example, individuals hunted animals, and collected vegetables and fruits, for their survival. Individuals in later generations entered into cultivation and produced specific farm and other products in surplus and supplied to others, and in turn expected others to fulfill their needs. Individuals who cultivated vegetables may have depended on individuals who cultivated rice or wheat or individuals who offered other services, and exchanged goods for goods or goods for service. Currency was introduced, simplifying transactions. Later, banking systems introduced cheque facilities, electronic money transfers, and credit cards, in place of currency in transactions.

The discussion can focus on the role of money in business. A question that can be repeated is how wealth is created or money earned. The aim here is to generate key insights, such as receiving payments for the quantities of goods or services rendered to others. Participants can be asked how they could prepare themselves to earn money and fulfill their needs. Questions can be repeated to explore the role of money. Was there any form of money when transactions began occuring? How does the barter system balance compensation for exchanges? Is cash always required to buy products now? How do bank checks or credit card systems enable transactions? The discussion should ideally conclude around key issues, such as equipping oneself to be productive and beneficial to others wherein the compensation fulfills one's own needs.

3.5.5 Outcomes

The following conclusions can be summarized:

- Exchange occurs to fulfill the needs of customers
- The nature of transactions has evolved over time, such as transactions from a barter system to the use of money and, now, electronic currency
- Technology, civilization, and evolution of human life lead to corresponding changes in goods, services, and transactional methods; however, the form that specific goods and services take are influenced by customer needs and how they are satisfied
- There are inevitable changes in needs and wants and influencing factors
- Many factors influence innovation and improvement in goods or services

3.6 Buyers, Users, and Customer Segments

3.6.1 Distinguishing Buyers and Users

3.6.1.1 Objective

Matching pictures to distinguish buyers and users.

3.6.1.2 Rationale

Discussions in the earlier session should highlight the purpose of producing goods and providing services; to fulfill the needs of others and to be compensated in return. It is important to understand the distinction between buyers and users or consumers, i.e., who is making a purchase, and who is using the product, from a business perspective. It would enable the participants to recognize the different players in the marketplace, a topic that is discussed in subsequent sessions. For example, spare parts and services are required to assemble and create a product. Sellers of such products are, in turn, buyers of these spare parts and services.

3.6.1.3 Input and Process

Four sheets of paper in different colors should be cut into circular shapes. The radius of the first sheet can be around 1.5 inches, the radius of the second can be two inches more than that of the first, the radius of the third two inches more than that of the second, and the radius of the fourth two inches more than that of the third. Four pictures that denote vegetation, four of animals (e.g., lion (wild animal), dog (pet animal), bird, fish), four of humans (e.g., baby, child, family, or people in a hospital), and four of objects (e.g., household articles – sewing machine, wall clock, and cupboard; motorcycle), are needed for this exercise. Each picture should be approximately 1.5–2 inches in width and length. On each sheet, pictures denoting vegetation, animals, humans, and objects can be placed at the outer end of the chart. Keeping the biggest circular sheet of paper with pictures at the bottom, setting the next smallest on this sheet, and fixing it with a pin at the center and so on would enable all pictures on all charts to be visible. The center pin should allow each sheet to rotate freely. A total of 21 such sets should be available to conduct this exercise, i.e., 20 sets for participants and one set preferably in larger size for the instructor to demonstrate in parallel during discussion (Figure 4).

The instructor's chart should be held on the board before starting this exercise. Each participant should be given a set and reminded that there is some relationship between the objects and the marketplace and that the circular sheets can be rotated. A few minutes should be allowed for participants to generate their ideas. They should be asked to arrange the sheets based on their discussion.

Once they complete the arrangement individually, the instructor's chart can be used for a demonstration (Figure 4). The instructor can ask participants for their thoughts and rationale. Two participants can be invited to repeat the procedure, using the instructor's revolving chart (demonstration set) displayed on a wall. Once these two volunteers complete the task, other participants can be asked whether they agree with the way the sheets are arranged. If there is any difference of opinion among the other participants, an opportunity can be provided to any two others and reconciled with the rest of the group until they reach consensus. Again they can be asked to explain what they did and why.

Participants may note that the pictures on the chart were initially haphazard and have now been arranged such that related pictures are in the same relative location from the center point of the chart. Participants can be asked what they understand from grouping these pictures and whether there are any links with the marketplace. Responses may be that one set of pictures represent nonliving (objects) and the other three represent life forms. The following questions can guide the discussion:

- Do all categories in different life forms need products that are in the market for their survival (e.g., fertilizers are produced for vegetation, special food items in the market for pet animals)?
- Who actually demands the items that are in the market?
- Who actually consumes it or who are the end users?
- Who actually compensates the seller?

Among the life forms, vegetations and animals may consume goods or services and they may be end users but they are not participating in the business directly and compensating the provider. Buyers are engaged in the exchange process. Buyers are potential customers for all items that are available in the market and actual users for many items. Hence, sellers target buyers of the business and try

Chart at the Beginning of the Assignment

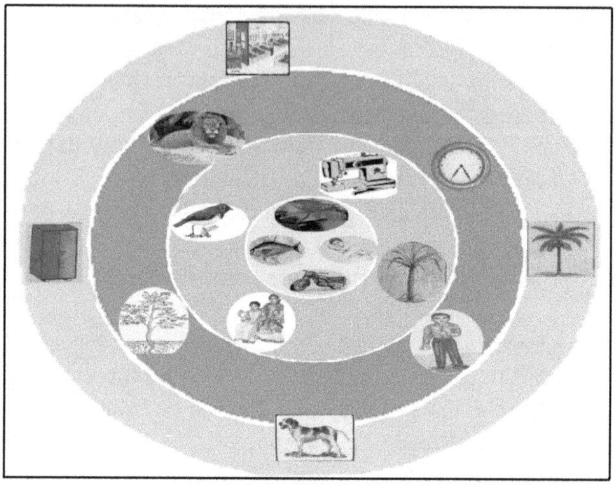

Chart with Matched Pictures After the Assignment

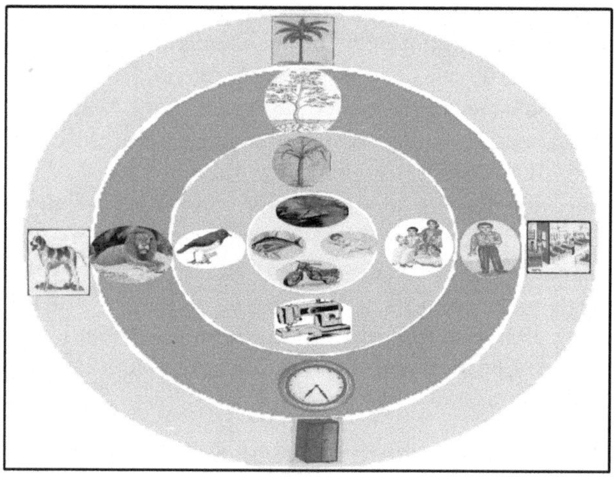

Figure 4 Distinguishing Buyers and Users

to satisfy their needs, though the actual end users or consumers may be different from the buyers. The use of categories, such as animals and plants, enables rudimentary treatment of content and an understanding of the key issues involved here.

3.6.2 *Customer Segments*

3.6.2.1 Objective

Understanding goods, services, and customer segments.

3.6.2.2 Input and Process

Pictures representing the categories of goods, services, and customer segments are required. Six sets of pictures with a picture from each category in each set are required along with three charts (Figure 5). Examples include medical drugs, doctor, and patient, clothes, tailor, and customer, and food, restaurant, and customers. Charts can be placed on a wall or board and 4- or 5-member groups of participants can be formed. One set of pictures should be given to each group. The instructor should use one set of pictures for demonstrating the procedures to be followed in this exercise. First, the instructor should show the three pictures and ask participants what they mean (Figure 5). Responses may include naming the good, or pointing out the occupation that is depicted in pictures that symbolize specific services. The discussion should be directed by providing leads, such as paraphrasing, (e.g., mentioning the name and occupation, what each symbolizes, how they relate to, and differ from, each other, and how they satisfy the needs of customers). The instructor should ask participants what the label for each picture is from a business perspective and use this opportunity to differentiate and define the good or service and the customer segment. For example, participants can be asked to explain a picture of medicines, doctor, and patient. Participants should be asked how a service fulfills one's needs, through whom and for whom. Responses may include the following:

- Patients are the beneficiaries and customers for medicine and medical service
- Drugs are goods, tangible products manufactured to fulfill the need of patients

Figure 5 Sample Picture of Good, Service, and Segment

- Medical personnel, such as doctors, nurses, and counselors, apply their technical skills to provide treatment for patients – a service
- Patient needs can be fulfilled through goods, such as medicines and drugs, or through services of medical personnel, such as physiotherapy

The title of each category can be written on the top of each chart with the picture placed on the respective charts. Once the demonstration is over, members of each group can be asked to discuss the pictures assigned to them, identify their category, place them on a chart, and present their rationale. The discussion should be moderated as differences of opinion may arise among participants regarding their categorization.

The discussion can then move to defining segments. A broad question to start the discussion is whether all products and services are required by all persons at all times? The pictures of adults can be moved to the row of products, such as schoolbags and notebooks that fulfill the needs of children, to provide examples. This represents a very basic and rudimentary way of demonstrating customer segments. The reasons why specific customers seek certain goods and services can be explored. The discussion should be facilitated until some understanding of the notion of a segment is reached. Generally, the response may be that a segment consists of persons with unique needs, who are potential customers of a particular good or service.

Pictures can be used to explain common ways to segment, such as by gender, age, subculture, climate, or geographic location. A discussion using food items can be employed to analyze how it varies from place to place, and from generation to generation, and how factors, such as culture and climate influence it. Different types of clothing and respective segments can be related to such factors as gender, climate, and affordability.

3.6.2.3 Outcomes

Consumers are those who use goods and services; for example, women who buy and use saris, or children who use bags, notebooks, and other educational materials that may be purchased by their parents. Customers are the actual buyers and include organizational buyers, such as retailers buying from wholesalers and wholesalers buying from manufacturers. The following conclusions can be noted:

- Customer needs drive markets
- Goods and services fulfill customer needs (goods are tangible products, the broader term for goods and services is products)
- Goods are tangible products, e.g., clothes
- Services are intangible products, e.g., tailoring
- Everyone may not want, or be able to afford, all goods or services

- Each good or service has potential segments
- Segments are potential customer groups who share similar needs and are served by specific goods or services.
- Understanding customer segments enables understanding customer needs and designing better goods and services.

3.7 Value Chains

3.7.1 Exercise

Role-playing in groups to understand value chains.

3.7.2 Objective

Understanding the role of exchange, as it occurs between various parties ranging from producers to consumers or users including intermediaries; understanding how multiple exchanges form a value chain.

3.7.3 Materials and Process

- White board, chart, and marker pens
- Two sets of pictures for the instructor's use (Figure 6)

Participants are likely to have observed value chains in day-to-day life. This exercise is an opportunity to understand the process for a sample product in a group and present it in sequential order, instead of using a lecture mode. The instructor can facilitate presentations through paraphrasing and using pictorial displays. This approach may enable participants to evaluate their presentations.

Participants can be assigned to groups of approximately 4–5 individuals and each group asked to focus on a sample product, identify its segment, discuss how it is produced and how it reaches the consumer or user, and provide rationale for the nature of the value chain. For example, fruits or milk could be used as products to discuss these issues. Participants should be asked to discuss these issues in detail in their group and prepare for a presentation. Before the discussion, group members should have clear assignments of roles, such as facilitator, recorder, and presenter. In parallel, the instructor should use charts to note the relevant issues from the presentation. The instructor should summarize each presentation by explaining the outcome in detail and using pictures, such as in Figure 6, to display the sequences.

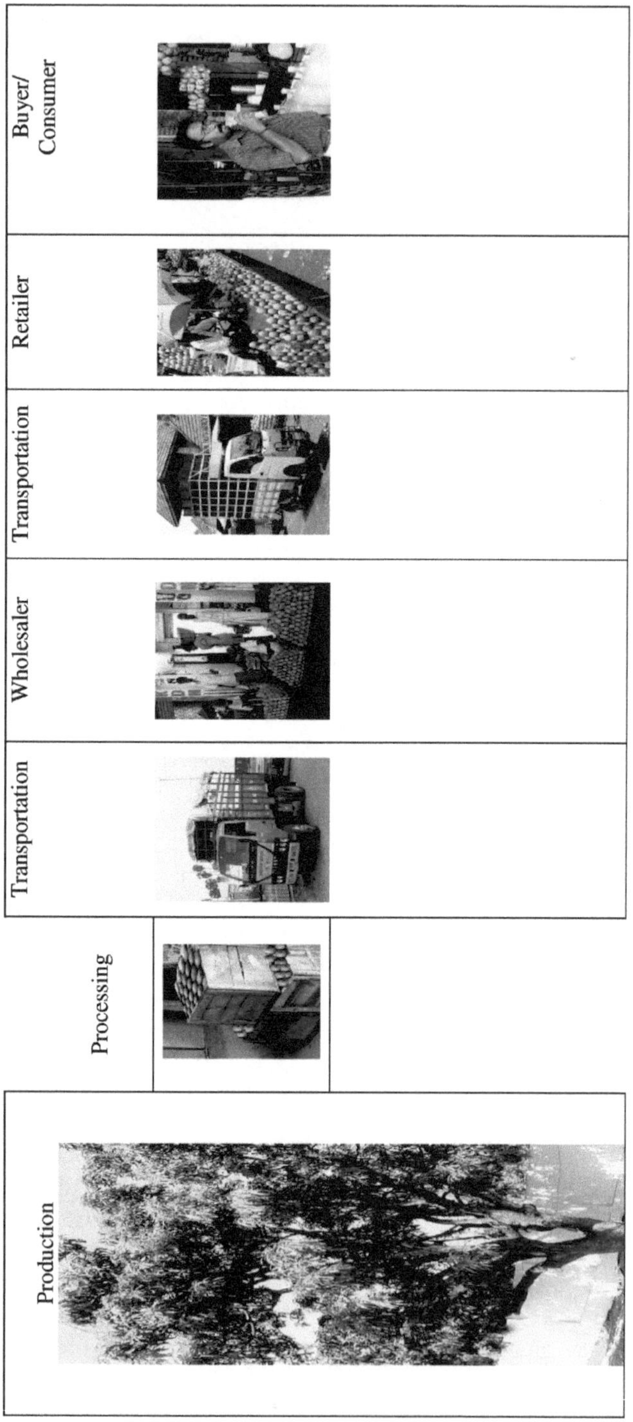

Figure 6 Elements of a Value Chain

3.7.4 Outcomes

A sample presentation is used to illustrate outcomes. One group identified fruits and fruit juice as their product for discussion. They presented vegetables and fruits as containing nutrients, and the special need they serve for pregnant mothers, children, and patients of all ages. Further, they stated that, generally, middle-class families would buy fruits regularly, and referred to them as a potential segment. They listed out the following and presented the process involved in the exchanges and the value chain in fulfilling the needs of the segment:

- Produced by farmers and harvested at the right time to ensure quality
- Collected and sorted by variety and packed
- Processed and transported to wholesale markets
- Cleaned, classified by quality; prices fixed by wholesalers
- Bought by retailers who resell to customers
- Fruits purchased by fruit juice shops from wholesalers or retailers, and fruit juices prepared by adding sugar and essence (flavoring) as ingredients

The instructor should use charts and facilitate grouping of the above process into categories as follows:

- Production
- Processing
- Transportation
- Wholesaling
- Retailing
- Consumption

The instructor should direct the discussion to enable further understanding of the exchange process. When discussing exchanges in different stages, a likely insight from participants is that products are not merely passed on to others but value is added at each stage, such as through adding other ingredients or transporting products, all aimed to fulfill the needs of the customer. For example, fruit vendors may buy fruits from the wholesale market and prepare fruit juice with fruits, sugar, and essence (flavoring) to add value and supply it to meet the requirement of patients or pregnant women or other customers. Both fruits and fruit juices have nutrition which serves the general need for nourishment.

The instructor can discuss the process and stages from production to usage, using the example of cotton clothes. Cottonseeds are planted to harvest cotton. Farmers collect the cotton from plants at fields. Quality cotton is sent to wholesale trading and then transported to textile mills, where it is processed and made into yarns and cloth. Cloth bundles are transported to wholesale traders and then to retailers. Customers buy clothes and get them tailored according to their needs. Finally, clothes may be delivered to members of customers' families who are the users.

The following can be used for discussion:

- How value is added from growing cotton through investing labor and applying fertilizers to ensure production
- How value is added from collecting and transporting the cotton at plants to collection centers to ensure it is available for sales
- How value is added through transporting cotton from collection centers to wholesale markets and grouping by quality to meet the process needs of different textile mills
- How value is added through transporting cloth from mills to wholesale and retail shops
- How value is added when customers buy clothes and get them tailored

The instructor can point out the main stages in value chains such as production, processing, transportation, wholesaling, retailing, and consumption, as highlighted above.

3.8 Summary

The instructor should enable a discussion to summarize the topics covered and paraphrase it as listed below:

- Expectations of participants at the beginning of the educational program
- Prioritizing elements of a business
- Marketplace exchange and the evolution of technologies, products, and transactions over time
- Goods – tangible products produced to fulfill the needs of customers
- Services – intangible products to fulfill the needs of customers
- Segments – groups of customers who share similar needs
- Value chains consisting of multiple exchanges, with value being added at each stage

At the end of the day, participants should be reminded that they are going to be taking the perspective of customers for the entire second day of the educational program.

Chapter 4
Consumer and Entrepreneurial Literacy Program – Consumer Literacy

4.1 Introduction

4.1.1 Overview

On Day 2, participants take on the role of customers. Simulated shops and role-playing by instructors are used to "cheat" participants or to mimic situations in local marketplaces that lead them to commit mistakes. The tasks are carefully designed to reflect pitfalls for customers. Our previous research identified a host of issues, which we cover here. A quiz in which stimuli are recorded statements covering different situations faced by customers is used to cover various issues. These issues include bargaining, weighing, buying wholesale versus retail, making versus buying, saving, understanding interest rates, switching stores and questioning sellers, being aware of rights, understanding discounts, paying in installment versus cash, checking prices and totals, planning purchases and preparing shopping lists, checking expiry on packages, and understanding MRP (maximum retail price). The overriding concept on Day 2 is that of the value of an exchange in terms of what is given versus what is got and the need to make informed choices.

4.1.2 Recap of Previous Day

The instructor should ask participants to share what they learned the previous day. Each participant should be encouraged to share their understanding in their own words. The instructor should facilitate the discussion and paraphrase the conclusions drawn to provide a smooth transition to the topics to be covered on Day 2. Participants' summary should include the sessions and topics covered on Day 1.

The instructor should provide an opportunity for participants to raise any general questions or seek clarifications before moving to the next session. Participants should be reminded that they will be taking the perspective of customers on Day 2.

4.2 Consumer Literacy: Skills, Knowledge, Rights, and Responsibilities – Role-Plays

Day 2 can start with a game, to enable participants to relax. The game may be a variation of "musical chairs", or asking participants to form a circle and pass a ball or any other small object around. When the instructor whistles, the participant who holds the object has to withdraw from the game. This could be repeated for five to six rounds.

The instructor can begin the discussion and ask participants what they understand about the purpose of producing products and of value chains. Exercises from the previous day may be referred to in explaining the basic concepts. A key conclusion from this discussion is that exchanges and value chains are centered on satisfying customer needs, leading to mutual benefit for buyers and sellers. The instructor should ask participants what their understanding from the first day's discussion is about gaining wealth or earning money and why customers pay suppliers of products, and paraphrase their responses. Issues to cover include the role of money as being payment for benefits received, and how wealth is created through exchanges involving payment for goods or services provided.

The instructor should reverse the question as to why customers buy a product and ask whether they lose their wealth or money for the value of goods and services. Participants may state that their purchase is to satisfy customer needs and their payment is for benefits received from the product. The instructor can remind the participants about how a customer should evaluate a product; whether it serves the purpose the customer seeks, and whether payment is in proportion to the benefit received from the product.

The key concept for the day should be explained, namely (perceived) value, the trade-off between what customers give up and what they get from an exchange.[1] Customers should be asked to list what they give up in a purchase and what they get in return. They should be informed that they will be explicitly comparing the value of different products later in the program. The key to being a skilled consumer is in assessing value carefully. A figure should be used to illustrate the concept of value later in the day.

4.2.1 Consumer Literacy: Skills, Knowledge, Rights, and Responsibilities – Role-Play in a Vegetable Market

4.2.1.1 Exercise

Role-play in a vegetable market - 2–3 competing vegetable shops are used wherein instructors role-play as sellers and participants purchase vegetables.

[1] *Pricing: Making Profitable Decisions* (McGraw-Hill Higher Education, 2002) by Kent B. Monroe.

4.2.1.2 Objective

Learning pitfalls in functioning as customers.

4.2.1.3 Rationale

This simulated shopping exercise has limitations, such as not fully capturing a realistic marketing environment in the classroom. When individuals buy goods through this type of role-play, some participants may be more cautious than normal while others may be less cautious. However, the exercise provides opportunities to point out positive and negative practices of customers in the buying process and creates awareness about the rights and responsibilities of customers.

4.2.1.4 Input & Process

- 6 kg of vegetables of any one variety but of same quality
- A perfect weighing machine
- A tampered weighing machine, which would show 850 g as 1 kg
- Two tables to create an artificial vegetable shop/market environment
- Three persons to play the role of sellers, two as shop owners and one as pavement (sidewalk) seller/street vendor

Shops can be organized at different corners of a hall to create three artificial vegetable shop/retailer settings. Two shops should look like vegetable retail shops and one should look like a roadside shop. Instructors or assistants should be assigned to role-play as sellers in each shop. They should use common tactics of typical sellers of local markets. Here, the shops are named Shop A, Shop B, and Shop C, respectively, to explain the process, with Shop C being the roadside shop.

A total of 6 kg of vegetables should be divided into three sets of 2 kg each. Shop A is given 2 kg, the selling price fixed at Rs. 9/kg, and the perfect scale used here to weigh vegetables. Shop B is given 2 kg, the selling price fixed at Rs. 8/kg, and the tampered scale used to weigh vegetables. The seller should use various distractions, including conversations with customers, to keep the focus away from the weighing process. Shop C is given 2 kg, which the seller divides into ten sets and sells for Rs. 2 each. This is often done in the real world to make a set affordable for low-income buyers. Once the shops are arranged and sellers assume charge, participants can be given money and asked to visit the shops and buy vegetables as they wish. Those participants who are not interested in making any purchases can be asked to observe the process and the transactions. After 10-15 minutes or as soon as the stock at the shops is sold, the instructor should ask participants to take their seats with the purchased vegetables.

The instructor should begin the discussion by asking participants whether everyone has bought vegetables. A variety of responses may be forthcoming. Some participants may say that they had planned to buy but the stock was over before they could to do so. Some participants may say that they preferred to observe due to fear or lack of experience. The instructor can explore and list the reasons for their fear, such as lack of experience or education, shopping in a new place, or fear of deception.

The instructor should pose the following questions; whether everyone who had made purchases used the same shop, whether they bought vegetables after visiting all the shops, and whether they decided on the shop based on any specific factors. Again, a variety of responses may be forthcoming. Some may say that they bought quality vegetables. Some may say that they preferred pavement (sidewalk) shops and bought vegetables at a cheaper price and some may say that they bought larger quantities for a lower price. The instructor should ask participants to justify their statements. The buyers who bought from Shop C may say that they bought larger quantities of vegetables for minimum price, they preferred to give business to a poor seller, or they preferred to buy minimum quantity. Those who bought from Shop B may say that they bought for a lower price when compared to others or that they chose the shop due to the seller's conduct toward the customer. Those who bought from Shop A may state that they preferred quality vegetables and bought them without being concerned about the price. The instructor should note these issues on a chart.

The instructor should invite a person who has bought the vegetables from Shop C to repeat the reasons for choosing that particular shop. One of the responses may be that the buyer obtained more quantity for minimum price. The instructor should ask participants the number of sets they bought and the amount paid to the seller. Assuming the buyer had bought two sets for Rs. 4, at Rs. 2 per set, the instructor should use the perfect scale and weigh the vegetables and calculate the net price per 100 g. Because the seller of Shop C divided the 2 kg of vegetables into ten sets, each set may average 200 g. So, two sets would weigh 400 g and the cost per 100 g would be approximately Rs. 1. Now, the instructor should ask participants to calculate the price per kilogram at Rs. 1/100 g and compare it with the prices of other shops. They may say that the selling price of Shop C was higher than it was at the other shops because the rate per kilogram is Rs. 10. Further, they may say that the price at Shop B was lower than at other shops.

The instructor should invite a person from those who have bought vegetables from Shop B to state the reasons for choosing the particular shop. One of their responses may be that they chose the particular shop due to lower price when compared to other places. The instructor should ascertain the amount they bought and the price paid to the seller. Assuming the buyer had purchased 1 kg for Rs. 8 to keep stock, though needing only 500 g for two days, the instructor should use the perfect scale and weigh the vegetables and calculate the net price per 100 g. Because the seller of Shop B used the tampered scale, the actual weight of vegetables in a perfect scale would be around 850 g only. Therefore, the cost per 100 g may come to around Rs. 0.94 [(8/850)*100 = 0.94].

The instructor should ask participants to compare the price between shops and confirm whether their earlier assumption was correct. This time, they may say that the price at Shop A is lower than at other shops. The instructor should invite a person from those who have bought vegetables from Shop A to state the reasons for choosing that particular shop. One of their responses may be that they chose the particular shop because they believed that the quality and weighing would be perfect where the price is high. The instructor should ascertain the quantity bought and the price paid to the seller. Assuming the buyer had bought 1 kg at Rs. 9, the instructor should use the perfect scale and weigh their vegetables and calculate the net price per 100 g.

Because the seller of Shop A had used the perfect weighing scale, there would not be any change in the actual weight of vegetables. Therefore, the cost per 100 g would be Re. 0.90 [(9/1000)*100 = 0.90]. Regarding quality of goods, the instructor should reveal the fact that all 6 kg of vegetables were of the same variety purchased at a single shop.

- Shop A: Rs. 9/kg – for perfect scale (therefore, cost is Rs. 0.90/100 g)
- Shop B: Rs. 8/kg – for tampered scale (actual weight is only 850 g; therefore, [8/850*100] cost is Rs. 0.94/100 g)
- Shop C: 2 kg divided into ten sets of 200 g each, rate per set is Rs. 2 (therefore, cost is Rs. 1/100 g)

The discussion should cover the following elements:

Cost – The instructor should ask participants to study the cost comparisons listed above and note the variations from their original assumptions.

Quality – Participants should be asked whether the quality depends on the goods and service or the type of shop. The instructor should invite a person who bought first from any shop and had the option to select quality goods, and a person who did not have the option to select quality goods but had to buy the remaining stock, to explain effective practices.

Cheating – Participants should be asked whether they could trust sellers and shops or they should be cautious in the selection of goods and shops and safeguard their own interest.

Quantity, storage life, and usage – The instructor should ask participants whether the vegetable (e.g., brinjal/eggplant) is perishable or non-perishable and whether it could be stored for many days. Everyone may agree that it is a perishable good and it could be stored and used for a maximum of a few days. The instructor should ask whether buying more than one's need just because of low price or quality or any other reasons is advisable. For instance, a buyer who knew that 500 g is sufficient to fulfill their need for two days buys 1 kg for reasons such as the particular product being available in the market for a cheaper price, to please the seller, to maintain their status in front of others, because they buy from the wholesaler, or because they feel that they are getting good quality. Participants may agree that the extra 500 g would be wasted. The instructor can use this opportunity to explain the utility of goods as well as the need to plan purchases over appropriate time frames.

4.2.1.5 Outcomes

Participants should be asked to list the best practices of informed customers that they learned from the exercise. The instructor should summarize the issues on a chart that can be referred to in subsequent discussions. Participants should be given the opportunity to think beyond the available options, and analyze and compare the benefits for a customer on price, quality, and other factors. Participants may have a tendency to draw narrow conclusions, such as how it is not a good idea to buy in a set for Rs. 2. They should be discouraged from drawing such conclusions. It should be pointed out that the key here is to understand what they are getting for what they are giving and to be careful about weighing and other issues. The set for Rs. 2 has benefits for customers who have severe constraints in their ability to pay, particularly if the identical, small amount cannot be bought elsewhere by weight.

4.2.2 Consumer Literacy: Skills, Knowledge, Rights, and Responsibilities – Role-Play with a Provisional Store/Retail Shop

4.2.2.1 Exercise

Role-play in a provisional (grocery) store/retail shop.

4.2.2.2 Objective

Learning pitfalls in functioning as customers

4.2.2.3 Rationale

This exercise provides opportunities to point out beneficial and detrimental practices of customers in the buying process and creates awareness about the rights and responsibilities of customers.

4.2.2.4 Input & Process

A provisional (grocery) store-like atmosphere should be created to stimulate the experience of shopping for provisions. A few locally available varieties of bathing soap and washing soap representing different brands, a few cosmetic items generally used by women in their day-to-day life, and a few packed condiments, such as mustard seeds, dhal (lentils), and chili powder, should be arranged. Each variety may have its own offers, free gifts, packing styles, and brand names. A few packages with fake brands and one or two packets with an expiry date that has elapsed should also be arranged on the table. A few packages of the same brand in different sizes or quantities should be available, e.g., 75 and 100 g. Some drugs and medicines should also be available.

The following represents one possible set of products to use:

- Major brand (Brand X) of toothpaste 40 g – MRP = Rs. 12.50
- Brand X toothpaste (80 g) – MRP = Rs. 25.00
- Major brand (Brand Y) of toothpaste (50 g) – MRP = Rs. 10.00
- Brand Y toothpaste (100 g) – MRP = Rs. 16.00
- Major brand (Brand Z) of bath soap (100 g) – MRP = Rs. 12.00
- Brand Z bath soap (100 g; 3 nos. in a pack) – MRP = Rs. 36.00 + (free gift of a brand of washing powder consisting of 4 sachets worth Rs. 3 each)
- Major brand of coffee powder 50 g – MRP = Rs. 32.50 + (free gift of a cup)
- A leading brand of some household item, e.g., washing powder
- An imitation with a similar sounding name as the leading brand of the same item
- Major brand of chili powder (50 g) – MRP = Rs. 6.25
- Major brand of chili powder (100 g) – MRP = Rs. 12.50
- Condiments such as mustard seeds, cumin, and coriander, in packets of different quantities, e.g., 100, 200 and 500 g
- Few medicines with expired dates
- Few tablet strips

These are illustrative examples, and specific products chosen should, of course, reflect the local context.

Instructors or assistants should play the typical role of retail shopkeeper/cashier and service person in the retail shop. They should sell the goods and take care of the entire provisional business including billing, collection of payments, and delivery of goods. Sellers should use both intentional and seemingly inadvertent errors common in the local markets, such as nonissue of bill for purchased goods, totaling mistakes, provision of wrong goods or brands, selling of fake brands, and supply of expired goods. Ten participants can be asked to play the role of buyers and the remaining asked to observe the exercise. Participants who volunteer to play the role of buyers should be instructed that they should have their family needs in mind, select their favorite brands, and buy the goods as they would in day-to-day life.

The seller should make some intentional mistakes and use deceptive practices, such as discrepancies in the billing and totaling, in goods provided, and in the supply of offers and gifts. There could also be mistakes in the goods provided. Some buyers may pay the amount after receiving the bill, or may demand the bill. Some buyers may verify the bill and the total, whereas others may not check the bill, i.e., they would order the goods and pay the amount asked by the shopkeeper. Some buyers may not verify MRP, expiry dates, offers, or brand details. Some buyers may come back to the shop and inform the shopkeeper of mistakes and get them rectified by the seller, whereas others may ignore mistakes. Some may quarrel with shopkeepers.

When the participants complete the purchase of provisions (groceries), the instructor should invite two or three persons and explain that they are going to be prescribed a few medicines, which they should buy from the shop as they do in normal life. The instructor should write the names of one or two drugs that are not available in the shop. The vendor should commit mistakes in price calculation and in providing the correct medicines.

4.2.2.5 Outcomes

After completing the exercise, instructor should ask participants to share their observations. The instructor should facilitate the discussion by identifying the strengths and weaknesses of customer practices that were observed in the exercise and listing out their responses. These responses can be paraphrased and captured as rights and responsibilities of buyers, and should be noted on a chart for further discussions.

Participants may list out the following:

- Buyers should have knowledge about the product to be purchased, e.g., ingredients and usage
- Buyers should enquire about different shops before deciding on the shop to buy from
- Buyers should assess value by comparing the price with quality and various product attributes
- Buyers should compare price and amount or package size to determine the size to buy
- Buyers should decide whether to buy, or make a particular product from ingredients, e.g., chili ready mix powder versus such ingredients as chili, pickle versus lemon and garlic, and readymade dresses versus cloth
- Buyers should see an actual need for a product and for a certain amount of the product before they buy (e.g., whether they should buy a wet-grinder or use the services of grinder mills, whether they should buy more of a perishable item than they would use before it spoils, and whether they should buy large quantities beyond their normal usage because of reasonable price)
- Buyers should check the weighing scale and be vigilant about the weighing method.
- Buyers should plan in advance for purchases and avoid wasting time
- Buyers should avoid spending their money and time unnecessarily for traveling to distant places to make purchases
- Buyers should request and, if necessary, demand, a bill from the vendor for goods purchased
- Buyers should verify the bill amount, totaling, and the products/goods supplied, before leaving the shop
- Buyers should check the price for each packet and should not pay more than the MRP but can pay less (this is an important issue because MRP is widely misunderstood)

- Buyers can demand that the vendor supply the offers or gifts announced by a company that makes a product
- Buyers should verify the manufacturing date, weight, expiry date, and usage of the product
- Buyers should be vigilant about fake brands
- Buyers can seek information about the product from the vendor or supplier
- Buyer can seek others' help to get technical advice or clarification or information before as well as after the purchase (e.g., buyers can seek the help of their doctor about dosage and the names of prescribed drugs, and seek the help of suppliers or service providers about operating electronic goods)
- Buyers should check the company's commitment on guarantees, warranty periods of the product, and other post-sales services

4.3 Consumer Literacy: Skills, Knowledge, Rights, and Responsibilities – Audio Quiz of Statements Relating to the Marketplace

4.3.1 Exercise

Quiz – Recorded quotes that typify marketplace interactions are played for participants, who should identify and explain them (Table 1).

4.3.2 Objective

Identifying, understanding, and overcoming common pitfalls in daily functioning as customers.

4.3.3 Input & Process

- A tape recorder
- Recorded cassettes with different marketplace quotes
- Charts to note down the scores of each group

Participants should be divided into groups and assigned names, such as Groups A, B, C, and D. The instructor should referee the quiz. Recorded tapes with conversational quotes from the marketplace are played one by one. Group members should discuss and identify the situation where the quotes could occur and discuss the problems or issues from the perspective of the customer.

Equal opportunities should be given to all groups to answer questions. A maximum of five points can be awarded to the group that provides the right answer and points

Table 1 Marketplace Quotes

Statements/Marketplace quotes	Explanation	Issues
"Look, you should have verified at the moment you bought it. What can I do if you ask me now?"	The seller makes this statement when the buyer returns later and complains of problems in the bills or products previously purchased	Totaling, counting, and checking goods purchased
"Madam, first please take a look at what I have given to you."	The seller makes this statement when the buyer complains while leaving the shop, of problems in the bill or products delivered	Billing and checking goods delivered
"You should have informed me when I left (to the market). What can I do, if you tell me now that we don't have this or that?"	The person who buys for the family makes this statement out of frustration that the list of items to be bought was not planned and he/she was not informed before going to the shop/market which is at some distance	Planning, making shopping lists
"What do we know? You say something and we listen to it. What do we do?"	The customer who depends on a seller expresses lack of knowledge or dependence due to factors, such as seller monopoly, credit, or literacy.	Searching for alternatives, switching stores, dependence
"We used to buy here because this shop is known to us. Why have you done this to us?"	The customer expresses anguish over breach of trust because the seller made mistakes or cheated in some way	Awareness and exercise of rights, making complaints
"You should state your preferences at the time of buying."	The seller advises the customer when he/she revisits the shop to return products	Pre-purchase evaluation and careful decision-making
"You can get only this for the money you paid."	The seller argues with the buyer who complains about the shortage in weight or quality of the purchased product	Justification for prices and quantities, bargaining and negotiating
"This costs only this much in that shop, (but) you say this much?"	The customer quotes the price in other places and tries to negotiate with the seller	Comparison, questioning, and bargaining
"You would know only when you go and buy there."	The seller makes this comment when a buyer asks for a product at a low price or lower than its actual listed price, quoting the price charged elsewhere.	Market prices, bargaining
"Ok, neither for you nor for me, you take this (product) for this much."	The seller negotiates with the buyer and offers to change the price or quantity of a product, or the seller begins by quoting a very high price and then settles for a lower price, still getting a very good price	Negotiation, price adjustments

Table 1 (continued)

Statements/Marketplace quotes	Explanation	Issues
"Whatever it is and though paid in monthly installments, it should not be purchased for this high a price."	A neighbor or friend of the buyer makes this comment when they feel that the price (including interest) of the product purchased in installments is too high	Interest/installment rates, understanding final price
"What you enquired about is not available now; the supply was over last month."	The seller replies to a customer who asks about the offer, discount, credit, or other issues	Offers, discounts
"It is yet to be available in the market. I will inform you once it arrives."	The seller replies to a customer who asks about a specific brand, items, offer, or other aspects related to products	Brand, product, offer
"This is better than that one. I say this not just from the perspective of children but considering other factors as well."	The seller or a friend recommends a particular product, compares and highlights the benefits	Assessing products and product quality, assessing value
"We need not buy this now; we could buy it during the festival time."	Family members or friends may suggest the time to buy and make use of special offers and savings	Offers, seasonal discounts, planning, buying based on needs
"Instead of buying here, you could have bought this at [area with big bazaar]."	Neighbors or friends of a customer suggest that the product could have been bought at a different place	Retail options, price, savings, value
"If you calculate both buying here and there, everything would come out the same."	Either a customer analyzes the time, travel, and price involved in the purchase of a product from two different places, or a customer who buys locally justifies the decision	Value assessment
"Instead of buying here you could buy from there because everything would be available there."	A friend or neighbor suggests the place to buy and shares market information	Market information, word-of-mouth, seeking advice
"I had no experience buying from there. With this shopkeeper, he would provide what we asked. Even if he does not have it, he would give something else that would be good."	A customer justifies the reason to buy from a particular place and highlights the benefits	Dependence, trust, customer satisfaction
"When a rate is printed on this, he would quote a different rate. There seem to be different laws for him alone."	A customer criticizes the seller who quotes a price for a product that is more than the MRP	Questioning, understanding meaning of MRP, price verification
"If we aren't a little cautious, that's it! These are times for the cheaters."	A customer comments out of frustration when finding some problem in a product	Cheating, informed decision-making
"It was not up to our taste. Therefore, I prepared it at home. It would be little more too (more quantity when made at home), wouldn't it."	A customer talks to friends or neighbors about making rather than buying products and associated benefits	Make or buy and related benefits and savings

(continued)

Table 1 (continued)

Statements/Marketplace quotes	Explanation	Issues
"What do I do? It is the end of the month; I can't be seen there. We should learn to buy when we have money and keep things in stock."	A customer who owes money to a seller expresses the inability to visit the shop again and reiterates that importance of planning	Planning, credit
"This type of picture won't be there and it won't be in this color."	A low-literate customer expresses doubt with the seller about the authenticity of the brand or product after verifying its symbol and color	Brand matching
"I could recognize from the first letter."	A low-literate customer expresses ways to confirm a brand or product	Pattern matching
"I used to buy during the season and keep sufficient stock."	A customer discusses best practices and feels proud of it	Planning, product and market information
"That is why I show the purchased medicines immediately to the doctor."	A patient/customer states the need to immediately seek the doctor's help to confirm the medicine purchased	Asking for help, technical information
"I would buy only a small quantity of the prescribed drugs."	A patient/customer talks about practices, such as rationing purchases, in buying drugs for treatment of illness	Importance of taking care of health needs, dangers of trading off health for money
"What is the use of buying this much quantity for just a family of three?"	Either a customer analyzes need and turns down the seller's request to buy larger quantities of goods or neighbors/friends comment about the purchases made by a customer which appear to exceed their need	Value, careful planning before purchase
"What can I do? I bought it without checking the date."	A customer discusses a mistake either due to lack of knowledge or oversight about the expiry date	Expiry date
"Sign boards are on each street and if you switch on the radio or TV, they are talking about this product everywhere."	Potential customers discuss details about a product	Evaluating marketing communications
"I thought the product would be of good quality because it cost more."	A customer discusses details about the lack of a relationship between price and quality in some instances	Price–quality relationships

could be deducted for incomplete answers. To begin, the opportunity to answer can be given to Group A and their score noted on the chart. If they do not provide the correct answer, the opportunity can be given to the next group in the chosen sequence. When all groups have had an opportunity or the correct answer has been stated, a score can be assigned to the group, and the next quote can be played for the next group in the sequence to answer. Simultaneously, the instructor can capture the main points from the quotes and write them down on a chart for subsequent discussions. Finally, total scores for each group should be announced and all participants recognized.

Sample marketplace quotes or statements are listed in Table 1. Relevant issues covered by each quote are also indicated. These quotes are examples and should be modified to fit different contexts. The following issues can be covered with the quiz: totaling, counting, rechecking, options, planning, quality and price, brand, pattern matching, offers, discounts, advertisements, short- and long-term health needs, thrift, cheating, cost analysis, tradition and influence of customs, dependence, seeking help, making or buying, installments, borrowing, interest rates, switching, questioning, and buying wholesale versus retail.

4.3.4 Outcomes

Issues discussed above could be summarized as shown below to orient participants on consumer rights and responsibilities:

- Right of access to a variety of goods and services at competitive prices
- Right to information on ingredients and usage of products
- Right to protest and protect oneself from unfair trade practices or exploitation
- Right to be informed about market information including details of the product, price, quality, quantity, and company or brand names
- Right of protection against dangerous products
- Responsibility to check products and negotiate prices before purchasing
- Responsibility to fulfill agreements

The guiding concept to summarize the discussion is value, i.e., what is given versus what is obtained in an exchange, and the need to carefully assess value in an exchange.

4.4 Summary

The instructor could refer to the key lessons learned from earlier sessions and compile them as given below to orient the participants on the rights and responsibilities of consumers:

- Customers should plan purchases carefully
- Customers should search for, and learn about, products, prices, and stores

- Customers should ask for a bill, receipt for payment, and warranty card
- Customers should check the product before receiving it
- Customers should exercise their rights when bargaining or interacting with shopkeepers
- Customers should understand and follow instructions when using products
- Customers should follow the accepted conditions in the contract
- Customers should discourage unethical trade practices
- Customers should be able and willing to pay for the cost of the product and services received from the seller or service provider

The instructor could pose the following questions in a summary discussion:

- Whose perspectives were covered today?
- What is the need to know and exercise the rights and responsibilities of customers?

The instructor should facilitate discussion and encourage participants to share their concerns, such as safety, timely services, available locations, or reasonable prices, and remind them that the customer should evaluate the product and the benefits it delivers, and whether they get benefits proportionate to the money paid in exchange as well as time spent and other costs to the customer.

The guiding concept to summarize the discussion is value, and the need to carefully assess the value of an exchange. The instructor can use Figure 1 to explain the concept of value, i.e., the trade-off between what customers get and what they give up in return, to conclude the sessions for Day 2.

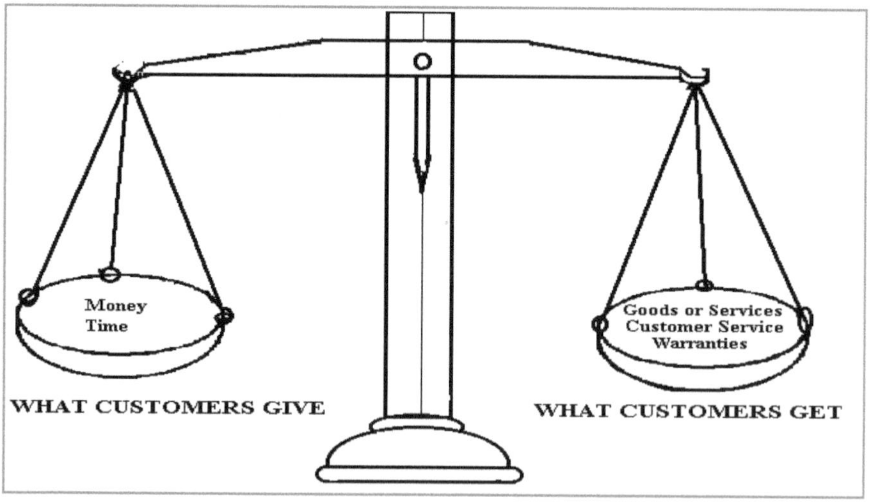

Figure 1 Balancing "Give" and "Get"

The instructor should encourage participants to summarize the topics covered from the first two days of the educational program. The instructor should then paraphrase responses and summarize the topics covered in the first two days.

Day 2

- Effective practices of customers
- Consumer rights and responsibilities
- Value, the trade-off between what customers give and what they get in an exchange

Participants should be reminded that they will be taking the perspective of sellers on the third day and focus on aspects of running a business.

Chapter 5
Consumer and Entrepreneurial Literacy Program: Day 3 – Entrepreneurial Literacy

5.1 Introduction

5.1.1 Overview

From Day 3 onward, participants take on the role of a seller. An issue that is covered is identifying and evaluating a business opportunity through a relative assessment of one's own strengths and weaknesses, and competitors' strengths and weaknesses, in light of the customer needs to be addressed. Emphasized here is the need to carefully evaluate a business opportunity and work through it before deciding to pursue it. Another central issue covered is the basic business philosophy of being customer-oriented and engaging in mutually beneficial exchanges as a means of making a profit. Different philosophies are covered here to highlight distinctions, such as a focus purely on selling or on production without paying attention to customer needs. These two broader issues set the stage for a discussion of more specific issues. The next topic covered is information gathering and research. The importance of carefully collecting and evaluating information is emphasized. Included here are ways of gathering information, such as through talking to people, observing the competition, conducting an analysis of costs, and obtaining feedback on specific ideas. Also covered here are some basic issues in asking questions when gathering information, such as planning questions beforehand, avoiding leading questions, and attempting to obtain accurate information. Role-playing is used to bring out these issues. The importance of asking oneself tough questions and looking for accurate information is emphasized. This is followed by a general introduction to consumer behavior in terms of steps in decision-making, such as need recognition, search for alternatives, and evaluation of alternatives, and the various influences on consumer decision-making.

The next major topic covered is product design, which includes basic issues, such as what a product is and what customers look for in specific products. The purpose is to understand how physical product characteristics and ingredients translate to psychological benefits for customers. The concept of customer orientation runs through all the topics discussed, such as through linking product design to benefits received by customers. Also important is the abstract benefit being served.

The distinction between goods and services is also reemphasized here. The importance of packaging to preserve the product and provide an attractive exterior is also covered. Exercises are used where participant-groups choose a product category and design a product.

5.1.2 Ice-Breaking Exercise

A game can be conducted as the first activity of Day 3 to involve participants. The instructor can write four or five names of goods or services, such as fruit juice, pickles, chili powder, and radio, on pieces of paper, which can then be folded and kept in a box. The instructor should ask participants to form a circle and pass a small object to the person standing to their left. The person who is holding the object when the instructor blows the whistle should be selected. That person should pick a piece of paper from the box and communicate about the goods or services written on the paper by acting it out without using or spelling any words to enable other members to identify the product. The person should communicate nonverbally until the others identify the good or service. The entire process can be repeated four or five times.

5.1.3 Recap

Participants should be asked to summarize the topics covered over the first two days. The recap can be organized by activity or session, which generally appears to maximize effectiveness, with each day being summarized by key concepts. The instructor should facilitate participants' understanding by summarizing key concepts, such as exchange and value chains on Day 1, and value on Day 2. They should be reminded that they are going to discuss issues, such as evaluating business opportunities, product, pricing, promotion, and distribution from the seller's perspective on Days 3, 4, and 5. They should also be reminded that the typical businessperson not only sells, but also buys, raw materials or ingredients, and other products. A seller oriented around serving customers and understanding how they judge value, the trade-off between what customers give and what they get in exchange, is likely to make a profit while serving customer needs.

5.2 Prioritizing Elements in Business (from Day 1)

The instructor should ask participants whether they suggest any changes to an earlier assignment from Day 1 where they placed pictures depicting money and various stages in the value chain for a product in concentric circles on a chart according to their importance. There may be changes in participants' perceptions after going through two days of the program and they may prefer to move the customer to the center. This is a major juncture in the educational program where participants realize the importance and centrality of customer needs and the importance of organizing a business around serving customer needs.

At this point, the instructor should summarize the philosophy of running a business that will be used in the educational program, to create mutually beneficial exchanges and make a profit as a result of satisfying customers. There are many ways to make a profit, by selling whatever one produces, or by producing whatever one wants to, without heed to customer needs. The philosophy of running a business covered here is one that is customer-oriented. A figure of a balancing scale with one side showing the buyer and the other showing the seller introduced in Day 2 should be used to illustrate this philosophy (Figure 1 in Chapter 4). The remainder of the educational program elaborates on various aspects of a business using this underlying philosophy. This philosophy is ethical in the sense that it is mutually beneficial, and also makes good business sense. From the point of view of the buyer, the important concept is value. The seller, on the other hand, should attempt to provide a valuable exchange to the buyer and make a profit as a result of providing value to the customer.

5.3 Evaluating Business Opportunities

The instructor should ask participants to assume they are business owners from Day 3 onward. They should be asked the very first thing to determine when considering whether to start a business. After the first two days of the educational program, participants usually understand the centrality of customers and customer needs for exchanges and for running a business, and, therefore, their responses may be that they should identify customer needs. The instructor should ask why and facilitate discussion. Asking the participants what they would do after identifying customers might yield answers, such as knowing the needs of customers and segments to which they aim to provide a good or service, understanding how their good or service would satisfy the needs of specific customers and segments, and fulfilling the needs of customers through delivering appropriate goods or services. The instructor should paraphrase responses and mark them on a chart, as shown in Figure 1.

Asking participants how a seller/businessperson can identify the right customers and their needs could lead to responses about studying customers and the marketplace. The instructor should ask participants such questions as what the next step after identifying the needs of the customer should be. The responses from participants may suggest that every seller or businessperson cannot fulfill everyone's need. The businessperson or seller should have adequate skills or strengths in a specific trade or product category to produce a product that would satisfy the needs

Figure 1 Step 1 in Evaluating Business Opportunities[1]

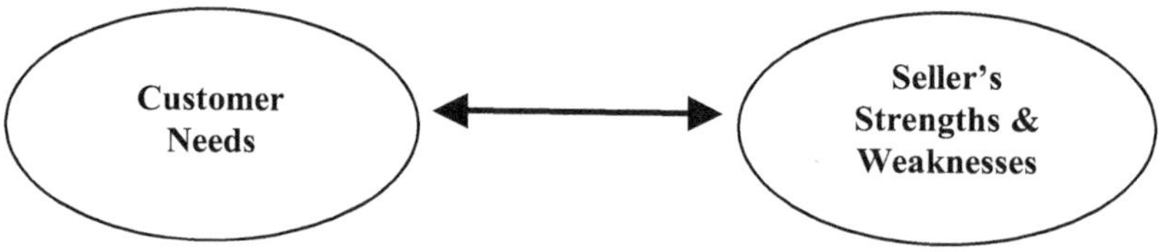

Figure 2 Step 2 in Evaluating Business Opportunities

of customers. The instructor should capture the words that connote skills or strengths from their statements and highlight it for further discussion and suggest that the assessment of strengths and weaknesses is central in deciding to pursue a business. The instructor should mark this as the second step and illustrate it as shown in Figure 2.

The instructor should ask participants whether this process could be stopped after finding customer needs and assessing the seller's strengths and weaknesses. The instructor should facilitate the discussion until participants raise issues about threat from competitors in the market to a particular product they decide to launch. The discussion should continue until a consensus is reached among the participants, that they should identify the competition and assess the competitors' strengths and weaknesses as well in order to evaluate a business opportunity (Figure 3). It would be preferable to research an opportunity thoroughly and decide not to pursue it rather than to hastily start a business and face a loss. This is an important theme to communicate in this session, and repeat in subsequent sessions, and in summarizing the learning points as well.

Although this process is discussed in discrete steps, the actual discussion may be iterative and the steps do not have to be covered in strict linear fashion. Moreover, though this approach aims to get the process of choosing a business started, a number of other factors need to be considered, such as business potential. Raw

[1]Figures 1, 2, and 3 are adapted with permission of the McGraw Hill Companies from Kenichi Ohmae, The Mind of the Strategist: The Art of Japanese Business, Figures 8.1, p. 92, copyright 1991, McGraw Hill.

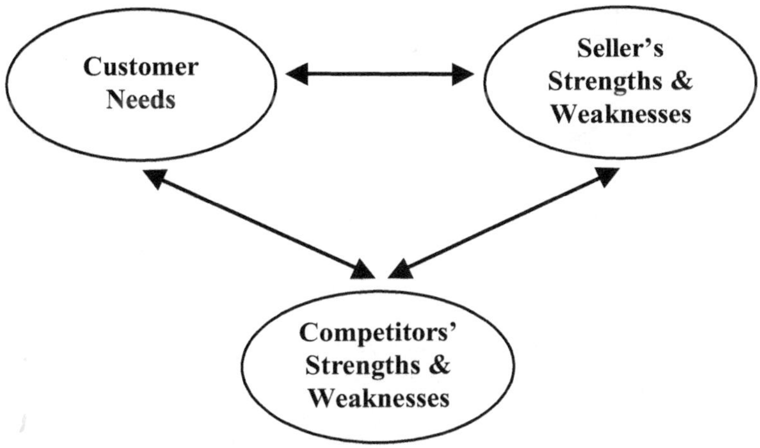

Figure 3 Step 3 in Evaluating Business Opportunities

material, capital, support services, and market potential are factors central to identifying viable income-generating activities.[2]

5.4 Gathering Information to Make Business Decisions – Elements of Research

5.4.1 Exercise – Gathering Information to Evaluate Business Opportunities

The instructor should repeat questions such as how the needs of customers or segments, and the strengths and weaknesses of competitors and one's own strengths and weaknesses should be identified. Responses from participants may include making enquiries, observing markets, and seeking others' help or technical advice. The instructor should ask participants what these activities are and what they should be called.

The instructor should ask participants whether it is advisable to carry on business-related activities based purely on their own assumptions and intuitions. The instructor can point out, using local proverbs where possible to enable participants to relate to the material at an intuitive level, that judgment based on thorough enquiries and verification is better than believing or trusting based on merely seeing or hearing. The instructor should facilitate the discussion to arrive

[2] We thank Kirti Prasanna Mishra for his insights on this issue.

at a consensus on the importance of ascertaining facts through systematic methods, i.e., to conduct research and carefully gather information. Participants' responses about sources of information and methods should be captured through brainstorming and discussion.

Information could be collected through informal interaction with the following sources:

- Introspection – experiences as a customer
- Relatives
- Friends
- Neighbors
- Individuals already making the product/running the business
- Retails shops who sell related goods or services
- Wholesale shops and markets
- Specialized institutions and departments for technical information

The instructor, in consultation with the participants, could classify the above as follows:

- Personal sources – family, friends, neighbors, and acquaintances
- Commercial sources – retailers and wholesalers
- Public sources – specialized institutions, departments, and media

The instructor should ask participants how they would seek information or conduct research and how they would ensure cooperation from the respondents and obtain accurate responses. For example, would they get accurate responses from a personal source when they are planning to start a particular business or would responses be biased either intentionally or unintentionally? The instructor should emphasize the importance of obtaining accurate information and discounting possible biases in information obtained.

The instructor should direct and facilitate the discussion about different ways of learning about consumer decision-making. As summarized in Table 1, approaches include considering how the participants would act as customers, asking potential customers about their experiences, asking customers about their purchase plans for the immediate future, and asking customers about ideal ways to buy products and ideal products.[3] The instructor should enable participants to recognize that research or information gathering does not end once a business is started but should be an ongoing process. Research or information gathering is a way of looking at the marketplace and understanding it. Research is akin to a lens through which one can view and understand the marketplace. Important here in identifying a profitable business is to ask oneself difficult questions before investing and facing losses. As mentioned earlier, it would be preferable to research an opportunity thoroughly and

[3] Approaches to learning about the stages of the decision process from Kotler, Philip (2003), Marketing Management, 9th Edition, Upper Saddle River, NJ, are adapted here to learn about buying processes as well as product preferences.

Table 1 Approaches to Learn About Customer Decision-Making

Considering how participants would act as customers in terms of the process they would follow to buy products and the products they would buy (would they buy from themselves?)	Introspective
Asking customers to discuss buying processes and outcomes of recent purchases, problems they faced, and their expectations	Retrospective
Asking potential buyers to discuss their likely buying process and expectations from goods or services	Prospective
Asking customers to describe the ideal buying process and the ideal product that would satisfy their need	Prescriptive

decide not to pursue it than to hastily start a business and face a loss. This is an important theme to repeat in this session and in summarizing the lessons learned.

Instructors could enact a role-play to highlight the issues. A role-play that can be used is one where an acquaintance encourages an individual to start a business without being thoughtful in providing advice. One of the instructors should act as a potential seller who wishes to start a business and collect market information and another instructor should play the role of retail shopkeeper and respondent. Their conversation should reflect the practical issues in informal research. The person who seeks information should have a very informal interaction with the retailer and try to gather information as it pertains to the new business. The instructor should orient participants on issues in collecting information through this role-play such as the following:

- The need to find multiple independent sources for information rather than rely exclusively on one source
- The need to supplement communication with people with other methods such as observation
- The need to understand individuals' motives and biases in providing information and discount accordingly (e.g., for a retailer, the threat of competition is an obvious motivation; for an acquaintance, lack of involvement or trying to please may be factors)

The instructor should caution participants that the method used in the role-play is one of many and not the only one. They should be asked to practice in a real world context where they may face different situations. The instructor should remind participants that research is not a one-time exercise in business but should be an ongoing process that results in improved practices.

5.4.2 Group Discussion and Presentation About Sample Research on a Selected Product

Groups of about 4–5 participants each should be formed and asked to discuss research methods and present how they would identify their segment and its needs, evaluate their strengths and weakness as sellers, and evaluate the competition. They could be given about 20 minutes to present and provided with clarifications as needed. The representatives of respective groups should present their conclusions. At the end of the group's presentation, the members from other groups could be given the opportunity to raise questions for clarifications. The instructor should moderate the discussion among participants. Issues that evolve from their discussion can be written on a chart for presentation. Groups may identify personal sources, such as neighbors and friends, from whom to seek information through conversations. They may list their own strengths and weaknesses and decide on the related product or service that could satisfy the needs of local customers.

They may identify the competitors and assume that the following attributes are areas of weaknesses for competitors, which could be translated into their own strengths:

- Price
- Models/Designs
- Variety in materials and price
- Courteous customer service
- Timings

Further, they may state that they would continue their research and listen to customers' views to fine-tune their product and improve their business.

The instructor should summarize each group's presentation and highlight the outcomes, gaps, practical difficulties, and potential errors. It may not be uncommon for groups to restrict themselves or show interest in businesses serving clientele they are familiar with. The need to be specific in describing potential segments in terms of geographic location and other characteristics should be emphasized. Table 2 presents a sample adapted from some group presentations.

The instructor should request participants to review the assignment completed during the first session on prioritizing elements of a business (Figure 2 from Chapter 3). The instructor should ask participants whether research is essential for a businessperson, and if so, where it could be illustrated in the diagram. The instructor should facilitate the discussion leading to research at the second circle from the center as shown in Figure 4. In other words, research is the means for understanding customers and the marketplace.

5.5 Consumer Behavior and Decision-Making

5.5.1 Consumer Behavior

The next topic is consumer behavior. The instructor should ask some participants to think aloud about how they purchased a product in a category the first time. The

Table 2 General Outcomes From Sample Research

Outcome from search	Group 1	Group 2	Group 3	Group 4
Potential goods/ service	Sari business	Agarbathi (incense sticks)	Notebooks	Tailoring for women's clothing
Potential segments	Women who are neighbors, friends, acquaintances, or employees of companies nearby	Middle-class families living in neighborhoods	School-going children living nearby, college students, employees and teaching staff	Women who are neighbors, friends, or acquaintances
Strengths (+) and weaknesses (–)	+ Friendly to customers + Material fitting customer's taste + Competitive price + Easy access to customers + Flexible timings to suit the customers + Speedy response – Lack of money to invest – Lack of experience	+ Technical know-how to produce the product + Competitive prices + Volume discounts – Lack of variety in product – Lack of money to invest – Lack of experience	+ Home delivery + Quality products + Consistency in supply and service + Convenient timing + Good price + Friendly to customers – Lack of variety in products – Lack of money to invest – Lack of experience	+ Tailoring skill + Timely delivery + Convenient timing + Post-purchase service – Financial resources for sewing machine or to hire extra help
Strengths and weaknesses of competitors	+ Size + Financial resources + Experience – High Prices – Unfriendly to customers	+ Size + Financial resources + Experience – High prices	+ Size + Financial resources + Experience – High prices	+ Modern Equipment + Size + Financial resources – High prices

Figure 4 The Role of Research[4]

responses should be summarized using the model shown in Figure 5. The instructor should use this model to present the stages in the customer buying process.[5]

5.5.1.1 Problem Recognition

The buyer recognizes a need or problem that is triggered by internal or external stimuli. Internal stimuli include the physiological needs of a person, such as hunger and thirst. External stimuli include the physical appearance of a product, which sparks interest in the good or service.

5.5.1.2 Information Search

The buyer searches for information. General sources of information include the following, as discussed in Session 3:

- Personal sources
- Commercial sources
- Public sources

---

[4] Adapted from Kotler, Philip, and Gary Armstrong, Principles of Marketing, 9th Edition, © 2001, p. 64, Figure 2.5. Reprinted by permission of Pearson Education, Inc., Upper Saddle River, NJ.

[5] Adapted from sources including *Marketing Management* (Prentice-Hall, 11th edition, 2003) by Philip Kotler. Other sources include *The Theory of Buyer Behavior* (Wiley, 1969) by John A. Howard and Jagdish N. Sheth, and *Consumer Behavior* (Harcourt College Publishers, 9th Edition, 2001) by Roger D. Blackwell, Paul W. Miniard, and James F. Engel.

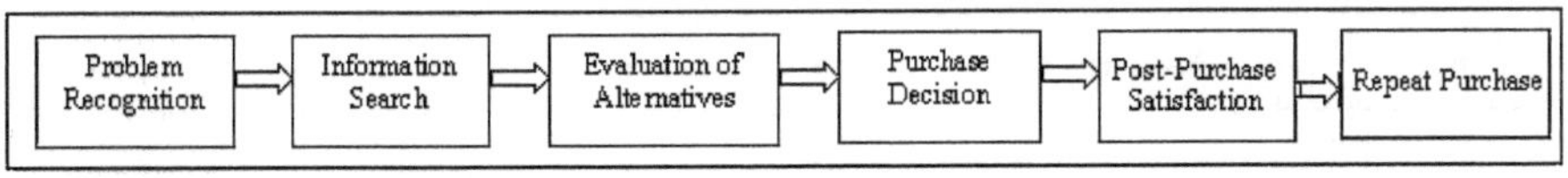

Figure 5 Stages in the Buying Process[6]

5.5.1.3 Evaluation of Alternatives

There is no single process used by all customers or by one customer in all buying situations. Customers may consider several factors while evaluating the alternatives. They try to satisfy their needs and look for certain benefits from the product. They may see each product as having multiple attributes and varied benefits. The attributes of interest vary by products and across buyers. Customers vary as to which product attributes they see as most relevant and the importance they attach to each attribute. They likely pay the most attention to attributes that deliver the sought benefits. The market can often be segmented according to attributes that are salient to different customer groups. The instructor should elicit examples from participants to convey the key issues above.

5.5.1.4 Purchase Decision

The actual decision to purchase is made following evaluation of alternatives.

5.5.1.5 Post-Purchase Satisfaction

Following purchase, the product is used and evaluated by customers. This step influences repurchase of the product and sustained sales for the seller.

5.5.2 Evaluating Alternatives

When evaluating alternatives, it is important to understand that, although there are many alternatives, customers may be aware of only a subset of them, and in turn consider only a subset of the alternatives that they are aware of. Only a subset of the alternatives in the consideration set may be in the choice set that receives close attention before an alternative is chosen. Participants can be asked to relate how they considered alternatives for specific product categories and arrived at the choice

[6] Adapted from Kotler, *Philip, Marketing Management*, 11th Edition, © 2003, p. 204, Figure 7.4. Reprinted by permission of Pearson Education, Inc., Upper Saddle River, NJ.

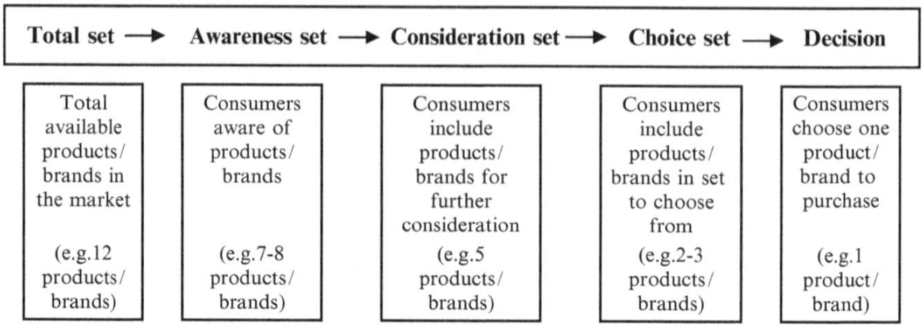

Figure 6 Sets of Products or Brands in Consumer Decision Making[7]

of one alternative. Such an approach of beginning with examples and then providing a broader summary is likely to be effective (Figure 6).[8]

5.5.3 From Evaluation of Alternatives to Purchase Decisions

After providing an overview of the decision-making process, some nuances in terms of how customers reach decisions can be covered. At least two sets of factors can intervene between the purchase intention and the purchase decision: attitudes of others and unanticipated factors. Infomediaries, such as published reports, can also play a key role. Unanticipated situational factors may also change the purchase intention. A customer's decision to modify, postpone, or avoid a purchase decision is likely to be influenced by perceived risk, such as the money at stake, amount of uncertainty about products, or financial difficulties (Figure 7).[9]

5.5.4 Sub-Decisions

Customers may make many purchase sub-decisions that sellers need to understand:

- Brand decision
- Vendor/dealer decision

---

[7] Adapted from Kotler, *Philip, Marketing Management*, 11th Edition, © 2003, p. 205, Figure 7.5. Reprinted by permission of Pearson Education, Inc., Upper Saddle River, NJ.

[8] Adapted from *Marketing Management* (Prentice-Hall, 11th edition, 2003) by Philip Kotler. Relevant sources include "Consumer behavior and product performance: An alternative conceptualization", *Journal of Marketing* (October, 1975), by Chem L. Narayana and Rom J. Markin.

[9] Adapted from *Marketing Management* (Prentice-Hall, 11th edition, 2003) by Philip Kotler. Relevant sources include "An investigation of relationships among evaluative beliefs, affect, behavioral intention, and behavior", by Jagdish Sheth, in *Consumer Behavior: Theory and Application* (John U. Farley, John A. Howard, and L. Winston Ring (eds.), Allyn & Bacon, 1974).

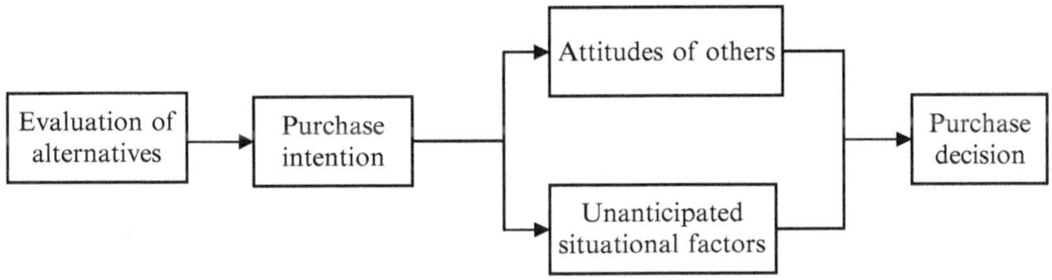

Figure 7 Stages Between Evaluation of Alternatives and Purchase Decision[10]

- Quantity decision
- Timing decision
- Payment method decision

5.5.5 *Buying Decision Process – Roles Individuals Play in a Buying Decision*

Often, the buyer may not make an independent decision to buy a product, though vested with ultimate decision-making power, either in a household or in an organization. The buyer may have to accommodate the interests of other individuals. An example, such as a household product used by everyone or a product being sold to a store or a small business, can be used as a starting point in the discussion. The discussion should be summarized by categorizing roles as[11]:

- Initiator Person who first suggests the idea of buying the product or service
- Influencer Person whose view or advise influences the decision
- Decider Person who decides on any component of the buying decision, whether to buy, what to buy, how to buy, or where to buy
- Buyer Person who makes the actual purchases
- User Person who consumes or uses the product or service

From a seller's perspective, it is important to understand how the decision to buy is made and the different roles that individuals may play in that decision. For instance, as a seller, it would be important to make initiators aware of products. It would be important to provide full information to the decider. For example, when selling to a wholesale or retail store, it is important to know the different individuals involved

---

[10] Reproduced from Kotler, *Philip, Marketing Management*, 11th Edition, © 2003, p. 207, Figure 7.6. Reprinted by permission of Pearson Education, Inc., Upper Saddle River, NJ.

[11] Adapted from several texts including *Marketing Management* (Prentice-Hall, 11th edition, 2003) by Philip Kotler. Relevant sources include *Organizational Buying Behavior* (Prentice-Hall, 1972) by Frederick E. Webster and Yoram Wind.

in various roles and to get information to the initiator. A fuller discussion of these issues is conducted under the topic of promotions. This discussion should be used to make participants aware that an understanding of consumer behavior is central as they continue to other topics, such as product design. If the business is to be oriented around the customer, the key is to understand consumer behavior.

5.6 Product Design

The instructor should begin the discussion with the question of how the needs of customers could be addressed by a businessperson. Participants may respond that it would be possible through providing goods or service. Figure 8 should be introduced to present the larger picture of the content being covered. The instructor should reverse the question and ask how a product could address the needs of customers, why a customer would be interested in buying a product, and how the product should be designed. Participants' responses for the first two questions may suggest that the product should primarily address the core needs of customers. Customers would prefer to buy a product if it is safe, cost-effective, and timely.

Responses about how to design the product may include fulfilling core and peripheral needs. The instructor should use a product, such as pickle, to provide an example and ask participants to list out the aspects to be considered when making the product. Products that participants are familiar with and can relate to provide a good starting point for exercises. Participants may explain the required ingredients, process, and packing methods. They should be asked whether the combination of ingredients, processes, and packing methods are common to all segments or would

Figure 8 Product Design[12]

[12] Adapted from Kotler, Philip, and Gary Armstrong, Principles of Marketing, 9th Edition, © 2001, p. 64, Figure 2.5. Reprinted by permission of Pearson Education, Inc., Upper Saddle River, NJ.

vary across segments. For example, a segment including construction workers may expect certain benefits from the product, such as a high degree spiciness and small, affordable package sizes. This may be different from the benefits expected by a segment consisting of middle-class families, who may emphasize healthy ingredients and larger package sizes.

The instructor can place pictures representing the senses/organs of humans, such as eyes, ears, nose, tongue, brain, and heart, on a chart and arrange participants' responses under respective pictures. For example, "taste" would be written under the picture of a tongue. The idea here is to bring out the different benefits of products in a concrete manner. The instructor should remind participants of the concept of a value chain and ask how and why value is added in the process of making pickles. Each ingredient and its blending with other ingredients provide specific benefits to customers from the final product. The discussion can be concluded by emphasizing that value is added to produce a customer-oriented product that satisfies the expectations and needs of customers. Products should fulfill the sensory and psychological needs of customers, and ingredients should not be included solely because the producer decides to do so but rather because they serve a benefit. The key here is for the seller to understand the link between each ingredient and each aspect of the production process, and the benefits delivered to customers. Participants should be reminded that a producer of a product should continue to research and make necessary changes in such aspects as ingredients, process, or customer service, and fine-tune the product to meet the needs of customers.

The instructor should ask participants to form groups and each group should select a good or service they wish to sell in the market, discuss it among themselves, and make a presentation about how they are going to design it and why they prefer such a design, e.g., designing products, such as nutritional mix powder, pickles, and masala/chili powder. The groups may recall the value chain and present the following as the main stages in their respective product design and its production:

- Purchase of ingredients for the selected product
- Process of product preparation
- Packaging process
- Making or supplying products in a variety of sizes/colors/models

Their presentation may reflect the following as vital aspects in the product design:

- Visual appeal
- Fragrance/aroma
- Taste/flavor
- Safety and healthiness
- Affordable sizes/configurations/models
- Brand recognition among customers

Because it is a first exercise, participants may focus on production in isolation and not on other aspects such as post-production and after-sales service. Participants should be asked to draw a multilevel figure where ingredients are at the bottom level, which link to benefits received by customers, at the middle level, which then lead to

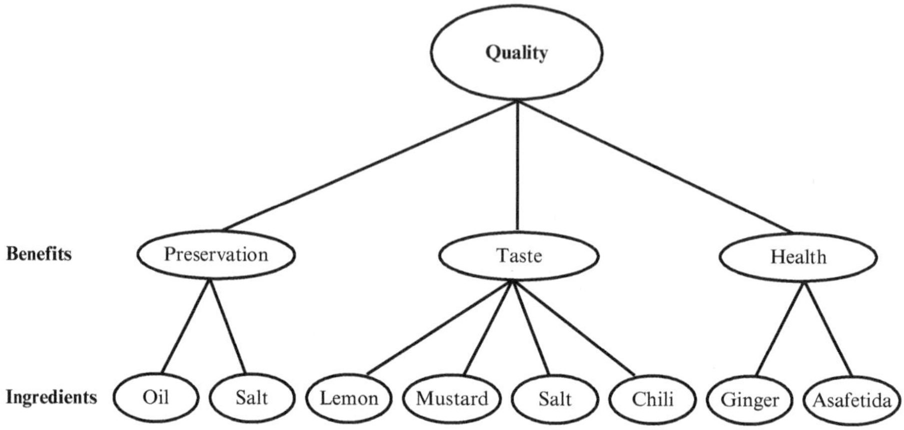

Figure 9 Understanding Customer-Oriented Product Design

overall perceptions of quality and satisfaction at the highest level. The aim here is to extend the implications of a customer orientation to product design. It is quite possible that a practical exercise may involve separating the task into two stages: first to list out ingredients and attributes, and next, to list benefits to customers (Figure 9).

Parallel to their presentation, the instructor should encourage discussion to classify the prescribed activities in product management and list them on charts as follows.

Input to product design and production:

- Updating knowledge on technology to make the product efficiently (e.g., how to make quality pickles)
- Identifying outlets to buy raw material or ingredients e.g., from retailers, wholesalers, or producers
- Deciding when to buy ingredients or raw materials, e.g., during periods of harvest or during periods when ingredients are cheaper in the market
- Mobilizing appropriate machinery, and labor, if necessary
- Using quality ingredients or raw materials
- Following a careful process of product design
- Ensuring hygienic (safe) preparation of the good or service
- Applying eco-friendly methods in the preparation
- Improving the attributes of products, e.g., spice, color, or aroma in the case of food items
- Providing information on usage of the product
- Packing and delivering products with adequate safety
- Using different package sizes and product type depending on the segment to be supplied
- Finding ways and means for storage, distribution, and delivery of the products

The instructor should remind participants of the relationship between product, pricing, distribution, and promotion. The instructor should also remind participants that the product design process does not end with determining the ingredients, but may need to be modified as issues of pricing, distribution, and promotion covered in subsequent sessions are considered. The central issue to emphasize here in product design is the need to understand the customer segment that the product is being made for, how customers will use the product, and what benefits they will derive from it. This understanding should form the basis for product design.

5.7 Summary

The instructor should facilitate a summary of topics covered in the last three days including Day 3:

- Understanding a customer-oriented philosophy of doing business, balancing buyer and seller goals through mutually beneficial exchanges
- Evaluating business opportunities through systematic assessment of needs, strengths and weaknesses, and competitors' strengths and weakness
- Understanding the role of research or information gathering
- Understanding customer behavior
- Product design

Chapter 6
Consumer and Entrepreneurial Literacy Program: Day 4 – Entrepreneurial Literacy

6.1 Introduction

6.1.1 Overview

Day 4 continues from the perspective of a seller. Factors to consider when setting price, the notion of value from the customer's perspective, the relationship between price and quality, and the relationship between price and volume are covered under pricing. Distribution is covered by using the concept of a value chain introduced on the first day. Again, participant-groups are asked to choose a particular product and work out various steps in the value chain from purchase of ingredients to distribution to wholesalers, retailers, and the end user. Exercises require participants to choose from distribution alternatives. Different types of promotions, ranging from banner advertisements to fliers, are discussed and related to different objectives, such as gaining awareness, generating interest, and encouraging purchase. It should be noted that the order of discussion of topics can be changed to cover pricing at the end as well. This provides the advantage of a fuller understanding of distribution and promotion costs. However, the current sequencing also has advantages in that the discussion of distribution and promotion can be used to revisit expenses and overall pricing issues.

6.1.2 Recap

The instructor can begin the discussion on price in the first session of Day 4, after summarizing the discussion of the previous three days by paraphrasing the main conclusions. The instructor should remind participants that information gathering or research is not a one-time exercise in business. It is an ongoing process to understand the marketplace and thereby provide quality products and improve service to customers. Such information gathering will be needed for pricing, distribution, and promotion as well.

6.2 Price

6.2.1 Assessing Value as Customers

The first major topic is understanding how to set prices. Figure 1 can be used to present the larger picture of the content being covered. The instructor can ask participants to list what they expect from a product when they analyze its price as a customer. Their views can draw from their life experiences as well as the learning from the first three days of the educational program.

Participants' responses may include:

- Value
- Usefulness
- Affordability
- Quality

The instructor should anchor the discussion on value from the customer's perspective, reinforcing its definition as what customers give and what they get in the trade-off. The instructor can remind participants that sellers have to acquire goods or hire services for manufacturing/producing a product and are, themselves, likely to be customers in their role as sellers. For example, to make batter, a seller has to buy goods such as rice, and urad dhal/black gram (type of lentils), and hire the services of wet-grinder mills. Participants can be asked to discuss what they give and get from the customer's perspective and then from the seller's perspective. Here, again the notion of value and how it is added at each step can be used to illustrate how costs accumulate.

Figure 1 Price[1]

[1]Adapted from Kotler, Philip, and Gary Armstrong, Principles of Marketing, 9th Edition, © 2001, p. 64, Figure 2.5. Reprinted by permission of Pearson Education, Inc., Upper Saddle River, NJ.

The instructor should ask participants in the course of the discussion as to what they expect from a product purchased from the market. Their responses may include:

- Satisfaction of core needs
- Affordable price
- Flexible quantity purchases
- Availability on time
- Availability at a convenient location
- Attractive design

The instructor should ask how a product fulfills customers' expectations and focus the discussion on value.[2] Responses may include the following. Value is added to a product as it passes through the value chain through such means as blending, adding ingredients, packing in different sizes, moving to different locations, and branding. Value includes benefits from the good or service, e.g., selling rice or grinding rice with other ingredients to prepare and sell batter, selling television sets or repairing them. Value includes other benefits such as customer service, and whether a particular product is available at a convenient place and time, in appropriate quantities, and with reasonable payment options. Value also includes psychological benefits; acquiring a product may enable customers to feel better about themselves. The instructor should highlight customers' statements that they buy only a certain brand of a product, such as soap or rice, to provide examples. The instructor should use customers' practices, such as exclusively buying and using eco-friendly products, to provide examples of psychological benefits.

The instructor should raise the question whether all customers would need or expect all benefits in a product and whether all sellers could provide such benefits to their customers. The instructor should remind participants of the discussion from the first day on segments and enable participants to understand different benefits in a product that may fit different segments. The instructor should explain to participants how customers may vary as to which product benefits they see as most relevant, the importance they attach to each benefit, and how they would pay most attention to benefits that deliver the sought advantages.

An example is presented below:

- Enabling mobility is the purpose of a bicycle and it should have basic parts, such as wheels, brakes, handlebar, and bell, to ride safely. However, a company may offer bicycles with additional features, such as gears and rear carriers.
- Pickles are used as a side dish, and can contain lemon or mango, oil, and spices, to provide taste. A seller may add ginger and asafetida for digestion and health reasons, and flavors for fragrance and attractiveness.
- A grinder is used to grind flour and some models may have a motor and a stone bed. A company may offer a tilting feature to collect ground flour, and motors with different capacities.

---

[2] Material on pricing is adapted from several sources including *Pricing: Making Profitable Decisions* (McGraw-Hill Higher Education, 2002) by Kent B. Monroe.

- A hotel room offers a place to stay and rest during travel with space, ventilation, beds, and toilet facilities. A service provider may offer spacious rooms with air-conditioning, room service, and a television, in addition to the basic needs served.
- A conventional vegetable cutter is made of steel with a wooden platform. A seller may add features, such as a coconut scraper and a steel platform, to make it useful for multiple purposes with a longer-lasting life.

The instructor can draw the diagram of a conventional vegetable cutter and another diagram with a coconut scraper as additional features to explain customer benefits. Further, the instructor can discuss two types of hospitality service providers in a category (e.g., lodges or motels), list out the customer benefits from both, and discuss the potential differences in price, as shown in Table 1. The instructor should ask what the charges of each provider would be, and whether they would be identical or different. Different colored chalk on a board or different colored ink on a chart can be used to draw a bar graph of benefits and price as shown in Figure 2.

The benefit bars of both providers can be hidden and participants asked which is costly and which is beneficial to customers (Figure 2). They may respond that the price of X is high and service provider Y might be beneficial to customers. The instructor should hide the price bar and ask participants which service provider gives more benefits (Figure 2). Responses from participants might point to brand X. The instructor should show both benefit and price bars, explain the differences, and remind the participants that the analysis should be based on the value of exchanges. Customers can choose the product which provides them with features or dimensions depending on their need and purchasing ability. Customers usually have to pay more or give more when they get more benefits from an exchange, and sellers could increase the price of a product depending on the benefit provided to the customer through additional features and dimensions. For example, better-quality rice can be priced relatively higher. There may be a relationship between price and quality, although this relationship may not hold often or may not hold for the entire range of prices. From a customer's point of view, it may be worthwhile to pay a little more to get better-quality rice but not too much more. Hence, the customer has to determine the price and quality levels at which there is best value, with affordability being the key constraint.

The instructor should raise a question whether a purchased product needs to be processed further with additional expense to the customer (e.g., purchase of raw chili, rice, or cloth, with additional or subsequent expenses, such as grinding

Table 1 Comparison of Two Types of Service Providers

	Customer benefits	Service provider X	Service provider Y
A	Rooms/space	Double room	Single room with limited space
B	Toilet	Individual attached toilet	Common/shared toilet
C	Air-conditioning	Air-conditioned room	Non-air-conditioned room
D	Phone connection	Intercom with telephone	Not available
E	Room service	24-hour room service	Not available
F	Food availability	Restaurant attached to hotel	No food service or restaurant inside the lodge

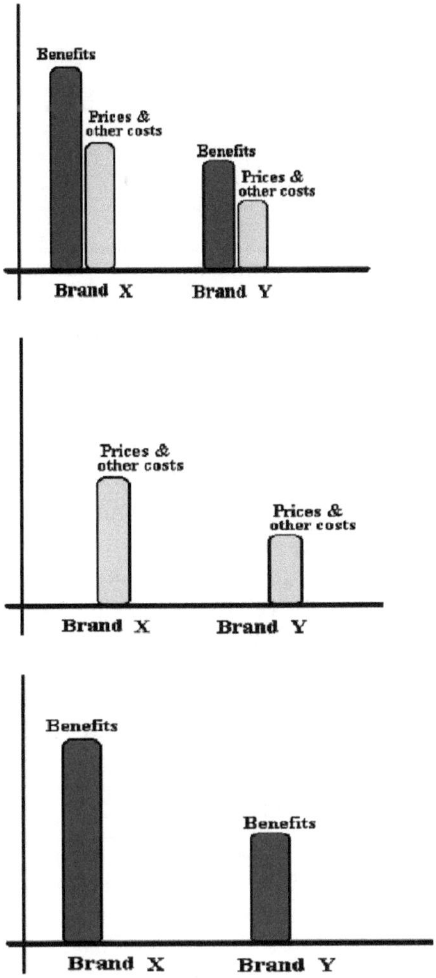

Figure 2 Understanding Value Trade-offs

charges for flour and tailoring charges for clothes). Here, an informed customer would compare and analyze the cost and consider options, such as making versus buying, and buying from local stores versus at larger markets. The discussion can be directed to understand various aspects including customer costs as shown below from the perspective of customers and the need to consider these costs while fixing the price of a product as a seller.

In addition to the purchase price, customer costs include the following:

- Costs for acquiring the product: e.g., entry ticket to a market, membership fee to join customer groups, registration charges for motor vehicles, transportation charges to buy from a distant location

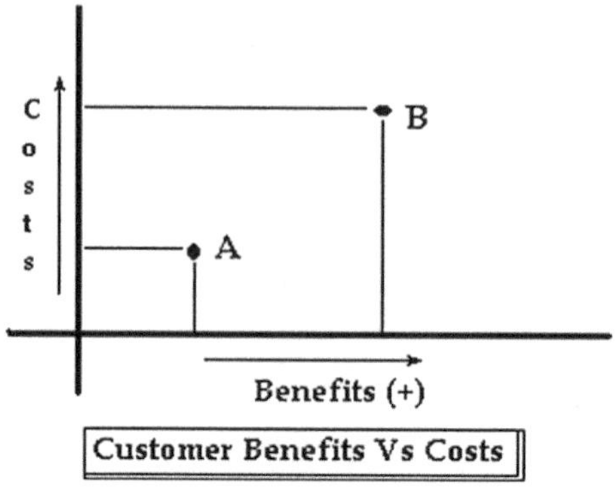

Figure 3 Customer Benefits vs Costs

- Costs for usage of a product; e.g., kerosene, firewood, or electricity to use an oven, fuel to use motor vehicles, and electricity or batteries to use radio sets
- Costs for maintenance of the product; e.g., wet-grinder, motor vehicles, and cycles
- Costs of ownership; e.g., tax for vehicles and assets, or license fees for shops
- Costs of disposal; e.g., veterinary waste and industrial waste

Figure 3 can be used to explain customer benefits versus costs.

6.2.2 Assessing Value for Sellers

The instructor should now shift the focus and ask participants to take the perspective of the seller. The instructor should ask what expenses are involved in each stage of adding value to the product, such as mobilization of ingredients, processing, manufacturing, packing in different sizes, transporting, wholesaling, and retailing. Having covered price from the buyer's perspective, the discussion can be directed toward why sellers charge different prices. Because participants have assumed the role of a businessperson from Day 3, the instructor should ask them what they understand about setting price. The instructor should facilitate the discussion and summarize it on a chart. Responses can be summarized to include the following general issues:

- Sellers may charge higher prices if they provide particular goods or services with unique product benefits, service benefits, or personal and image benefits to customers
- Product benefits for customers may vary for different products sold by different sellers, and, hence the prices may also vary

The instructor should ask participants why a seller charges a price for goods or services. The responses from participants should be paraphrased, such as that the seller charges for the value of goods or services exchanged in the trade-off, having invested money, goods, or service in each stage of adding value to the product reflected in the following costs:

- Ingredients
- Transportation
- Manufacturing machinery and equipment
- Processing and manufacturing
- Labor
- Commission
- Advertising, offers, and discounts
- Interest on the money invested
- Other overheads, such as electricity, phone, and rent
- Fees, charges, and taxes

The instructor should now ask participants to think about price from the seller's perspective. The instructor should ask participants what the objectives of the seller should be in setting price. Their responses may include providing quality products at affordable prices for different segments, making profits, or winning customers from competitors. The instructor should facilitate the discussion and note the key issues on a chart. Objectives may include the following:

- Meet or beat the competition
- Maximize profit
- Achieve return on investment

The time frame for these objectives may also vary from the short term to the long term. For example, low prices in the short term may lead to profits in the long term due to a large customer base and lower costs of producing in larger quantities. These objectives could be achieved in several ways including:

- Superior benefits to customers to expand the customer base
- Affordable, competitive pricing to attract more customers and maximize profits

The instructor can use the diagram in Figure 3 to explain how price may be lower when benefits are reduced and other customer costs are increased, as well as how price may be higher when customer benefits are increased. Price decreases should not sacrifice sellers' investments but rather enable them to compete by improving value. The instructor should remind participants that customers may assess the value of each exchange, i.e., customer benefits and costs, compare the prices of goods or service that are available with those of competitors in the market, and consider the price to pay. Customers may be willing to pay a higher price for a product with superior benefits.

The instructor should ask participants which type of expenses should be included or taken into account and which excluded while fixing the price. The instructor should facilitate the discussion and explain that expenses are not only costs associated with manufacturing goods or providing services, but also *all* other costs incurred for the production of goods or services including the following:

- Labor (paid and nonpaid) – e.g., one's own labor, relatives' labor
- Rentals for places and machinery used in the process of production

At the same time, the seller cannot expect the customer to pay for expenses that are not related to the product. The seller should distinguish personal from professional expenses. For example, a businessperson taking loans for family expenses or investing in family assets should keep such expenses distinct from business costs. A person who is running a flour grinding business at home and using electricity from the house cannot treat the entire electricity bill as investment in the production of batter. But the apportionment of electricity expenses should be equivalent to the actual consumption for the business or usage of the wet-grinder for business activities. The point here is to keep costs distinct and accurate to possess accurate information and enable effective and efficient functioning as a business. It is also important to factor in unpaid labor because there is an opportunity cost associated with working elsewhere and earning wages versus working for free in one's own business.[3]

Sellers should also distinguish between fixed and variable costs in setting price. Here, an example using products, such as pickle, can be employed to make the point (Table 2). Sellers could try to reduce their margin of profit or compromise on short-term profits to broaden the customer base and stabilize their business. Consider a flower seller who enters into an agreement with a shopkeeper or an individual family to supply two feet of garland (for worship) at a fixed price throughout the month or year. Although the market price of flowers is high, this particular seller may have to adjust the profit margin during the period when market price is lower, such as during specific seasons. This would enable the seller to retain customers in the long run. However, the seller should gather information and analyze costs to forecast long-term profits and fix the price accordingly.

The instructor should ask the groups who discussed product design the previous day to select the same product they focused on, discuss and present how they are going to fix the price, and how they arrive at the final price. Although different products could be used for different exercises, it is preferable to strongly encourage groups to stay with the same good or service to understand the linkages between product, price, promotion, and distribution.

Each group should explain their pricing methods and present rationale. They may anticipate the following expenses and treat them as investment costs of a product that they expect to recoup along with profits:

- Ingredients
- Transportation
- Processing and equipment
- Labor

[3] It should be noted that a central element of the adaptivity of subsistence entrepreneurs is in their ability to seamlessly move between personal and business domains (e.g., in using left over inventory, such as perishables, at home). Therefore, this broader issue should be factored into the discussion about the need to maintain distinctions between personal and business domains and subsistence entrepreneurs' adaptibility in this regard highlighted as being important and necessary.

Table 2 Example of Costs and Profits

Product identified for the business: Lemon pickle		
I. Product design		
a. Purchase of ingredients		
Condiments	Units/Qty (kg)	Estimated cost
Lemon (300 × Rs. 0.25)	300 Nos.	75.00
Gingili oil (2 × Rs. 80)	2.0 kg	160.00
Dry chili (1 × Rs. 25)	1.0 kg	25.00
Fenugreek (100 g)	0.1 kg	4.00
Mustard seeds (100 g)	0.1 kg	6.00
Asafetida (1 pack)	1 packet	10.00
Vinegar		10.00
Salt (1 kg)	1 kg	5.00
Ginger		5.00
Transportation & labor		120.00
b. Process		
Details	Units/Qty (kg)	Estimated cost
Chili – grinding charges		10.00
Kerosene for boiling & tempering		12.50
c. Packaging		
Details	Units/Qty (kg)	Estimated cost
Plastic covers (different sizes)	1 kg	25.00
Packing bottles	25 Nos.	100.00
Labels/wrapper sheets		25.00
Printing charges for product information		50.00
Candles to heat plastic covers for packing (local methods)		1.00
Paper cardboard (readymade) to clip pickle packets		5.00
Stapler & pins		15.00
Total	**10.0 kg**	**663.50**

II. Pricing		
a. Average production cost		
Details	Units/Qty (kg)	Estimated cost
Total quantity of product produced from the above ingredients & process	10.0 kg	663.50
Average cost	1.0 kg	66.35
Average cost (100 g)	0.1 kg	6.63

b. Tentative selling price

Details	Estimated units	Units cost	Estimated cost
0.50 kg bottle	8	60.00	480.00
0.25 kg bottle	10	30.00	300.00
0.10 kg packets	15	12.00	180.00
0.01 kg packets	200	1.00	200.00
Total			**1160.00**

(continued)

Table 2 (continued)

III. Promotion			
Details	Estimated units	Units cost	Estimated cost
Advertisement board	1	100.00	100.00
Labeling with product information			Covered earlier
Fliers			100.00
Commission charges (vary depending on the size of product/amount of sales)	[8×3 + 10×2 + 15×1 + 15]		74.00
Total			**274.00**

IV. Distribution			
Details	Estimated units	Units cost	Estimated cost
Delivery charges			Combined with commissions

V. Summary			
Details	Estimated units	Units cost	Estimated cost
Product (total expenses until production of product)			663.50
Promotion			274.00
Distribution			0.00
Total expenses/investment			**937.50**
Expected revenue			**1160.00**
Tentative profit margin			**222.50**

- Commission charges
- Other overheads such as electricity
- Packaging
- Advertising
- Offers and discounts

During the presentations, the instructor should use a chart to classify and note down the categories in which costs are incurred as shown below:

- Purchase of ingredients for the selected product
- Product preparation or manufacturing costs
- Packaging process and costs
- Distribution costs including assigning agents and delivery points
- Promotion costs including advertisements, commissions, gifts, offers, and discounts

The instructor should encourage participants to review the issues presented by all groups and summarize them as shown in Table 3. The key point to make here is to include all costs, direct and indirect, toward making and selling a product.

Improvements may be seen in participants' analysis when compared with the earlier exercise on product design. They may consider distribution and promotional aspects while fixing the price, in addition to the cost of the product. The

Table 3 Analysis of Costs

Product	Ingredients	Manufacturing & packaging	Distribution	Promotion
Pickles	Cost of lemon, oil, chili, mustard seeds, and other ingredients, labor, and travel	Expenses for grinding for chili, boiling, packet covers, printing labels, packaging, labor, and travel	Expenses for labor, transportation, and post-sales collections	Expenses for advertisements, commissions, gifts, offers, and discounts
Batter	Cost of rice, black gram, and fenugreek, labor, and travel	Expenses for grinding flour or wet-grinder, electricity, packet covers, printing labels, packaging, labor, and travel	Expenses for labor, transportation, post-sales collections, and shop rent/advance	Expenses for advertisements, commissions, gifts, offers, discounts, and interest on credit
Flower selling/ vending	Cost of flowers, yarn/fibers, labor, and travel	Expenses for packing leaves and covers, labor for weaving and countersales if needed	Expenses for labor, transportation, post-sales collections, and shop rent/advance	Expenses for display boards, offers, discounts, interest on credit, and investment
Masala/chili/ gravy powder	Costs of ingredients, such as chili, coriander, turmeric, and gram, labor, and travel	Expenses for grinding, electricity, packet covers, printing labels, packaging, labor, and travel	Expenses for labor, transportation, post-sales collections, and shop rent/advance	Expenses for advertisements, commissions, offers, and interest on credit

instructor should facilitate the discussion and remind participants about the relationship between product, price, distribution, and promotion. For example, producing pickle and packing it in identical quantities in very attractive bottles may not serve the purpose across different customer segments. The needs of different segments may vary and customers in different segments may expect different prices and different quantities, through different distribution channels. Hence, product design and price should be based on customer needs.

6.2.3 Discounts

The instructor should ask participants why sellers offer discounts and how discounts are decided in the marketplace. The instructor should use general practices of small-scale sellers as examples and direct the discussion to enable participants to understand price discounts and allowances[4]. Key issues to be covered include the following. Generally, sellers are more willing to reduce the price for buyers who pay their bills/dues promptly or who are regular customers. A typical example is an installment seller who offers different prices to buyers who settle the installment ahead of the agreed time. A seller is sometimes ready to reduce the price for those who buy large volumes. A typical example is a flower seller who sells woven flowers for Rs. 2.50 per 12 inches and is ready to provide an additional six inches free of cost to those who buy for more than Rs. 10. This is a quantity discount. A manufacturer generally offers discount to distributors and other agents to perform certain functions. For example, a manufacturer or wholesale distributor offers resellers money or additional goods free of cost. These are functional discounts. A seller may provide a small vessel for every purchase of a big household article. This is a free sample offer. A seller offers price reductions to those who buy goods or services off-season or in slow selling periods. Lemons would be costly in summer seasons but available for lower price in winter seasons. A parallel is with laborers being willing to work for lower wages off season. These are seasonal discounts. An extra payment may be designed to gain reseller participation in special programs, such as exchange melas (fairs), or promotional allowances may be paid for participating in advertising and sales support programs. A small scale pickles producer or sales agent may fix some margin for the reseller in addition to the general commission or labor charges to increase interest and participation in sales promotions.

Sellers may use several additional pricing techniques to stimulate early purchase:

- Price reduction on a few fast moving goods to draw in customers
- Special event pricing in certain seasons, such as festivals, or the new year, to draw in more customers
- Cash rebates to encourage purchase of specific products within a narrow time frame, which enables the seller to clear stock
- Loans offered over longer periods lowering monthly payments

[4] Many of the discounts discussed here are described in *Marketing Management* (Prentice-Hall, 11th edition, 2003) by Philip Kotler.

- Psychological discounting, such as by setting a high price and offering the product at a significant discount
- Loss-leader pricing where a store sets a very low price for one or a few products in order to influence customers to visit the store to buy other products.

It should be noted that the seller may forego short-term profits to build a customer base and achieve long-term profits. The instructor should remind participants that a seller could use one or more of the above but it is not necessary to provide any of the price discounts and allowances discussed. A seller should add manufacturing costs, service costs, and reasonable profits in the price of products, and should offer price discount and allowances if there is a short-term or a long-term advantage to doing so.

The instructor should discuss the consequences of price discounts. A customer may analyze prices and discount offers of different sellers based on market information. Lack of awareness of different pricing methods or poor experiences with this type of promotional pricing may lead to confusion and create an impression that all discounts are dubious. It is important for sellers to provide factual information about their product and pricing to their customers.

6.3 Distribution

The instructor should ask participants what is meant by distribution. Figure 4 should be used to present the larger picture of the content being covered. Distribution enables customers to use a good or service. It is the process of moving goods and services from production to consumption. Distribution involves various elements, such as transportation, and warehousing (one common set of stages is provided in Figure 5[5]).

Figure 4 Distribution[6]

[5] *Marketing Management* (Prentice-Hall, 11th edition, 2003) by Philip Kotler.

[6] Adapted from Kotler, Philip, and Gary Armstrong, Principles of Marketing, 9th Edition, © 2001, p. 64, Figure 2.5. Reprinted by permission of Pearson Education, Inc., Upper Saddle River, NJ.

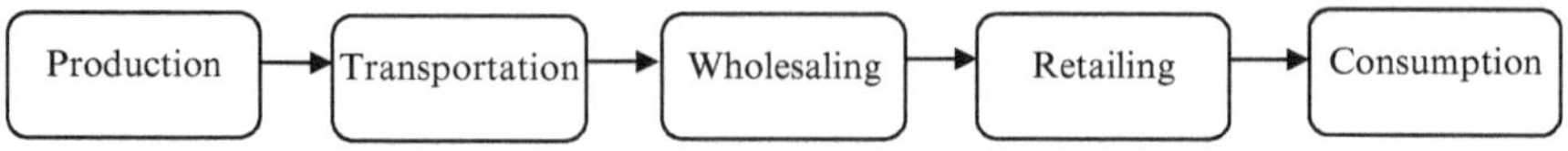

Figure 5 Stages in Distribution[7]

The instructor should link this discussion with the concept of a value chain, which was discussed on Day 1 and remind participants about the different stages they have listed out and their purposes. The instructor should ask participants to use these stages in completing the following exercise. Participants should work in groups and discuss distribution methods for a selected product, identify the segment, analyze how they are going to distribute the product and explain why they prefer the chosen method. To do so, they should first be asked to trace the entire value chain for the product. They should be encouraged to use the same product chosen for earlier exercises. Although different products could be used for different exercises, it is preferable to strongly encourage groups to stay with the same good or service to understand the linkages between product, price, promotion, and distribution. The instructor should facilitate group presentations, and list key points on charts. The presentations may include products they chose for the discussion, how they designed the product, what their anticipated segment is, what the value chain for the chosen product is, and what distribution channels they propose, with supporting rationale. The groups may prefer and propose means of distribution that are practical for small-scale manufacturers and sellers of particular products.

The following is a sample presentation proposed by a group for pickle distribution:

- Buy quality ingredients
- Prepare tasty pickles
- Pack in different sizes/packages, such as Rs. 0.50 packets, Rs. 1 packets, Rs. 5 packets, ¼ kg bottles, ½ kg bottles, 1 kg packets, and 5 kg packets.
- Sell to different customers through different methods of distribution depending on the needs

For example, persons living in neighboring houses who are working for daily wages may prefer to buy packets priced from Rs. 0.50 to Rs. 5. The seller should prepare packets to suit their requirements and distribute them through personal selling, and perhaps not depend on resellers or agents for this purpose. The seller could visit markets or other places where there are a large number of potential buyers and use personal selling. The seller could hire delivery persons for wages or appoint agents on a commission basis for supplying the product to retail shops in the vicinity. The seller could contact civic organizations, such as self-help groups, and places, such

[7] Adapted from Kotler, Philip, Marketing Management, 11th Edition, © 2003, p. 507, Figure 17.2. Reprinted by permission of Pearson Education, Inc., Upper Saddle River, NJ.

Table 4 Sample of Distribution Exercise

Product design/package	Customer groups	Distribution channels
Rs. 0.50 packets	Neighboring houses	Personal selling
Rs. 1 packets	Markets/junctions where people assemble	Direct sales
Rs. 5 packets		
	Retail/petty shops	Commission agents
	Nearby streets and neighborhoods	Self-help groups
1/4 kg packs	Relatives and friends	Personal selling
1/2 kg packs	Retailers and hotels	Direct sales
	Retail/petty shops	Commission agents
	Nearby streets and neighborhoods	Self-help groups
1 kg pack	Hotels	Direct sales
5 kg pack	Marriage halls/parties	Commission sales
	Wholesale shops/stores	

as companies or construction sites, with many potential buyers. These customers may prefer small packets as well as ¼ and ½ kg bottles. The seller could prepare such packages to meet the requirements of these customers and hire commission agents or make regular visits to distribute the product. The seller could use bulk packaging and solicit orders from hotels and marriage halls and provide functional discounts or commissions to intermediaries for regular orders. The instructor should ask participants for their rationale and summarize their responses as shown in Table 4. The instructor should remind participants that they should continue to conduct research to identify the emerging needs of customers as well as strengths and weaknesses of competitors to fine-tune the distribution of their product. Participants should also be asked to revisit costs originally considered under pricing and incorporate changes.

6.4 Promotion

The instructor should ask participants what they mean by promotions, and summarize responses. Promotion involves sellers' communications with current and potential customers. The diagram in Figure 6 should be used to introduce the topic and show how it fits in the bigger picture.

The instructor should pose a question about how sellers could communicate with customers about their product. The responses from participants may be as follows:

- Fliers
- Advertising on media including sign boards
- Personal selling
- Sales promotions

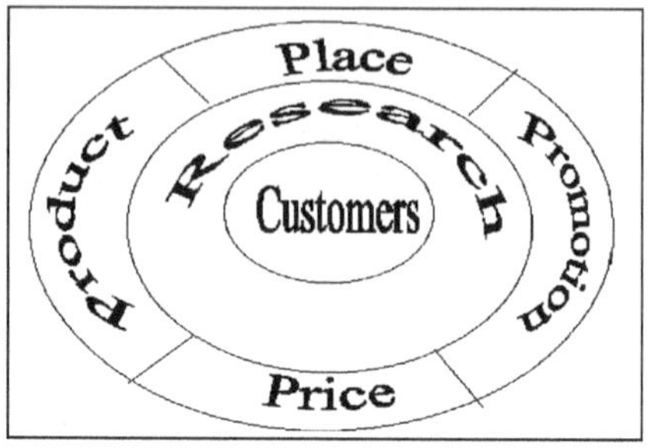

Figure 6 Promotion[8]

- Publicity
- Public relations
- Exhibitions
- Demonstrations
- Packaging

The instructor should group this list into major promotion methods, such as personal selling, advertising, sales promotion, and publicity. The instructor should pose the question as to why sellers have to communicate with their customers. The instructor should remind the participants of the purchase decision-making process of customers, such as problem recognition, searching for alternatives, evaluation of alternatives, purchase decision, and post-purchase satisfaction. The instructor should highlight searching for alternatives. The instructor should restate the definition for promotion after discussing the purpose of communications with customers.

The instructor should ask the same groups formed for earlier assignments on product design, distribution, and pricing to discuss viable promotion methods for a product and present how they are going to promote it and why they prefer specific methods. Again, it is preferable to focus on the products used in previous exercises. The presentation by each group should be noted on the charts. Some sample promotional methods covered in such assignments are listed below:

- Fliers, advertisement banners, and boards
- Advertisements through local periodicals
- Displays of materials and information
- Offers and discounts
- Free samples
- Public relations
- Incentives to dealers, retailers, and commission agents

---

[8] Adapted from Kotler, Philip, and Gary Armstrong, Principles of Marketing, 9th Edition, © 2001, p. 64, Figure 2.5. Reprinted by permission of Pearson Education, Inc., Upper Saddle River, NJ.

- Demonstrations and exhibitions at local and weekly markets, meeting halls, public celebrations of festivals
- Encouragement of word-of-mouth among customers

The instructor should use a sample product depending on the context and type of participants and facilitate the discussion as to how each of the following can be achieved through promotional methods. This is a modified series of steps based on the customer decision-making model, and can be elicited first through discussion about a specific product (Figure 7).

1. Customer awareness – How can customer awareness be promoted?

The instructor should ask participants why they propose to use fliers as a promotional method, what the fliers would contain, and whom they would be distributed to. Their responses may be that fliers should be distributed to the public to communicate with the potential segment and would contain information, such as the product and brand name, product usage, manufacturer's address for contact, outlets where the product is available, sizes/configurations/quantities and prices of the product, and customer service. Discussing whether everyone who received the fliers would buy the product should lead to specifying the promotional objective. For example, an objective may be to make customers aware of the product. This objective could be achieved through the use of a specific communication vehicle, such as a flier. The discussion should emphasize the importance of understanding what the promotional objective is before designing a communication. The instructor should remind participants about designing content related to the product that enables the seller to create awareness among the potential segments.

2. Customer interest – How can customer interest be promoted?

The instructor should pose the question as to how customers who are aware of the product can become interested in it. A variety of responses on different promotional means, such as visual displays with information, can be used to discuss this issue.

Figure 7 Hierarchy of Customer Responses[9]

[9] There are several examples of multi-stage processes similar to the one shown in Figure 7 in the literature. Several sources include *Marketing Management* (Prentice-Hall, 11th edition, 2003) by Philip Kotler, *The Psychology of Selling* (McGraw-Hill, 1925) by E. K. Strong, and "A model of predictive measurements of advertising effectiveness", *Journal of Marketing* (October, 1961), by Robert J. Lavidge and Gary A. Steiner.

3. Customer learning – How can customer learning be promoted?
The instructor should pose the question as to how customers who are aware of the product and interested in it can learn more about it. A variety of responses on different promotional means can be used to discuss this issue, including conducting demonstrations and exhibitions at local markets, at meeting halls, and at venues for public celebrations of festivals.
4. Trial – How can customers be encouraged to try a product?
The instructor should raise the issue of encouraging trial. Participants may propose free samples, personal contacts, and discounts to encourage customers to try a product. Free samples may achieve other objectives as well, such as awareness and interest.
5. Purchase – How can customers be influenced to buy?
The instructor should ask participants how customers can be encouraged to buy the product. Participants may suggest prominent displays to show product availability, low introductory price, and easy access to products. Here, different distribution methods listed in previous exercises can be reemphasized.
6. Repeat purchase – How can customers be influenced to repeat their purchase?
The instructor should ask participants whether the promotion methods aim for one-time purchases or repeat purchases. Participants may quote methods that would make the customers buy again, such as sharing business cards, providing post-sales services, providing incentives to dealers, retailers, and commission agents, increasing distribution centers and agents to reach the customers easily, entertaining advance orders, providing goods in advance and short-term credit facilities, providing quality products, and providing discounts to customers who influence others to buy the product.

The instructor should conclude the discussion by reminding participants of the importance of using specific promotional methods that are appropriate for specific products and customers and that are tied to specific promotional objectives. The instructor should also emphasize the importance of achieving all the promotional objectives leading to purchase and repurchase, such as awareness and interest. Having a quality product that no one knows about is not going to lead to purchase because of lack of awareness – the first promotional objective. Having a low-quality product is not going to lead to repurchase despite all the other promotional objectives being reached. These two scenarios, one where there is a quality product that no one has heard of, and one where customers are aware of and try a product but do not buy it again, can be posed as questions that participants should answer in terms of what the underlying causes could be. The instructor should also note that a promotional method may achieve multiple objectives. A free trial may achieve several objectives, such as awareness, interest, learning, and trial.

6.5 Summary

The instructor should emphasize the interrelatedness between various aspects, such as product design, manufacturing, pricing, distribution, and promotion, in developing a coherent approach to running the business.[10] The instructor should enable group discussion to summarize the key lessons in the last four days, and paraphrase the main points of each topic below:

- Understanding value and setting price
- Understanding value chains and making distribution decisions
- Fitting specific promotional methods to objectives such as awareness and interest

[10] Depending on the audience, a broader discussion of marketing and business strategy can be included. Similarly, a discussion of branding can also be provided in greater detail.

Chapter 7
Consumer and Entrepreneurial Literacy Program: Day 5 – Societal Responsibility and Other Miscellaneous Issues

7.1 Introduction

A number of miscellaneous issues are covered on the final day including the basics of accounting and finance, computing interest rates, and return on investments. Issues in organizational behavior, such as forming self-help groups and conducting negotiations would also be useful. Ethical issues in business should be discussed within the broader philosophy of balancing seller and buyer needs with societal good, including several topics, such as sustainable consumption and production, and environmental degradation. Discussion should also focus on seeking out opportunities proactively in an ever-changing world. Key issues learned from the first four days should also be summarized through discussion.

7.2 Ethics

7.2.1 Ethics as Buyers and Sellers

The instructor should invite participants to share their perspectives about ethics as buyers and sellers and note issues on a chart. Participants may use different words, such as justice, trust, honesty, and fairness. After discussion, the instructor should summarize that an important element of ethics is to follow the golden rule stated in many philosophies to "treat others, as you want to be treated". Hence, as a seller, one should treat buyers as one would like to be treated as a buyer and vice versa. The customer-oriented business philosophy covered on the previous days is based on mutually beneficial exchanges that are honest and fair. The figure of a balancing scale shown earlier should be used here (Figure 1 in Chapter 4).

7.2.2 Rationale for Ethical Practices

The instructor should then encourage participants to discuss the rationale for engaging in ethical practices. Participants may present different reasons for the need to be ethical, such as legal implications, social obligations, moral responsibility, healthy attitudes, and spiritual consequences. The instructor should probe each of these reasons. Participants may respond with reasons such as respecting religious faith and fear of God. The instructor could quote statements on ethics from major religions and philosophies. For example, as mentioned earlier, the golden rule can be used, which appears in some form in many of the religions and philosophies.

7.2.3 Ethics in Business

The instructor should use the broader discussion of general ethics to lead to the topic of "business ethics" and ask participants what the role of ethics in business is. Soliciting participants' responses on how they wish to be treated could stimulate discussion on ethics. The responses may include the following:

- Respecting individuals' feelings and inherent dignity
- Providing honest feedback
- Listening carefully
- Being polite and honest
- Avoiding cheating and deceptive behavior
- Engaging in sincere partnerships or relationships
- Tolerating/pardoning inadvertent mistakes
- Avoiding unnecessary suspicion
- Living up to commitments
- Extending help in times of need

The instructor should ask participants whether customers and sellers expect such treatment from their respective partners in business transactions. To stimulate further discussion, the instructor should ask participants to recall any arguments between sellers and customers that they may have witnessed in the past and to explain it further without revealing identities of individual sellers or buyers. They should be asked to list out the potential reasons for quarrels or conflicts between buyers and sellers, such as when each one considers the other's actions as unjustifiable. Participants may present potential reasons for arguments or quarrels that may lie either with sellers or buyers as listed below:

- Disrespectful behavior
- Overcharging
- Quality of purchased product not good
- Product not delivered on time or at the requested place
- Products delivered not matching buyer's order
- Seller or service provider not taking responsibility for poor goods or services
- Return or exchange of defective goods not accepted
- Payments not made as per agreement
- Buyer not accepting goods previously ordered

The instructor should facilitate the discussion and ask participants why conflicts happen. Responses can be paraphrased in terms of a buyer or seller failing to fulfill expectations. The instructor should ask participants what general expectations are and highlight responses. As some of these expectations are common to everyone, as a seller, one should treat buyers as one would like to be treated as a buyer and vice versa.

The instructor should clearly distinguish ethics from legality and ask what participants mean by legal implications and why there are codes and rules. For instance, some actions may be legal but unethical. The responses from the participants may include the following:

- Codes reflect the moral, social, and cultural obligations of citizens to their society
- Codes/rules provide guidance to resolve disputes between two or more persons

The instructor should request participants to list out ethical practices in business and underlying rationale. Answers and keywords about business ethics should be noted on a chart. Responses are likely to include aspects, such as trust, honesty, professionalism, concern for customer need, polite treatment of customers, accurate weight/measurement, and respect for customers.

Responses about the rationale for application of ethics in business include the following:

- Treat partners with respect
- Promote the business
- Create trust among the stakeholders
- Widen the customer base
- Maximize/increase profits
- Establish/create brand name
- Avoid disagreements and comply with legal and social obligation
- Create trust and repeat business

The instructor should paraphrase responses that suggested that an ethical way to consistently create wealth is by mutually beneficial exchanges. Profits and rewards would be the result of fulfilling legitimate expectations of customers and business partners. Therefore, ethical behavior can also make good business sense. This issue needs to be emphasized in summarizing the rationale provided by participants for ethical behavior.

The instructor should remind participants of a customer-oriented business philosophy, and contrast it with a production orientation or a selling orientation. With a customer orientation, customer needs are balanced against profit-making (Figure 1 in Chapter 4). The figure of a balancing scale can be used to emphasize mutually beneficial exchanges through ethical business practices. The instructor should point out the need for sellers to view themselves as customers and assess whether they would accept certain unethical behaviors. This is akin to sellers viewing their own products or ideas for products from the customer's perspective to see if they would buy the product.

7.2.4 Ethics, Business, and Society

The discussion can be broadened to include the third element in addition to buyers and sellers, i.e., society. An example should then be used to bring out the importance of this third factor. For example, trees are cut to use wood for basic human dwellings and other purposes. Customer-oriented products, such as wooden furniture, have been introduced in the market. However, overuse of wood leads to deforestation and affects the ecology.

Agrarian societies produced vegetables that were consumed by the people at large. Growing high-yielding varieties and using fertilizers are some of the ways through which production and sales of products have been increased. Foods are processed for transportation over long distances and storage for extended periods of times. However, chemical fertilizers and stimulants used in the cultivation of vegetables and chemical flavors used in processing can have negative effects in a variety of ways. Customers are now encouraged to buy vegetables cultivated from organic and eco-friendly farming methods.

More generally, the instructor should draw attention to the negative effects of over-consumption and the need to balance customer-orientedness and profits with the effects on society. The importance of sustainable production and consumption should be emphasized. The instructor should draw a diagram as shown in Figure 1 to explain the need to balance three elements: customers, profit, and society.[1] The instructor should state that a seller may follow business methods to gain high profit without concern for the other two elements in the figure and ask participants whether specific practices, such as those listed below, are acceptable:

- Selling rotten fruits/vegetables or defective products
- Selling adulterated goods
- Storing and selling food items in unhygienic places
- Selling banned drugs
- Using production methods that cause pollution
- Using and disposing materials while running a business without concern for the environment

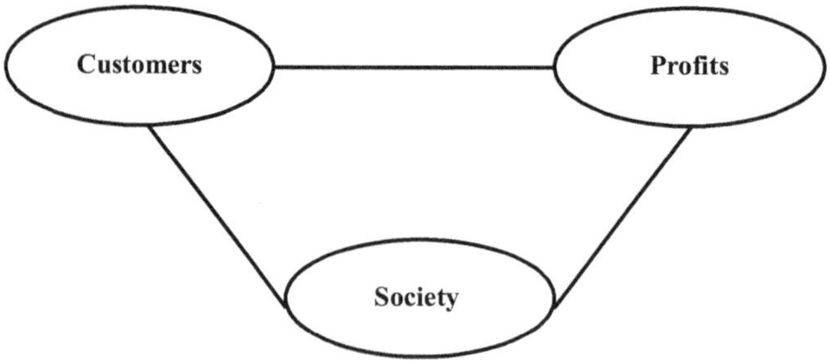

Figure 1 Balancing Customers, Profits, and Societal Responsibilities

[1] *Marketing Management*, 11th edition (Prentice-Hall, 2003) by Philip Kotler.

The instructor should ask participants what they consider as right ways of running a business when considering societal responsibility. The discussion should focus on examples of unethical practices, which would be against the interests and well-being of customers, sellers, and society. It should also be pointed out that good ethics can make good business sense, establish trust among customers, and lead to repeat purchase and loyalty. Examples from participants can be used that show trust in specific sellers because of ethical practices.

Examples that can be discussed include the following. Customers and sellers enter into written or oral agreements. Written communications, order forms, and bills, are examples of business activities based on written agreements. Oral enquiries and normal buying practices in the vegetable, fruit, and flower markets, provision stores, and roadside or small-scale eateries, are examples of conducting business based on oral agreements. Disputes may arise when the parties to the agreement fail to comply with it.

Customers approach tailor shops with the trust that their clothes would be tailored according to their requirements. Customers buy packed food items or wheat flour in plastic packets, sealed electronic products, or colored cloth, with the trust that they would meet the specifications and quality indicated by the producers. Often, the quality of the product may not be verifiable during purchase. Some disputes may arise when customers cannot expect and act on the premise that sellers will perform their roles competently and provide products of acceptable quality. Customers should also have reasonable expectations from products. In this regard, buying or selling a product should not be viewed as not a one-time event by customers or sellers.

The instructor should invite participants' responses on how sellers and customers can avoid disputes and maintain ethical relationships in business. Their responses may include honesty, trust, and avoidance of deceptive practices. The instructor should facilitate the discussion to enable participants to understand the role of clarity, equity, and justice in achieving ethical exchanges. Buyers and sellers should have clarity as to what they could expect from other persons and what they have agreed on. For example, as discussed on Day 2, a seller should clearly inform buyers about the warranty period on products, and buyers should also enquire about such issues before making purchases. Buyers should have clarity about the details of the product to be supplied. Sellers or buyers should not discriminate based on gender, caste, creed, income or literacy level, and religion. Buyers and sellers should provide an opportunity to the other party to present their views and concerns. Sellers and buyers should avoid coercive language, such as "Do this or else", and instead develop a language of choice, such as "Let's try this". Principled negotiations will occur only when there is trust, candor, and forthrightness in a relationship where both partners spell out their wants. Sellers should be ethical in transactions, take initiatives to continuously improve value, and avoid taking unfair advantage. Buyers and sellers should create opportunities to resolve their differences through one-to-one interaction, and respect for others' views and problems.

The instructor should ask participants whether buyers and sellers should identify and understand who is right and who is wrong, or what is right and what is wrong. The discussion should be facilitated to conclude that a workable ethical business system is based on mutually beneficial exchanges with full information, mutual respect, and empathy. Central here is concern about fellow human beings and society as a whole. Through consistent ethical behavior, trust can be established, which allows genuine business partnerships to form and grow. Lacking such ethical behavior, customers, profits, and society may suffer, i.e., all three elements in the triad that need to be balanced.

7.3 Costs and Accounting

Participants should be asked to study the chart with their expectations that were noted on the first day. The instructor should ask participants whether all expected topics and issues were covered in the last four and a half days. A likely response is that all the necessary topics were covered with the exception of specific skill training to produce a product. The instructor should underline participants' expectations on how to run a business without loss or how to identify and run a profitable business to lead the discussions on cost and accounting. The instructor should revisit the charts that present the issues and topics covered in the last four and a half days and ask participants whether the material covers all aspects of running a profitable business. The instructor should also ask participants how an entrepreneur could review the business to assess its profitability.

7.3.1 Cost Analysis

The instructor should ask participants to list out all expenses including product costs and administrative costs involved in running a business. Preferably, participants can work in groups with the product they have used on the previous two days and consider all the costs associated with running a business. The instructor should facilitate and summarize discussion to explain various costs. Participants should be asked to consider product and administrative costs, including the purchase of ingredients, processing, manufacturing, transporting, distribution, and promotion of products.

Another area that should be covered in detail is the distinction between fixed and variable costs. Using the example above, costs should be divided into fixed and variable costs. Understanding the nature of these costs is important for making decisions about how many units to produce and how to break even. Again, the example above should be fully worked out to explain break-even analysis.

7.3.2 Return on Investment

Sellers need to compute the return on their investment when running a business. For example, a seller could invest Rs. 300 in a plastic bucket business and make Rs. 40

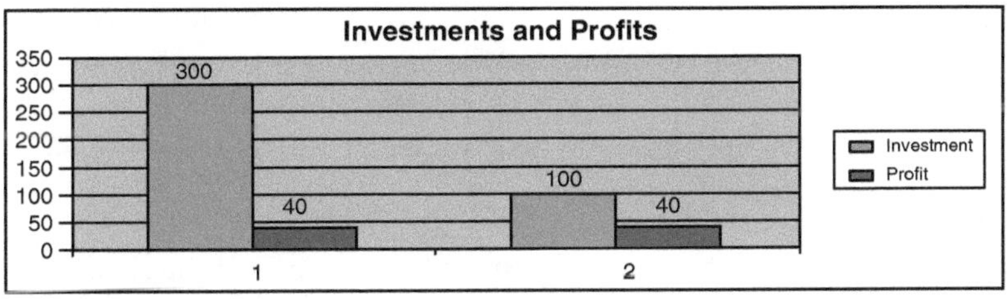

Figure 2 Understanding Investments and Profits

as average daily profit. The same seller could invest Rs. 100 in selling tender coconuts and receive the same Rs. 40 as average daily profit, using the remaining Rs. 200 for investment elsewhere (Figure 2).

7.3.3 Opportunity Cost

Opportunity cost is the cost of not pursuing an alternative opportunity. It is the income that individuals forego when they cannot pursue a specific alternative because they choose another. For example, a person may earn a salary of Rs. 2,500 per month by working for a company and an additional Rs. 500 per month in interest on a savings deposit of Rs. 10,000, for a total income of Rs. 3000 per month. Alternatively, this person could earn Rs. 2,500 on average per month from starting a new business with an investment of Rs. 10,000, currently in a savings account. By choosing to start a business, this person would have an income that is lower by Rs. 500 per month. However, the business may have potential to expand whereas the job may be uncertain in the future. The point here is to consider all costs in a decision along with various factors and time frames that cannot be easily reduced to rupee amounts.

7.3.4 Accounting

The instructor should pose the question whether business persons need to know the answers to the following:

- Whether their business is profitable?
- How their investment was used?
- What are the outstanding dues from customers or suppliers?
- What are the amounts payable to suppliers or financiers?

The instructor should ask participants how they can find answers to these questions. The instructor should remind participants that there are sellers who assess their business performances without proper records. The common perceptions among those who run their business without maintenance of records may be the following:

- Spending significant time or investing in more manpower will yield profits
- Buying cheaper material and selling it in the market will lead to profit and sustain the business
- Broadening the customer base will help to expand the business and lead to more profit
- High turnover will help the seller to increase profit
- "Rotation", i.e., increasing capital through borrowing or buying more products through credit and selling to customers on credit, will help achieve profits

However, just as conducting research and gathering information from the marketplace is important for making informed decisions, it is also important to maintain careful internal records to provide a sound basis for decision-making. Accounting records enable informed financial and other business planning. Because sellers run businesses to make a profit, they should analyze costs associated with various aspects, such as product, promotion, and distribution. This would be possible if they have accurate records for periodical analysis. This is no different than a buyer asking for a full listing of products purchased and money paid.

Sellers may seek the help of their siblings, relatives, or acquaintances to maintain and analyze records periodically. This would help them to keep control of resources needed to maximize profits and sustain the business. The instructor should facilitate a wide-ranging discussion and summarize responses, which may include the following:

- Record keeping may not have been prevalent when commercial activities were based on the barter system
- Recording business transactions likely became important after the introduction of money
- A seller has to extend customer service as a means of expanding the customer base or retaining current customers and may have to depend on credit transactions
- Sellers receive cash or materials in exchange for products supplied or machines or manpower and have different types of expenses (e.g., loans, credit purchases, credit sales).

It would be useful to revisit cost analyses from previous exercises, such as the ones on product design and pricing, to emphasize the inclusion of *all* costs, e.g., transportation or use of electricity at home for business purposes. Accounting enables systematic planning by providing accurate information. Moreover, in preparation for Day 5, half the participants can be asked to maintain accounts on paper on Day 2 for the next three days. In the current session, these participants as well as the other half of participants can all be asked to recall their expenses in order to show that writing down expenses provides a more reliable summary.

Purposes for maintenance of records include the following:

- To have reliable records of all the business transactions to refer to as needed
- To prevent or minimize misunderstanding or conflict with customers, sellers, and intermediaries
- To maintain records of income and expenses in order to calculate profit and loss, and assets and liabilities, and ascertain the progress of the business

- To monitor and control expenses, to maximize profits, or to minimize losses
- To maintain records of customers and suppliers and track pending dues
- To have information for legal and statutory requirements, such as registration with departments, and for tax purposes

7.4 Open Session for Clarifications

The instructor should invite participants to organize aspects, such as customers, research, product, price, distribution, and promotion in concentric circles to reflect the orientation of the educational program (Figure 6 in Chapter 6). The instructor should pose questions and suggest different configurations as a way of drawing out arguments about the figure. The instructor should display the charts completed on Day 1 that pertain to prioritizing elements of business at the beginning of the educational program and ask participants whether they find any changes in their perspectives. It could be used as one way of evaluating the effectiveness of the educational program. It would serve to evaluate effectiveness of teaching methods on issues and topics covered over the five days and assess the value of the program to participants.

The instructor should once again ask participants what should be the first step in evaluating business opportunities using Figure 4 from Chapter 5. The instructor should use this session to explore possibilities of introducing innovative goods or services and encourage the participants to exploit the potential in the marketplace, such as selling sliced, readymade vegetables for cooking, or delivering goods and services to customers' homes. This session should explore livelihood opportunities in the specific context where the program is conducted. This is particularly important in an era of globalization characterized by large changes that impact individuals living in subsistence. A brainstorming session customized to specific contexts can be very useful in this regard. Although we use products that participants can relate to in various exercises as a starting point, they should be encouraged to discuss a range of products, including those involving high technology. The importance of sustainable consumption should also be reiterated in this context with the need to balance societal concerns with profits and customer needs. Production methods that use resources in sustainable ways should be highlighted in this discussion.

7.5 Summary

The instructor should facilitate a group discussion to summarize key conclusions and lessons learned from all five days, and paraphrase the main points as shown below. Participants should be reminded of the concepts to be applied to facilitate mutually beneficial exchanges between buyers and sellers. A diagram of a scale with the customer on one side and the seller on the other used on Day 2 should be shown to conclude the discussion.

Day 1

- Expectations of participants at the beginning of the educational program
- Marketplace exchange and the evolution of technologies, products, and transactions over time
- Prioritizing elements of a business
- Goods, services, and segments
- Value chains consisting of multiple exchanges, with value being added at each stage

Day 2

- Effective practices of customers
- Consumer rights and responsibilities
- Value, the trade-off between what customers give and what they get in an exchange

Day 3

- Using a customer-oriented philosophy of running a business.
- Evaluating business opportunities through systematic assessment of needs, strengths and weaknesses, and competition
- Using research to gather information
- Basics of consumer behavior
- Customer-oriented product design

Day 4

- Understanding value and setting price
- Understanding value chains and making distribution decisions
- Promotional methods – fitting specific promotions to objectives, such as awareness and interest

Day 5

- Ethics
- Relationships between customers, profit-making, and society
- Sustainable production and consumption
- Costs and cost analysis
- Accounting and records
- Opportunities in an era of globalization

7.6 Conclusion

As a conclusion to the educational program, the following elements can be covered:

- Participants' feedback about the educational program
- Valedictory note and distribution of certificates if applicable
- Distribution of incentives to participants if applicable
- Vote of thanks

The program described here is the longest version we have conducted to date in order to provide as much detail as possible. However, in practice, what is currently being offered is 1- or half-day marketplace and consumer literacy programs, which cover what is presented on Days 1 and 2 in terms of basics of marketplace exchanges and consumer literacy, and a 1 or 2-day entrepreneurial literacy program. In a 1- or half-day marketplace and consumer literacy program, much of the discussion can be compressed to cover the following. Introductory remarks can be shortened and ice-breaking exercises and other games can be eliminated.

Registration
Introduction – ice-breaking exercise omitted
Expectations – compressed statement by instructors
Prioritizing elements of business
Evolution of products, technologies, and transactions
Customers, consumers, and end users
Goods, services, and segments
Value chains

In our experience, it is possible to cover these topics in about 2.5–3 hours and then move to the second major topic of consumer literacy. Here, the role-play for vegetable shops and for a grocery store, as well as the quiz, can be completed in about 2.5–3 hours while emphasizing the points below:

Consumer literacy
Understanding and assessing products
Value in exchanges
Skills and knowledge for consumer decision-making
Consumer rights and responsibilities

In sum, these two major topics can be covered either in a 1-day program or in half- or three fourth of a day program as needed. These topics provide the basis for the entrepreneurial literacy education. All aspects of the entrepreneurial literacy education need to be covered and can be done so within time constraints, averaging about an hour per topic:

Review of business perspectives
Evaluation of business opportunities
Elements of research
Consumer behavior
Product design
Price
Promotion
Distribution
Ethics
Costs and accounting

A marketplace consumer and entrepreneurial literacy program could be conducted in one, two, or three days depending on time constraints. A number of approaches are being tested in this regard. In conclusion, our comprehensive 5-day program has provided a sound basis with which to experiment and create different configurations in terms of duration and content, as well as envision other modes of delivery, such as the electronic medium, that we discuss subsequently.

Chapter 8
Implications for Nonprofit Organizations

This chapter briefly summarizes the implications of this educational approach for social initiatives by nonprofit organizations. These implications extend to both governmental organizations and NGOs. We begin by emphasizing the distinct aspects of our program in terms of a focus on the know-why followed by the know-how. We then discuss how consumer and entrepreneurial literacy programs can complement other initiatives. Another section highlights the need for nonprofit organizations to adopt marketplace literacy education for their employees and volunteers and view developmental approaches from the perspective of satisfying "customers." We then discuss operational aspects of our program. The chapter concludes with a discussion of scaling and customization issues based on our experience to date.

8.1 Addressing The Know-Why and The Know-How

A number of resources are needed to function in the marketplace including financial resources and know-how. Having finances alone without the know-how, or a specific vocational skill can often lead to failure of an enterprise. Our focus is on the know-how which could be categorized at three levels; at the lowest level in terms of vocational literacy, at the middle level in terms of the know-how to run aspects of a business, such as keeping accounts or designing products, and at the higher level in terms of the know-why, an understanding of marketplaces and aspects, such as understanding the need to satisfy customers to succeed, or deciding how to choose a business. This higher level provides deeper understanding and a basis from which to learn about specific aspects, such as product design and pricing, that are all related back to a customer orientation. Our program is unique in this respect, in focusing on the higher level know-why as the starting point. We found many programs that address the lowest (vocational) level, few that addressed the middle (know-how) level, but none that addressed the highest (know-why) level.

Unique to our approach in terms of content is a focus and a discussion of the know-why as a basis for the know-how. In other words, an understanding of aspects, such as marketplace exchanges and the need for customer orientation, form the basis for the "how" of product design and promotion and other such topics.

Central to our approach is a learning sequence that begins with a deeper understanding of the marketplace and then moves to middle level "how to" issues which are then applied to lower level trades or products. The sequence of learning in our educational program begins at the highest level of understanding and is followed by the "how" of various aspects of running an enterprise, with examples of specific products or trades being covered in the application of the know-how. A central objective of this approach is to enable some degree of choice for individuals to proactively influence the marketplace, rather than being exclusively reactive in terms of their choice of business or how they conduct their business. We envision individuals with the know-how to use the existing set of livelihood opportunities, and also to innovate in a variety of ways to fit in the value chain, particularly important in an ever-changing world. As discussed, a poor individual who knows how to cook may set up a food shop, using available resources or by taking a loan. Our aim is to enable somewhat more abstract thinking based on an understanding of the marketplace. Perhaps, the food shop is the wrong business to be in, and a broader set of options need to be considered. Perhaps, the right location needs to be chosen for the food shop. Perhaps, it may be preferable to be in the business of supplying food ingredients, such as dough for snack items, to families and hotels. Alternatively, the microentrepreneur may not know how to run the business. Therefore, the know-why as a basis for the know-how can provide such entrepreneurs with the broader background to enable more abstract thinking in the marketplace realm and to learn how to learn about marketplaces.

8.2 Consumer and Entrepreneurial Literacy as Complementing Other Initiatives

Consumer and entrepreneurial literacy programs can supplement a number of initiatives and a few examples are discussed below.

8.2.1 Complementing Financing Initiatives

Numerous nonprofit organizations across the world provide financing and small grants to enable entrepreneurship. Often, such loans or grants are preceded by assessment of a number of factors, such as likelihood for success and repayment of loans. A version of our educational program can be considered as a prerequisite to such initiatives that can increase the likelihood of success for microentrepreneurs. Completion of the program, in addition to serving as a screening device, could provide the skills and confidence necessary to run a microenterprise.

Our experience with conducting these programs is that it can be used as a means to identify individuals interested in pursuing entrepreneurial activity, although proper procedures should be in place to maintain fairness, as well as transparency regarding the purpose of the program. Our approach has sometimes been to provide a 1-day marketplace and consumer literacy program, and then seek out individuals who complete this program to self-select into the entrepreneurial literacy program. Our program could also be customized wherein individuals come up with a plan for a microenterprise at the end of it that represents a part of the application process. Our approach also attempts to address some of the failures from financing efforts, such as lack of know-how or even apparent lack of interest and motivation, which may be related to know-how or self-confidence. A vast literature on microfinancing has documented the phenoemenon and its benefits and weaknesses (e.g., Ackerly, 1995; Conroy, 2003; Kabeer, 2001; McDermott, 2001; McGuire and Conroy, 2000). Our recommendation that marketplace literacy programs complement microfinancing efforts is consistent with the need for integrative development strategies that address needs in a variety of realms, such as education, health and sanitation (Fairley, 1998). A number of issues, such as the narrow livelihood opportunities that individuals consider or lack of previous entrepreneurial experience (Kabeer, 2001) or lack of sufficient skills to run a microenterprise, are addressed by our approach.

8.2.2 Complementing Livelihood Initiatives

Our educational approach is ideally suited to organizations that can also provide a range of entrepreneurial opportunities. Organizations that can provide a backbone of entrepreneurial opportunities for subsistence individuals would benefit from our approach which provides the know-how. Although only a limited number of entrepreneurial opportunities may be feasible, understanding the know-why as a basis for the know-how can enable individuals to innovate and create new opportunities and think outside the box. As discussed, our goal is to enable individuals who are contemplating a business closely tied to their existing skill set to think more abstractly about where they could fit, whether in terms of geographic location or in the value chain, and to proactively influence the marketplace and innovate in a variety of ways in an ever-changing world. For example, for the individual who runs a food shop and makes snack items, opportunities may lie in preparing an ingredient (such as the dough used to make snack items) and delivering it door to door or to hotels, or in locating the business in an optimal place and so forth. The skills and self-confidence that underlie proactive thinking need to be provided through marketplace literacy educational programs.

8.3 Marketplace Literacy for Employees and Volunteers of Nonprofit Organizations

Our marketplace literacy program also has relevance for employees and volunteers who implement developmental efforts and delivery of services in nonprofit organizations. The notion of serving "customers" and understanding the marketplace has implications for socially driven organizations as documented in the literature on social marketing (e.g., Andreasen and Kotler, 2002). Our program can enable low-literate employees and volunteers to understand customer orientation and market orientation and apply it in their day-to-day activities.[1] A number of issues, such as product design, pricing (in terms of costs to potential beneficiaries that are usually other than money and expenses for nonprofit organizations), distribution, promotion, and performance (measured through efficiency and effectiveness in delivering social value) can be considered along with an understanding of consumer behavior through market research. Also pertinent are the strengths of the organization in delivering a specific service, such as adult education, and the range of issues that arise from a customer orientation. Our program can be customized to include such examples of services offered by nonprofit organizations to educate their employees and volunteers, using input from a variety of stakeholders. The program can also be customized to different contexts, such as for leaders of self-help groups or operators of computer kiosks.

8.4 Operational Aspects of the Marketplace Literacy Program

Much of our experience has come from working with community-based organizations. Our approach has been to undertake all educational expenses but expect such organizations to recruit interested participants and provide space for conducting the program. We have not agreed to terms, such as paying a certain amount for each participant recruited in our program, but rather requested that organizations seek out interested participants. Our emphasis is on investment and commitment from the organizations we work with and from participants as well, usually in terms of time.

Our central cost relates to salaries for instructors. Additionally, for each program, our expenses are for stationary (e.g., charts, pens) and other requirements (e.g., vegetables and weighing balances for setting up simulated shops). Our approach as it relates to incentives for participants has been to recruit them, usually without offering any incentives. On occasions when we have voluntarily given out gifts at the end of the program, we have usually done so without announcing it up front. Our proposition to individuals has been that we would provide an educational program for which we ask for their time and attention. In our experience, levels of attendance have been very high and individuals who have attended our educational program have displayed a sincere interest in learning.

[1] Interestingly, this possibility was raised by employees of a non-profit-organization in the course of learning how to impart our marketplace literacy program to the communities they serve.

8.5 Scaling and Customization

A number of macro level issues are relevant to the process of scaling up this approach. At the outset, it should be noted that the very notion of scaling as in taking a single model and applying it in all situations needs to be viewed with much skepticism. Rather, the approach needs to be customized to different situations, while retaining the key elements of the program, such as the design of instructional methods, the emphasis on concepts and basic understanding of marketplaces, and the dual approaches to buyer and seller issues. Such a willingness to constantly adapt is necessary, given the myriad differences between urban neighborhoods, villages, states, and regions, as well as countries. These differences range from livelihood opportunities to sociological dynamics.

8.5.1 Scaling Through Self-Help Groups

A number of approaches could be adopted to scale such nonformal education. One promising approach is to train self-help group leaders or other individuals in a community to conduct the program with appropriate supervision. Such an approach would leverage the one-to-one interactional marketplace characterized by rich social networks. In carrying out such an approach, it should be noted that much of the learning arises from group discussions. Therefore, instructors would need clear guidance on introducing topics and tasks, supervising small group discussions, conducting class discussions, and reiterating key issues and lessons learned. The supervisory level is important in that it should ideally consist of individuals who have a good grasp of the curriculum, and combine knowledge of the content with knowledge of instructional methods. Such scaling assumes organizational support to reach a large number of self-help groups. This approach could also be supplemented with video- based or computer-based exercises and educational material. With the increase of televisions in subsistence contexts, video-based exercises and instruction could be used to supplement the efforts of program coordinators.

8.5.2 Scaling and Customization Through Large Organizations

Another approach to scaling is through working with a large organization that provides comprehensive services. Our experience currently in progress with one such organization, the Byrraju Foundation, in the state of Andhra Pradesh in Southern India, is noteworthy. This organization provides a variety of services to numerous villages, including adult literacy programs and livelihood opportunities.

Our initial interaction involved a demonstration of an abridged version of our program with a translator who spoke the local language, i.e., Telugu. Our audience included potential participants and instructors, as well as facilitators from the organization. Our team consisted of the three authors and a translator. We commenced with a brief discussion of expectations followed by two picture based exercises to bring out the centrality of exchanges in the economic realm and the importance of serving customer needs to succeed as a business, respectively. We then explained distinctions between types of customers and also discussed customer groups or segments through pictorial tasks. We briefly introduced the notion of a value chain where exchanges add value at each stage. We then covered consumer literacy and the guiding notion of value. We used simulations of vegetable shops, and a grocery shop, and conducted an audio quiz to cover issues in a participatory fashion. In the next part of the program, we emphasized that participants were to take the role of entrepreneurs. We discussed topics such as choosing a business, conducting research, and understanding consumer behavior. We then discussed product design for specific products chosen by groups. This was followed by a discussion of promotion, distribution, and pricing. We emphasized the interconnections between the previous sessions and the entrepreneurial literacy sessions and the need to design valuable and mutually beneficial exchanges.

Some general observations are noteworthy. Although the audience consisted of rural participants from a different state in India, their reactions were typical, emphasizing the value in our approach. The translation emphasized the importance of terminology in Telugu, the language spoken in Andhra Pradesh. It also emphasized the need for an instructional manual for instructors and handouts to participants in Telugu. The active participation of facilitators who combined knowledge of content with knowledge about the audience was invaluable.

The next stage involved conducting a full 5-day program where the audience consisted of 24 trainers-of-trainers, i.e., individuals who would train the actual trainers who deliver the program. These trainers-of-trainers, in turn, would train and supervise trainers in a total of approximately 150 villages. The trainers would provide the program to groups of individuals in villages, eventually directly reaching 40,000 to 50,000 individuals, and indirectly reaching the members of the households these individuals belong to. This approach can also be supplemented with video-based or computer-based exercises and other instructional material. At the end of this 5-day program, tentative plans to move forward to facilitate the process of trainers-of-trainers training the trainers were developed and are presented in Appendix 1.[2] These plans provide an exemplar of the gradual development of content as the piloting moves forward and communication with facilitators, trainers-of-trainers and trainers required for implementation.

8.5.3 E-Educational Programs in Consumer and Entrepreneurial Literacy

Another promising approach to scaling and customization is through e-education. A confluence of several factors suggests attempting to scale our current efforts through computers and computer centers. These factors include the spread of computer centers to rural areas (e.g., in India), their use for adult education, and the use of computers for simple transactions or to search for information. Computer kiosks can be considered

[2] Our activities in this regard will be continuously updated at www.marketplaceliteracy.org.

as hubs for a computer led e-learning approach. Computer portals can be used for an electronic version of our program, with coordination by, say, the leader of a self-help group or an employee of a computer center. Unique here is computer-led in-depth education for low-literate audiences, an approach with the potential to scale non-formal education in general. Such scaling typically requires overcoming challenges associated with the instructor-intensive nature of educational efforts.

Whereas such an approach appears possible in theory, there are a number of elements to consider. We envision a number of possibilities posed as questions.

- Can the program be completely online?
- Can the program be online but coordinated by self-help group leaders or computer center owners?
- Can the program be online but actively taught by self-help group leaders or computer center owners?
- Can the program be in the form of support for direct instruction (self-help group leaders or computer center owners), such as through slides and other instructional support?

Much of the learning that occurs in such an educational program is through interactions among participants and discussions. Therefore, the e-educational approach would need to retain these important elements. Thus, topics could be initiated through a computer animation or game, used as a basis for group discussion, followed by group interaction with the computer and conclude with feedback from the computer interface. Essential here is the need to keep interactions with the computer interesting and brief. Also of relevance here is perhaps the need to consider alternatives to delivering a single educational program, such as a series of sequential exercises or games that build on each other to cover specific topics. Such an approach allows flexibility for participants to learn over a long period of time as well as flexibility in using the computer facilities. However, such flexibility may come at a cost in terms of the intensive learning that can occur through a program where topics are covered contiguously in a short time frame. For illustrative purposes, a description of a possible computer administered program focusing on the first two days of the 5-day program, marketplace literacy and consumer literacy, is presented in Appendix 2.[3]

Finally, an important issue here is related to scaling and the need for a model that would enable and incentivize organizations and individuals to participate in this initiative. The e-educational program could provide added content in computer kiosks that are run as sustainable businesses, as social initiatives, or as supplementing the value chain for businesses providing goods and services.

A constant challenge in this as well as other efforts to reach larger audiences is the need to separate what "sounds good" from the actual benefit that is reaching participants through careful design and assessment. The promise of reaching wide audiences through the use of technology is difficult to ignore. However, promise may not become reality because of a variety of reasons, such as dilution because of the mode of delivering the program.

---

[3] We thank Susan Byrd for designing this e-educational program for illustrative purposes and preparing the appendix.

8.5.4 Marketplace Literacy in Advanced Economies

Although this book is focused on subsistence marketplaces using research in India, our experience has implications for developing marketplace literacy programs for low-literate, low-income individuals living in advanced economies, such as the USA. For example, in the USA, functional low literacy is sizable, as is poverty. Adult education programs represent excellent examples of providing individuals with marketplace skills, as do other programs, such as nutritional education, which provide skills in specific domains. However, there is a need for systematic development of a marketplace literacy program that is customized to the customer-to-large-corporation context that characterizes advanced societies, as well as the nature of entrepreneurial opportunities available. A few key issues are highlighted here.

Central to such an approach, and in stark contrast to our approach in India, is the need to enable marketplace skills in an environment that is rich in symbolic information, such as on packages. Therefore, considerable emphasis has to be placed on understanding symbols and using printed information, such as on packages and advertisements. This is in contrast to the generic nature of products and the need to evaluate them in experiential ways that characterize the subsistence marketplaces we studied in India as well as the frequent face-to-face communications. In this regard, our work in the USA has emphasized developing user-friendly nutrition educational materials that do not assume processing of complex text and abstract information (Viswanathan and Gau, 2005). This is all the more pertinent in the larger context of a plethora of products in a western context, and the need to make sense out of the complex environment filled with textual and visual information.

Also relevant here is the need for counting skills in an environment where technologies are used for adding and other computations needed in interacting with the marketplace. In contrast to the widespread verbal counting methods that we found in our research in India, low-literate individuals in the USA have considerable difficulties with computational tasks (Viswanathan et al., 2005). This causes a number of problems in negotiating the shopping environment, such as in totaling shopping baskets, ordering from a menu, and so on. Low-literate individuals display ingenuity in confronting these problems, such as devising pictorial ways of adding and subtracting, for example, using images of currency notes (Viswanathan et al., 2005). However, central to marketplace literacy education is the need to enable the development of computational skills in a shopping context.

Central to the problems that low-literate consumers face in the USA are issues of self-esteem. Therefore, increasing self-confidence and awareness of rights should be central to the goals of marketplace literacy education. This is particularly difficult, given the stigma attached to low literacy and associated low income in advanced societies. In contrast to the rich social networks that we can leverage in subsistence contexts in India and the camaraderie and empathy that develops due to shared adversity in a one-to-one interactional environment, the challenge for marketplace literacy education in advanced societies is to overcome the isolation that low-literate individuals feel in environments where certain levels of literacy are assumed. Noteworthy is the lack of two distinct marketplaces in advanced societies to the extent that is found in subsistence contexts in India. As a result, businesses, such as large retail stores, may not cater to the needs of low-literate, low-income customers to the degree that small outlets in subsistence contexts in India do.

On the entrepreneurial side, the customer to large corporation relationship that characterizes advanced economies provides another contrast with the subsistence marketplaces we studied in India. Often, employment opportunities are in narrowly defined capacities within a large organization. The two-sided nature of buyer and seller in subsistence marketplaces in developing contexts may not fully transfer to such a setting, nor do many of the aspects of the marketplace literacy program based on this notion. Shared learning and shared adversity between low-income buyers and sellers in the same neighborhood may not translate to an environment characterized by large businesses. Nevertheless, because of the experience that individuals have as customers, the approach of using consumer literacy to engender entrepreneurial literacy has intuitive appeal. Also important in developing entrepreneurial literacy is the need to enable ways of proactively finding self-employment opportunities in an advanced economy. The key to an entrepreneurial literacy program is to filter down the relevant business concepts and convey them in a manner that relates back to individuals' lived experiences. Just as livelihood opportunities need to be provided by organizations in the subsistence contexts in India, organizations that proactively create livelihood opportunities in advanced economies can enable entrepreneurial activity.

Although a number of unique challenges need to be confronted in developing marketplace literacy programs for low-literate, low-income individuals in advanced economies, the presence of infrastructure, such as in terms of adult education centers or public libraries, offers some unique opportunities as well. For example, the potential to scale efforts through e-educational approaches are substantial. As is the case with our work in India, there are many innovative examples of marketplace related educational programs to draw from. There is much to learn from the work of instructors in literacy and nutritional education programs in designing marketplace literacy programs or adapting existing ones.

Finally, it should be emphasized that subsistence contexts with extreme poverty does exist in advanced economies, such as the USA. In such contexts, the need to be entrepreneurial is critical. Depending on the level of poverty and literacy, different types of approaches to marketplace literacy education may be needed that range from approaches that resemble our program in India in some ways to ones that are considerably different. The systematic research-based process that we used is instructive in this regard as are the curriculum development and delivery issues.

8.6 Conclusion

Our educational approach has important implications that extend to both governmental organizations and NGOs. Our distinctive focus on the know-why as a basis for the know-how offers a number of advantages. The consumer and entrepreneurial literacy programs can complement other initiatives, such as microfinancing. Marketplace literacy education is also relevant to employees and volunteers of nonprofit organizations in viewing developmental approaches from the perspective of satisfying "customers." A number of operational aspects of the program and issues relating to scaling and customization provide insights about its implementation in different contexts.

References

Ackerly, B. A. (1995). Testing the tools of development: Credit programmes, loan involvement and women's empowerment. *IDS Bulletin*, 26(3), 56–68.
Andreasen, A. and Kotler, P. (2002). *Strategic Marketing for Nonprofit Organizations*, 6th edition. Prentice-Hall.
Conroy, J. D. (2003). *The Challenges of Microfinancing in Southeast Asia*. Institute of Southeast Asian Studies, Singapore.
Fairley, J. (1998). New strategies for microenterprise development: Innovation, integration, and the trickle-up approach. *Journal of International Affairs*, 52(1), 339–350.
Kabeer, N. (2001). Conflicts over credit: Re-evaluating the empowerment potential of loans to women in rural Bangladesh. *World Development*, 29(1), 63–84.
McDermott, P. (2001). Globalization, women, and development: microfinance and factory work in perspective. *LBJ Journal of Public Affairs*, 13(1), 65–79.
McGuire, P. B. and Conroy, J. D. (2000). The microfinance problem. *Asia-Pacific Review*, 7(1), 90–108.
Viswanathan, M. and Gau, R. (2005). Functional illiteracy and nutritional education in the United States: A research-based approach to the development of nutritional education materials for functionally illiterate consumers. *Journal of Macromarketing*, 25, 187–201.
Viswanathan, M., Rosa, J., and Harris, J. (2005). Decision making and coping of functionally illiterate consumers and some implications for marketing management. *Journal of Marketing*, 69(1), 15–31.

Appendix 1

An Example of Scaling Through Large Organizations

The listing below captures key issues relating to the educational program in the process of scaling.

General educational suggestions

- Begin with simple goals
  - 1-day marketplace and consumer literacy program described below could be sole focus initially
  - Most meaningful exercises could be used as starting point as suggested below
- Use a pilot training conducted by trainers-of-trainers to fine tune
- Customize examples and group exercises to livelihood opportunities in villages

- Configure program in terms of duration and content
- Develop support materials including computer based material over time

Program configuration

- 1-day (or 6-hour) marketplace literacy and consumer literacy program
  - This content is usually useful to all low-literate, low-income individuals and also provides the basis for entrepreneurial training
- 2-day (or 1.25 days in compressed form) entrepreneurial literacy program for interested participants who complete the 1-day program

Program content

- 1-day marketplace and consumer literacy program:
  - Marketplace literacy and a focus on exchange
    - Expectations
    - Exercise on prioritizing elements for a business and discussion
    - Exercise on evolution of technologies, products, and transactions followed by conclusion about customer orientation
    - What is a value chain? What are goods versus services? What are market segments?
    - Summary of exchanges as being central to marketplace activity; multiple exchanges and the formation of value chains; serving customer needs and its centrality to success
  - Consumer literacy and a focus on value
    - Grocery store exercise and illustrative issues
    - Audio quiz and illustration of issues
    - Summary of value
- 2-day entrepreneurial literacy program:
    - Expectations
    - Repeat of prioritizing elements of a business briefly leading to a customer oriented business philosophy
    - Choosing a business
    - Market research
    - Consumer behavior (market segments could be introduced here if needed)
    - Product (goods and services could be introduced here if needed)
    - Price
    - Distribution
    - Promotion
- The four elements of product, price, distribution, and promotion can be simplified initially through a combined discussion where groups work through the various issues for a single good or service. These assignments can be customized to reflect livelihood opportunities in villages. Over time, details and educational materials could be added to this part to make each element distinct:

- Accounting – a topic that could be built in over time
- Ethics and societal responsibility (including environmental issues) – a topic that could be built in over time
- Open-ended discussion of livelihood opportunities – a topic that could be built in over time

Communication and facilitation

Continuous communication with trainers-of-trainers through a discussion forum and prescheduled electronic chat meetings as needed:

- Continuous interaction during program configuration through learning material development
- Direct or technology-enabled observation of trainers-of-trainers pilot program for purposes of support and feedback
- Visit to village setting for our own education as needed for observation of training and for learning first-hand about livelihood opportunities

Appendix 2

Proposed Model for e-educational Marketplace Literacy and Consumer Literacy Program

Prepared by Susan Byrd

I. Introduction

1. Welcome the participants to the session
2. List the stakeholders: e.g., organizers, facilitators, instructors
   (a) Use a voiceover with images (e.g., pictures of the instructors, company logos) to familiarize participants with the idea that there are tangible persons behind the educational tool.
3. State the rules:
   (a) Encourage open involvement and the expression of views with group.
   (b) Discuss importance of completing the program.
   (c) Explain the length and format of the program including timing and duration of breaks.
4. Explain basic computer usage: how to handle a mouse, how to move images on a screen (assume no previous knowledge of computers).

5. Icebreaker activity:
   (a) Goal: make everyone feel comfortable and facilitate sharing.
   (b) Suggested activity: Have each participant state their name as well as their expectations for this program.
6. Discuss expectations:
   (a) State that there are many things that can be learned from this seminar, but that participants cannot expect answers to their specific problems.
   (b) State the title of each section of this seminar. (Display a "menu" type screen where each session's title is in a quadrant. As the session is spoken through the voiceover, the quadrant lights up. For familiarity, the "menu" screen should be shown before the start of each session. This will give the participants an idea as to how far they've progressed.)

General format for each session:

1. *Introduction*: Introduce the idea with a voiceover and images.
2. *Animation*: Animate the activity (video or moving pictures).
3. *Group time*: Allow for time to complete the activity (in groups or individually).
4. *Presentation time*: Allow for group presentation time.
5. *Computer simulation*: Make a simulation where the group moves objects on the screen to match the conclusions they reached in their discussion.
6. *Summarize findings/verify results*: Voiceover to summarize findings and verify results.
7. *Transition*: Transition to the next idea.

II. Session 1: Prioritizing the Elements of a Business

Objective: Assess how participants prioritize various elements of business.

Input and process: Materials to be used include four sets of pictures relating to fishing, flowers, rice, and clothing. Each set of pictures includes those of a product, wholesale distribution, retail distribution, and final consumer usage as well money/currency notes.

Supplies: Pictures and a diagram of concentric circles.

1. *Introduction*: Describe how this activity is prioritizing the different aspects of a business.
2. *Animation*: Show a computer animation depicting the placement of certain images within a set of concentric circles.
3. *Group time*: Allow for groups of 4–6 individuals to discuss and place their pictures in the circles.
4. *Presentation time*: Each group should be given time to present their findings to all the participants.

5. *Computer simulation*: When the groups have formed a dominant answer to the activity, they will enter the results into the computer simulation. The computer will then be able to determine if the group has reached the correct conclusions. If not, it will present alternatives.
6. *Summarize learning*: With a voiceover, the computer will summarize desired outcomes of tasks and key lessons. Explain that there will be time later to change the results of this activity.
7. *Transition*

Outcomes: Usually, money, or in rarer instances, the product, is likely to be placed in the innermost circle. Other elements are generally given less importance and placed in outer circles. This session is difficult to summarize because there are many possible outcomes at this point in the training. Later on in the sessions, it will become apparent that the customer moves to the center.

III. Session 2: Evolution of Technologies, Products, and Transactions

Objective: Understand the process of exchange and the evolution of technologies, products, and transactions over time.

Input and process: Each group should be asked to arrange a set of pictures in chronological order, according to their evolution, place them on a chart and then present a narrative. Possible topics for the pictures are different stages of evolution of transport vehicles, of cooking devices and of transactions or transactional methods.

Supplies: Sets of pictures of different objects and paper to place it onto.

1. *Introduction*: Explain why products and ideas evolve over time. State possible reasons for this evolution.
2. *Animation*: Show an animation of the evolution of a certain idea or object. This will help the participants understand what they should do.
3. *Group time*: The groups will be given time to decide the evolution of their category and provide an explanation. Each group will be given a different category.
4. *Presentation time*: Time should be given for each group to present and describe their category to all the participants.
5. *Computer simulation*: Once the groups have had time to present, they will be asked to apply their knowledge to a different category. They will enter the results into the computer simulation. The computer will then be able to determine if the appropriate conclusions have been reached. If not, it will suggest alternatives.
6. *Summarize learning*: Explain the evolution of products. Ask participants to consider the evolution of transactional methods as an example. (How did people move from barter to the use of currency and then to electronic currency?)
7. *Transition*

Outcomes: At the completion of this activity, participants should know that:

- Exchange occurs to fulfill the needs of customers
- The nature of transactions has evolved over time from a barter system to the use of money, and now, electronic currency
- Technology, civilization and evolution of human life lead to corresponding changes in goods, services, and transactional methods; however, the form that specific goods and services take is influenced by customer needs and how they are satisfied
- There are inevitable changes in needs and wants and influencing factors
- Many factors influence innovation and improvement in goods or services

IV. Session 3: Distinguishing Buyers and Sellers

Objective: Matching pictures to distinguish buyers and users.

Input and process: Use a moveable tool to facilitate the understanding of categories of types of buyers, sellers and consumers.

Supplies: Pictures glued onto disks that rotate to allow the participant to match groupings.

1. *Introduction*: Explain the difference between buyers, consumers and sellers using examples of storeowners (sellers), parents (buyers) and children (consumers).
2. *Animation*: Using computer animation, demonstrate how the circles in the tool can be moved to match up the categories.
3. *Group time*: Allow enough time for each individual person to complete the activity.
4. *Presentation time*: Allow a few participants to present their categorizations. Then allow time for discussion and time for the participants to reach consensus that a certain grouping is correct.
5. *Computer simulation*: Once the groups have had time to present, they will be asked to apply their knowledge to a different category of buyers/sellers/consumers. They will enter the results into the computer simulation. The computer will then be able to determine if the group has reached the correct conclusions. If not, it will suggest alternatives.
6. *Summarize learning*: Link the categories to business ideas by classifying each category as a buyer, seller or consumer.
7. *Transition*

Outcomes: Participants should be able to group the different categories and understand the distinctions between buyers, sellers, and consumers.

V. Session 4: Customer Segments

Objective: Understanding goods, services, and customer segments.

Input and process: Using pictures of prototypical goods, services, and customers/segments, participants will examine interactions between the groupings.

Supplies: Pictures of related goods, services, and customers/segments, and paper to glue the pictures onto.

1. *Introduction*: Explain the idea of goods versus services. Then describe how certain customers and customer segments are interested in specific goods or services.
2. *Animation*: Using representative images, animate the process of distinguishing goods and services, and linking them to related segments.
3. *Group time*: Allow time for each group to perform the activity with their own pictures.
4. *Presentation time*: Allow time for each group to present and explain how they differentiated the pictures into categories.
5. *Computer simulation*: Once the groups have had time to present, they will be asked to apply their knowledge as a group to a different sample of goods and services. They will enter the results into the computer simulation. The computer will then be able to determine if the group has reached the correct conclusions. If not, it will suggest alternatives.
6. *Summarize learning*: Introduce/explain these ideas:
   - Customer needs drive markets
   - Goods and services fulfill customer needs
   - Goods are tangible products, e.g., umbrella, fish, and sari
   - Services are intangible products, e.g., umbrella repair, and tailoring
   - Everyone may not want, or be able to afford, all goods or services
   - Each good or service has potential segments
   - Segments are potential customer groups who share similar needs and are served by specific goods or services
   - Understanding customer segments enables understanding customer needs and designing better goods and services
7. *Transition*

Outcomes: The participants understand the difference between goods and services, and understand the notion of segments.

VI. Session 5: Value Chains

Objective: Understanding the role of exchange, as it occurs between various parties ranging from producers to consumers or users including intermediaries; understanding how multiple exchanges form a value chain.

Input and process: Participants can be assigned to groups of approximately 4–5 individuals and each group asked to choose a sample product, identify its segment, discuss how it is produced, and how it reaches the consumer or user, and provide rationale for changes over time.

Supplies: None

1. *Introduction*: Introduce the idea that raw products are given value through exchanges.
2. *Animation*: Depict a generic product through the value chain showing how each exchange adds value. Describe value added in each step.
3. *Group time*: Give each group time to discuss their products and perhaps prepare a short skit or presentation describing the exchanges necessary for a valuable product.
4. *Presentation time*: Allow time for each group to present value chains to the group.
5. *Computer simulation*: Use an easily recognizable product to simulate the exchanges that it goes through. Allow for the participants to manipulate the order of the value chain or the nature of the value chain by taking different routes and also allow them to select what type of value has been added.
6. *Summarize learning*: State conclusions about how value is added.
7. *Transition*

Outcomes: Participants will be able to identify how value is added to products that they use everyday through multiple exchanges along the value chain.

VII. Session 6: Vegetable Market Experience

Objective: To learn pitfalls when functioning as customers.

Input and process: By watching a video that depicts customers in a market and then answering questions, students will learn possible pitfalls as well as tips they can benefit from.

1. Topics to address:
   (a) How sellers may manipulate weight to benefit themselves (e.g., using faulty scales; rounding weight up or down).
   (b) How to calculate actual value for different amounts of a product.
   (c) Possible distractions in the market (e.g., talking with sellers while they are measuring).
   (d) How to avoid overzealous sellers (e.g., those sellers who use persuasive techniques to encourage overconsumption and excessive spending).
   (e) How to decide the amount of a product to buy (e.g., even though it may be more valuable to purchase in bulk, perishables may spoil before they are used).

2. Medium:
   (a) The video should be filmed in a realistic but simulated vegetable market. This way, participants benefit from being able to directly relate the setting to their situation, and the instructors are still able to manipulate the behavior of "sellers" to address the topics above.

(b) The actors should be as close to the participant's demographics as possible, again, to make it easy for participants to directly relate it to their situation.

3. Follow-up:

(a) After the video, there should be time for participants to discuss what they have seen.
(b) To facilitate discussion, a voiceover should be provided that asks guiding questions about the specific topics that the video discussed:
   (i) Manipulation of weight
   (ii) Calculating value
   (iii) Distractions
   (iv) Issues with sellers
   (v) Amount of product needed.

(c) To ensure that the discussion helps participants reach the correct conclusions, a computer simulation will ask questions similar to the following:

   (i) "What type of error occurred in this scene?"
   Show scene of a seller using an invalid weighing machine.
   (ii) Show a screen with three distinct sections. Each section has a clip-art type image relating to the text and voiceover. When the screen first appears, each section will light up individually and a voiceover will read the text. Then, the second section will light up and be read. Then, the third section will light up and be read. Also, when the participant uses a mouse to go over the sections of the screen, the voiceover will play again. Once the participants have agreed on which section is the correct one (which type of error occurred in that scene), they will click and the computer will provide feedback if they are correct or not.
   (iii) Repeat with another question.

VIII. Session 7: Provisional Store/Retail Shop Experience

Objective: To learn pitfalls in functioning as customers.

Input and process: By watching a video that depicts customers in a market and then answering questions, students will learn about the rights and responsibilities of customers.

1. Topics to discuss:

(a) Offers or free gifts
(b) Packaging styles (how marketers may make a package look similar or dissimilar to a familiar product)
(c) Brand names/images/logos

(d) How to avoid fake brands
(e) Noticing expiration dates
(f) Differences in sizes between the same products
(g) The seller should make some intentional mistakes and use deceptive practices, such as discrepancies in the billing and totaling. There could also be mistakes in the delivery of goods. Customers can be depicted to behave in different ways, such as not checking products, not computing totals, and so on.

2. Medium:

   (a) This should also be in a realistic video format.
   (b) Again, the actors should be similar to the participant's demographics.

3. Follow-up:

   (a) After the video, there should be time for participants to discuss what they have seen.
   (b) To facilitate discussion, a voiceover should be given that poses pointed questions that relate to the topics mentioned earlier.
   (c) A short set of "quiz" questions should be asked through a computer simulation.
   (d) It is important that this session focus on value and ensuring that customers retain their rights in the store.

IX. Summary/Conclusion

1. Summarize the learning from each of the sessions.
2. Thank the participants for attending.
3. Encourage them to provide feedback.
4. If sponsors subsidize this program, display information about them.

Chapter 9
Implications for Education

This chapter presents a number of issues that are relevant to education.[1] These issues are important in placing this educational program in the context of the literature and practice in education in general. A number of unique issues we faced are discussed in this chapter. Our discussion to this point has been grounded in the research, and the development of the educational program. This chapter draws out some broader issues relevant to education and discusses them in the context of the literature where relevant. We start out with a brief discussion of linkages with research and practice documented in the literature. We then emphasize some of the key distinctions in our program.

9.1 Linkages with Research and Practice

Generic issues that we highlight in our educational program have been used and written about in numerous contexts in education and more specifically, in adult and nonformal education. In designing instruction for adult learners, a number of frameworks have been presented. For example, a framework emphasizes assessing one's own skills, developing content knowledge, learning about learners and understanding the learning contexts (Dean, 2002), all elements of our approach. In learning about learners, Knowles (1980) distinguishes between basic and educational needs. An understanding of these two categories of needs and their relationship is critical in a subsistence context where needs are often basic and immediate and where education may offer a means to address these needs. Similarly, a number of methods can be used to assess learner needs. We used in-depth interviews and observations and immersion in the context as the basis for guiding our educational

[1] The material in this chapter is reprinted with minor editing with permission from Elsevier from Viswanathan, Gajendiran, and Venkatesan (2007). This article was published in the International Journal of Educational Development (2007), doi:10.1016/j.ijedudev.2007.05.004, Viswanathan, M., S. Gajendiran, and R. Venkatesan, Understanding and enabling marketplace literacy in subsistence contexts: The development of a consumer and entrepreneurial literacy educational program in South India, Copyright Elsevier, 2007.

program. A variety of learning methods have been discussed in the literature including role-play and simulation (Galbraith, 1998), which are used in our program. We also emphasize cohort and collaborative learning (Drago-Severson, 2004). In terms of our focus on nonformal education in a developing context, there are similarly numerous examples in the literature (e.g., Singh, 2005). We highlight some distinct aspects of our educational program.

9.2 Working with Existing Skill Sets and Literacy

Our philosophy was to take the participants as is in terms of their levels of literacy and work through the educational program. We did not require basic literacy in any form, nor did we teach it; rather, we assumed that our participants could not read or write. Many programs are similar in emphasizing, say, technical skills, rather than basic literacy (e.g., Krishna, 2006). We worked with the skill sets that participants brought to the program, which were unconventional but considerable, and often derived from the social context of frequent one-to-one interactions. Participants, individually and collectively, bring a number of skills to the program that we can build on, such as spoken language skills in the native language and number recognition skills. Some possess writing skills in the native language, although we do not assume this to be the case. As the program evolves, participants in various small groups pool their skills together to complete assignments, performing tasks that include assigning spokespersons and preparing charts for presentation. In a longer time frame, if women we train are from a community or a self-help group, this sharing continues, as we observed 3–6 months later in efforts to pool resources to buy staple items wholesale or to run a business. In a larger sense, women who participate in the educational program report sharing knowledge by informing others about their learning. Unique to these resource-poor but network-rich contexts is that a small educational effort can go a long way.

9.3 From Functional Literacy to Basic Literacy

The consumer and entrepreneurial literacy program can, in turn, facilitate basic literacy. Numerical and verbal skills play out in the economic realm and learning to bargain in a customer setting, or learning to analyze costs in a business setting can, in turn, enable basic literacy. Functional skills in the economic realm may lead to acquisition of basic skills. The economic realm provides a rich context where counting and reading skills play out and where individuals can draw on their experiences. In this regard, researchers have noted the relative ease of computation among low-literate individuals when dealing in dollars rather than abstract numbers (Viswanathan et al., 2005). Similarly, skills relating to budgeting, accounting, and other topics covered may lead to enhancement of basic counting skills. Some participants report developing confidence to read and count.

Some skills may be inherent and unrecognized, emerging in a context-rich setting, such as shopping. A key issue here appears to be difficulty transferring across domains. This is not surprising, given that the use of analogy and transfer has traditionally been considered the behavior of those who are comfortable with using structural information (Gentner, 1983), likely due to their well-developed schemas (Gick and Holyoak, 1983). Requirements to complete transactions, to avoid being cheated, and so forth may lead to the development of skills in marketplace contexts that may not transfer to basic settings, similar to the findings of Viswanathan and Gau (2005). By highlighting these skills, our educational program can serve to reinforce the notion that individuals possess some level of basic literacy and can build on it.

9.4 Breaking Barriers Between Individuals and Groups

A tendency in designing an educational program may be to assume that individuals will interact among each other, an assumption that is reasonable in many contexts. In fact, a homogeneous class may even be desirable (Carr-Hill, 2001). However, our effort, like other such efforts, is at the confluence of poverty and low literacy as well as culture. Although groups of participants in the specific programs we have conducted to date have mostly been homogeneous in terms of gender (i.e., usually exclusively women), they may be from different strata or different castes. Barriers that exist at the beginning of the program may come down over time, emphasizing the need for educators to understand the cultural context. For instance, we conducted a program in a village where women from different strata based on caste came from different locations in the village. Although, they started out the program staying with their respective groups, over time, there was more interaction among women from different castes, as the program ensued. We are, of course, not claiming that our program led to a social revolution in the village. Rather, it was interesting to observe the breaking of barriers in a small microcosm of social interactions, presumably through a learning environment with emphasis on equal treatment and respect for ideas. A lesson learned here is the need to possess an understanding of the underlying social relationships that exist, which may have to be overcome to some degree during the educational program. Learning about learner characteristics as well as the learning context is important to the design of an educational program (Dean, 2002).

9.5 Rights and Functional Skills

The rights approach versus the functional approach to literacy has been discussed in the literature (Robinson-Pant, 2003; UNESCO, 2003; Verhoeven, 1994). In reality, these two approaches are intermingled in our educational program. Our follow-up qualitative assessment suggests that much of the learning relates to self-confidence and awareness of rights. Following participation in our program, some women reported taking over purchasing duties from their husbands, bargaining, and switching shops, leading shopkeepers to identify them as the ones who participated in the program and providing them with better treatment and service. Consumer literacy education focuses on both functional skills and rights. In fact, the two are inseparable in some ways in that the exercise of a functional skill may follow from the awareness of a right. For example, at a broader level, making well-informed purchase decisions involves seeking information and being aware of several rights. The use of functional skills is in the context of being aware of one's rights. Acquiring functional skills and learning about rights combine to reinforce self-confidence. The inter-relationships between these elements are accentuated in the social context of myriad face-to-face interactions among individuals. Self-confidence is central to engaging in conversations and negotiating the marketplace of one-to-one interactions. Our program emphasized both the rights and the functional approaches. Relevant here is also the emphasis on "education for living and education for making a living" (Singh, 2005, p. 2; Gerasch and Duran, 2005). Also relevant is a holistic view of education in terms of learning to know, to do, to live together and to be (UNESCO, 2006; Singh, 2005). Rights embedded in consumer education and in awareness about the marketplaces have implications for these important objectives.

9.6 Curriculum Choices

Our focus at the lowest levels of literacy and income was the guiding principle in deciding on curriculum issues. How do we convey the central and most important concepts to individuals who have lived through the unique experiences of subsistence marketplaces but are at the lowest level of literacy and income? This was the guiding question that led to our choice of the concepts we describe in the program. In terms of content, our basic approach is guided by a customer-oriented philosophy of doing business based on mutually beneficial exchanges. There are a number of business issues we could have covered, such as managing human resources and so forth. However, for the audience we were targeting, an appreciation of exchanges, value chains and most importantly, customer needs, is perhaps critical as a starting point. We start out at the basic level of an exchange. We use multiple exchanges to illustrate a value chain. These are fundamental and intuitive concepts and provide the building blocks for then discussing the nature of these exchanges. Our focal concepts included value in exchanges, viewed from both buyer and seller perspectives. We cover topics, such as product design, promotion, pricing, and distribution, reinforcing a customer-oriented perspective. Such knowledge would enable conception of products and enterprises, with more specialized knowledge for carrying on these enterprises perhaps being acquired through experience or through subsequent education, using the learning from our educational program as a basis. Moreover, the notion of mutual fairness in exchanges resonates at a human level, as does the right of every person to make a livelihood. Understandably, abstract economic and business principles relating to competition and other issues are not usually contemplated, nor particularly relevant. Similarly, rudimentary financial and accounting knowledge may be sufficient, whereas much of the business literature aims to address the specific issues faced by large organizations.

We covered the broader issue of identifying a business by evaluating one's strengths and weaknesses, the competition, and customer needs, a translation of notions from business strategy tempered by reality on the ground. Our specific issues on the entrepreneurial side ranged from product design and distribution to pricing and promotion. However, our discussions of these topics were not restricted to the perspective of any single area of business, such as marketing. Rather, we discussed logistics and operations when covering distribution, and production when covering product design. Costs were front and center throughout the treatment of these topics and particularly in discussing pricing.

As discussed, we cover societal responsibility and issues of sustainability and the environment. We also address threats and opportunities in globalization. Our emphasis on basic understanding of the marketplace would ideally open up choices for participants. Coupled with our use of open discussions, our program can potentially encourage a proactive attitude toward the marketplace, rather than a reactive one, that we hope results in participants shaping and altering the economic reality that they face.

9.7 Conceptual Treatment of Content

Another broad issue relating to education was our emphasis on conceptual treatment. Researchers have argued that low-literate individuals have difficulties with abstractions, and engage in concrete thinking in the visual, graphic world of usage rather than the more abstract world of concepts (Luria, 1976; Viswanathan et al., 2005). Our goal was to enable longer-term learning, and essentially, to enable participants to learn how to learn. Therefore, we organized the material around some key concepts. One concept was value and valuable exchanges, to organize much of the material about buyer and seller behaviors. Other concepts included the philosophical orientation of a business. The key to implementing such an approach has been to relate the content and the instructional methods of the program back to participants' lived experiences, and leverage the social skills that they bring to the program in the design of classroom exercises.

There were many challenges in trying to illustrate the concepts. For example, when we use simulated vegetable shops to demonstrate how prices, quality, and weighing may differ, participants often draw conclusions that one type of shop was bad and another was good. We reiterate that our conclusions are not about types of shops, but that these are just examples created to illustrate broader issues, such as the need to make informed choices based on value in specific exchanges. When using the notion of value, which essentially involves a judgment of what is given and what is obtained in return, individuals may equate what is given with price. This requires elucidation in terms of the various give-and-get components, such as price, travel effort, and costs, versus quality, respectively. Understandably, individuals often do not consider the nonmonetary and indirect monetary costs associated with purchasing a product, given severe income constraints. Therefore, it is important to be vigilant in tempering the outcome of specific examples to avoid concrete conclusions and illustrate more abstract issues.

Both low income and low literacy can create a short-term orientation that is often practical but sometimes counterproductive. The importance of abstracting across time needs to be emphasized. For example, return on investment is an important issue but sellers may often not think beyond the next day and may not consider profits in proportion to investment. One seller noted that whether he invested Rs. 300 or Rs. 100 in buying vegetables, a profit roughly equivalent to his daily monetary needs was sufficient because "that is all that he needed," a refreshing lesson in contentment, but, nevertheless, one that is disadvantageous in the near future. Buyers may not plan ahead for the month and buy at cheaper prices from a large reseller for a number of reasons, such as buying daily at retail due to the credit offered and out of fear of the next crisis. However, a longer-term orientation would enable them to switch buying habits when circumstances allow.

9.8 Customizing Concepts

There are, of course, many assumptions built into the design of the program based on the unique context that we researched. Needless to say, actual customization in a variety of diverse settings will bring out many more issues that we do not anticipate, both in the content and the delivery of the program. However, we anticipate a number of issues in customizing this program to different settings, including subsistence marketplaces in advanced economies. At a concrete level, depending on the context, many examples need to be adjusted. Perhaps most important are the unique set of products and markets encountered in South India. They form the underpinning for materials used throughout the program. Our material showing evolution of products across long periods of time are generic enough to be used in most contexts. We use generic images of value chains, such as starting out with farmers and moving to consumers. However, images that are close to the reality that participants face, including appearances of people and objects in the educational materials that are used, would go a long way toward helping them relate to the program. Important here is the need to relate the content back to participants' lived experiences. Materials, shops, and procedures used for the consumer literacy program would need to be modified to capture different realities. For the elements of the entrepreneurial literacy program, examples of products and value chains that are from the context where the program is run would be necessary. Relevant to customization is translation into other languages. Our limited experience suggests that translation would require creating terminology to describe concepts and marketplace phenomena as well as stimuli that are relevant to specific cultures. Because spoken language is central to our approach, the need to capture the essence of the content would require careful translation with a full understanding of curriculum issues.

At a broader level, our conceptual treatment and an emphasis on the know-why serves to provide an organizing framework, with our procedures providing one exemplar of a viable program. Our orientation in terms of viewing buyers and sellers as two sides of the same coin applies to marketplaces characterized by small buyers and sellers and frequent one-to-one interactions. Our emphasis on conveying concepts also generalizes, provided appropriate attention is paid to leveraging lived experiences and skills that participants bring to the program. The larger purpose of enabling individuals to learn how to learn and move towards a path of lifelong learning is central here. Ideally, such an orientation enables individuals to understand the larger context, exercise choice, and proactively interact with the marketplace. The specific concepts we use are fundamental and apply in a variety of settings. For instance, the broader notion of value would be very useful to organize a number of issues. Our approach in terms of a research based program is consistent with starting out by educating ourselves about the potential recipients of an educational program before designing it. This is consistent with successful literacy programs that have initially researched the potential beneficiaries (Robinson-Pant, 2003; Rogers et al., 1999).

Another issue relates to subsistence marketplaces in advanced societies, such as the USA. As discussed in the previous chapter, there is much that can be done to provide marketplace literacy to low-literate, low-income individuals in the USA. Adult education programs represent excellent examples of providing people with marketplace skills. Similarly, other programs, such as nutritional education, provide skills in specific domains. However, there is a significant need for using a research-based approach to teaching marketplace literacy that recognizes the constraints individuals face due to low literacy and low income. Such a program would, of course, need to be customized to the customer-to-large-corporation context that characterizes advanced societies as well as the nature of entrepreneurial opportunities available.

9.9 Conclusion

This work has a number of implications for educational research and practice, particularly for areas such as nonformal education, adult literacy, and educational programs in subsistence contexts. This program has a number of implications for research and practice in education, as suggested by the discussion of distinct aspects, such as conceptual treatment of material. Generic issues relating to adult literacy include the linkages between functional literacy and basic literacy, and the balance between rights and functions. Issues specific to the realm of consumer and entrepreneurial literacy range from the concepts covered to the instructional method. The constraints that individuals living in subsistence face are substantial and their efforts to overcome adversity are heroic. Our intention is not to overstate the case for the type of educational program we have developed as much as to highlight its potential, particularly when coupled with other initiatives, such as financing and livelihood opportunities. The need for such educational programs aimed at enabling generic marketplace literacy, the unique issues that arise in the design of such programs, and the need to continually assess and improve their effectiveness suggests important avenues of future research and practice in education.

References

Carr-Hill, R.A. (ed.) with Okech, A. Katahoire, A., Kakooza, T., Ndidde, A., and Oxenham, J. (2001). Adult literacy programs in Uganda. *Human Development Africa Region*. Washington DC: The World Bank.

Dean, G. (2002). *Designing Instruction for Adult Learners*. Melbourne, FL: Kreiger.

Drago-Severson, E. (2004). *Becoming Adult Learners: Principles and Practices for Effective Development*. New York: Teachers College Press.

Galbraith, M. W. (1998). Becoming an effective teacher of adults. In: M. W. Galbraith (ed.), *Adult Learning Methods: A Guide for Effective Instruction*. Malabar, FL: Krieger.

Gerasch, P. and Duran, A. (2005). Training in modest housing construction for those who need it most: An example from Nicaragua. In M. Singh (ed.), *Meeting Basic Learning Needs in the Informal Sector*. Dordrecht, The Netherlands: Springer.

Gentner, D. (1983). Structure mapping: A theoretical framework for analogy. *Cognitive Science*, 7, 155–170.

Gick, M. L. and Holyoak, K. J. (1983). Schema induction and analogical transfer. *Cognitive Psychology*, 15, 1–38.

Knowles, M. S. (1980). *The Modern Practice of Adult Education: From Pedagogy to Andragogy*. New York: Cambridge.

Krishna, A. (2006). Pathways into and out of poverty in 36 villages of Andhra Pradesh, India. *World Development*, 34, 271–288.

Luria, A. (1976). *Cognitive Development: Its Cultural and Social Foundations*. Cambridge, MA: Harvard University Press.

Robinson-Pant, A. (2003). *Overview of Learning Programmes for Literacy and More General Life/Vocational Skills for Women*. Paper prepared for UNESCO EFA Monitoring Report Team. Paris: UNESCO.

Rogers, A., Maddox, B., Millican, J., Newell-Jones, K., Papen, U., and Robinson-Pant A. (1999). *Re-defining Post-literacy in a Changing World*. DfID Education Research Serial No. 29. London: DfID.

Singh, M. (2005). *Meeting Basic Learning Needs in the Informal Sector*. Dordrecht, The Netherlands: Springer.

UNESCO (2003). *Gender and Education for All: The Leap to Equality*. EFA Global Montoring Report. Paris: UNESCO.

UNESCO. (2006). *Literacy for Life*. EFA Global Monitoring Report. Paris: UNESCO.

Verhoeven, L. (1994). Modeling and promoting functional literacy. In: L. Verhoeven (ed.), *Functional Literacy: Theoretical Issues and Educational Implications*. Amsterdam: John Benjamins.

Viswanathan, M. and Gau, R. (2005). Functional illiteracy and nutritional education in the United States: A research-based approach to the development of nutritional education materials for functionally illiterate consumers. *Journal of Macromarketing*, 25, 187–201.

Viswanathan, M., Rosa, J. and Harris, J. (2005). Decision making and coping of functionally illiterate consumers and some implications for marketing management. *Journal of Marketing*, 69(1), 15–31.

Chapter 10
Implications for Business

This work has a number of implications for research and practice in subsistence marketplaces. The educational approach in itself has direct implications for business practice. The translation and modification of generic business concepts to an educational program focused on subsistence contexts highlights a number of issues of relevance to business education, research and practice. These issues are directly relevant to businesses that work with individuals in subsistence marketplaces along elements of the value chain as entrepreneurs and as customers. The research underlying the educational program also has important implications for business. Unique to this research in distinguishing it from other approaches to studying poverty is the bottom-up focus here that can be contrasted with a macrolevel economic focus or a medium level business strategy focus.

We begin by discussing implications of the educational program for business, covering potential applications. We then derive implications inherent in our translation of generic business concepts to subsistence contexts. We then cover implications of our research for business. We conclude with a discussion of the challenges that subsistence marketplaces pose to business research and practice.

10.1 Creating "Win-Win" Scenarios in Subsistence Marketplaces

A key implication of our work is the role of education in empowering individuals as customers and as entrepreneurs. The latter is particularly relevant when providing individuals living in subsistence the opportunity to participate in the production process, thereby creating buying power and win-win scenarios. A number of principles have been elucidated in the literature in terms of localizing production and deskilling processes in running businesses at the base of the pyramid (Prahalad, 2005). A key element that can empower individuals to participate and make a living is generic marketplace know-how. Our focus on the know-how would be useful for businesses considering ways of educating individuals as potential partners, employees, or customers. These are two sides of the coin; enabling consumption and entrepreneurship. Enabling consumer literacy can also lead to a thriving marketplace with informed customers. Given the lack of informational resources, consumer education often has to be part of the multifaceted solution that businesses devise to function in subsistence marketplaces.

Our philosophical orientation is to view consumption and entrepreneurship as two sides of the same coin in designing and delivering the educational program. Central here is the close relationship between the roles of being a buyer and a seller in a one-to-one interactional marketplace, in contrast to a customer to large corporation relationship. Frequent interactions through which buyers and sellers learn about each other, along with shared adversity and relatively easy transfer of skills from one domain to the other, are central factors here. A nuanced understanding of consumption and entrepreneurship is important for businesses functioning in subsistence contexts. Our approach of covering consumer literacy and the notion of value as a precursor to entrepreneurial literacy enables understanding of both sides of the equation. It also emphasizes the importance of filtering business relationships down to simple human values and exchanges. Being informed buyers can lead to being effective entrepreneurs and vice versa. In our research, we came across individuals who started out with almost no experience as buyers or sellers but who began to develop skills in one domain out of necessity and, as a result, developed skills in the other. Our experience in the USA suggests that the individual to large corporation relationship that characterizes both customers and employees is not as conducive to this type of diffusion of learning between consumption and entrepreneurship. The diffusion of learning in the subsistence contexts in India we studied occurs at the individual and group levels and supplements the more macro marketplace-level interactions and mutual reinforcement between consumption and entrepreneurship that can occur in a variety of ways. In the next section, we discuss specific business applications that expand on the notion of developing win-win scenarios.

10.2 Potential Business Applications of Marketplace Literacy Education

In this section, we provide an overview of a wide range of ways in which businesses can use marketplace literacy education that cover core business activities and social initiatives.

10.2.1 Employee Training in Corporate Settings

A stark contrast in developing contexts is the coexistence of rich and poor in a number of settings. This contrast is increasingly noticeable as successful companies in such emerging nations as India offer a variety of services geared to wealthy and upper-middle class customers that are delivered by low-literate, low-income employees. Employees of businesses in developing countries are often from low-literate, low-income backgrounds but interact with customers and the marketplace in unique ways. In an era where consistent customer service is increasingly valued, employee training to interact with customers is critical.

Our approach provides the basis to design such training programs. Beginning with the need for a customer orientation, our approach emphasizes the know-why that is important for potential employees to understand. Our approach can be customized to then address the know-how in terms of specific customer interactions. For example, when training employees in a retail setting, the educational program can be customized to provide a basic understanding of marketplace exchanges in such a setting and of the need for a customer orientation. Employees could take the role of customers to understand issues from the customers' perspective in sessions on consumer literacy, while relating specific situations back to their lived experiences. They could then be trained on specific customer interactions. Similar issues apply in a number of arenas where customer interactions are with low-literate, low-income employees.

An added benefit of our approach is that a comprehensive educational program can serve as a catalyst to enable employees to learn how to learn, thus, opening up avenues of advancement that are typically inaccessible due to the requirements of formal education. Clearly, the type of program we have outlined would be one of many factors that would be required to enable such opportunities. However, companies would benefit from identifying talented employees, who, despite the circumstances and constraints created by lack of literacy and resources, are fully capable of rising in the organization, but are prevented from doing so because of formal educational requirements.

In this regard, our approach also provides a framework for conveying the essence of aspects of a business administration program (such as a miniature MBA), without requiring formal educational prerequisites. By elaborating on various topics as needed, a comprehensive educational program could be developed. In summary, our approach can be customized through greater breadth and a more comprehensive business education program or through greater depth relevant to more specific positions that low-literate employees work in.

10.2.2 Entrepreneurial Education Along the Value Chain

Our educational approach is very relevant in enabling individuals and groups to contribute more effectively to value chains. For example, the agriculture sector is one of many where low-literate, small farmers interact with larger corporations. Well-informed farmers with knowledge of the big picture would be valuable partners in cocreating innovative products or innovative solutions to problems. Recent examples, such as ITC's (Indian Tobacco Company) e-choupal in India (Prahalad, 2005), illustrate the power of information in the agricultural context. Entrepreneurial education can be empowering in ways that benefit the individual and the company involved. In the case of computer kiosk-based approaches, an e-educational approach to entrepreneurial education could be designed to fit into ongoing activities. In this regard, our program has also been customized for educating computer kiosk operators and enabling them to create a sustainable business.

Low-literate resellers in urban and rural settings can also benefit from such education that provides a broader overview of the marketplace. For example, HLL's (Hindustan Lever Limited, a subsidary of Unilever) innovative distribution network involves woman entrepreneurs functioning as resellers in rural settings in India, selling health and hygiene products (Prahalad, 2005). HLL's management provides one-to-one supervision supplemented with group meetings that enables these entrepreneurs to perform effectively. Our approach of education about the know-why as a basis for the know-how would enable or increase input from low-literate resellers that cocreates solutions from the ground up. Such solutions may range from product design to promotional planning that then feeds into company strategy. Knowledge of the big picture in terms of marketplace exchanges can enable individuals along the value chain, often those closest to customers, to contribute and participate in planning and implementation. Our experience suggests that big picture know-why supplemented with know-how enables individuals to learn how to learn while also developing self-confidence to express their views. Far-sighted companies can develop these valuable resources that are available to them which can lead to insights about the marketplace and ideas for solving problems as well as for proactively innovating in terms of product design, promotion, distribution, and other issues.

10.2.3 Consumer Education as a Component of Marketing Communications

Given the lack of informational resources that subsistence customers face, businesses can use consumer education to emphasize the benefits of their products. Germane here is the large potential for such education to be synergized with product relevant business activity. For instance, consumer education can be customized to a variety of arenas, such as nutrition education. Our approach offers a general umbrella organized around common issues and emphasizes value in an exchange. A program customized to nutritional, health, or hygiene products could emphasize the complex trade-offs between health and costs that customers make, often to their detriment in the longer term. Our approach of using simulated shopping and audio-based quizzes, or similar approaches, could be customized to the nutritional arena. Such an approach is also consistent with the need to provide multifaceted solutions in environments where a variety of resources including informational resources are severely lacking.

10.2.4 Consumer and Entrepreneurial Literacy as Complementing Microfinancing

Microfinancing has been emphasized in recent decades in terms of its potential to transform lives through economic upliftment. Our emphasis on generic consumer and entrepreneurial literacy supplements microfinancing and addresses the need for know-how to succeed in running an enterprise. Financing alone may sometimes lead to failure of an enterprise and inability to repay loans, whereas the know-how to succeed in business can supplement microfinancing initiatives. Our approach of understanding both the buyer and seller perspectives is also relevant for individuals in evaluating microfinancing opportunities and making prudent decisions. When supplemented with consumer and entrepreneurial education, microfinancing can potentially be more effective from the perspectives of borrowers and lenders. In this regard, the role of information in decreasing inefficiencies in systems has been discussed in a number of arenas, such as ITC's e-choupal (Prahalad, 2005). Consumer education in a number of areas, can similarly lead to informed and efficient marketplaces. The discussion of microfinancing in Chapter 8 and the importance of integrative development in a nonprofit context translates to the need for multifaceted solutions in a business context where marketplace literacy education is used to complement microlending.

At the simplest level, two ingredients that individuals need to start a microenterprise are money and know-how, the former addressed by microfinancing and the latter usually addressed through a vocational skill. Such microenterprises may not succeed due to lack of generic know-how about running a business. In fact, a vocation skill could potentially be a disadvantage in this regard, in narrowing individuals' options. Our focus on the know-why as a basis for the know-how encourages individuals to consider the different enterprises they could create, although the options available to them are limited by the extreme constraints they face. A key here is providing a basis for individuals to explore the marketplace for opportunities and exercise the choices available to them. Our conjecture is that such know-how will lead to greater success for microfinancing approaches and could supplement these programs, a line of reasoning that we plan to test in the future.

10.2.5 Consumer and Entrepreneurial Literacy as Social Initiatives

Consumer and entrepreneurial education provide an ideal vehicle for businesses to engage in social initiatives. The net effect can be an informed marketplace with the potential for economic upliftment. Consumer education can also be provided to create a thriving marketplace with informed customers. The potential for win-win scenarios discussed earlier is particularly relevant in the educational domain. Entrepreneurial activity, in turn, leads to buying power or creates opportunities for businesses to partner with local individuals and communities.

10.3 Translating Business Concepts for Subsistence Marketplaces

In developing our educational program, we gained a number of insights in our efforts to translate relevant concepts developed in the context of large organizations to a one-to-one world of very small enterprises. What translates and why? And when are new concepts required based on new insights? The answers to these questions have important implications for business. The treatment of concepts in the business literature by and large assumes a worldview from the perspective of large organizations or from the perspective of small organizations with some resources, given the nature of organizations that exist in advanced economies and in the upper levels of developing economies to serve the varied needs of customers. However, a fundamental shift in thinking is required to take the perspective of the microenterprises that we studied and is the likely outcome of our educational program. There are several examples of this translation process, which in turn have implications for businesses.

10.3.1 Market Segments

The notion of market segments translates into groups of customers that individuals know and interact with or are at geographically reachable distances. Rather than think in terms of underlying dimensions of segmentation at an abstract level, there are constraints in terms of travel and access that necessitate consideration of proximate places and relatively concrete factors. A number of factors make a concrete, bottom-up notion of segments practical for the purposes of our participants. Therefore, we discuss segments by asking individuals about groups of people they could sell to, and then build up from there. We attempt to expand their notion of potential markets by examining ways in which they can sell at different points in the value chain.

This issue has important implications for larger businesses aiming to operate in such settings. Segmentation and market coverage strategies involving resellers may need to be built from the ground up, with geographic proximity and access being important considerations. This is a localized approach that has to take into consideration the unique situation in different locations, much more so than can be envisioned in an advanced society. In a sense, the market has to be stitched together one location or neighborhood at a time, rather than "scaled", assuming similar characteristics across the broader market. Similarly, market research has to be gathered from resellers while being cognizant of the local nature of segments.

10.3.2 Identification of Business Opportunities

The notion of identifying and evaluating a business opportunity presents another interesting example, in terms of customer needs, company strengths, and competition.

These are approaches developed for larger organizations but essentially are encompassing enough as to apply at an individual level in terms of one's own realistic evaluation of strengths or capabilities, the need being served, and who to compete with. However, raw material, capital, support services, and market potential are factors central to identifying viable income-generating activities. Larger organizations that work with individuals on the ground need to understand the strengths that these individuals bring in terms of developed relationships and intimate knowledge of the marketplace.

10.3.3 Customer Orientation

Customer orientation is another such notion that bears the test of translation to these markets. Fair exchanges are intuitive at a human level irrespective of levels of literacy although the nuances require elucidation here as they do elsewhere. In fact, fairness is a highly developed notion, given the daily adversities that individuals face and the sense of camaraderie in living through such adverse conditions. Individuals do, in turn, grasp the notion of providing valuable exchanges when they are sellers instead of buyers, perhaps more intuitively than in settings characterized by a large organization to individual customer relationship. There is a one-to-one correspondence between fair exchanges at a human level that are valued in these settings and fair exchanges in the marketplace. In turn, businesses need to pay particular attention to fair and transparent exchanges.

10.3.4 Perceived Value in Exchanges

Related to this discussion, value is another concept that translates to this setting, in encompassing what is given and what is received. Elucidating these respective components during the literacy program requires particular attention, such as in enabling individuals to understand that more is given than just money, such as time and effort, aspects that are usually neglected, and often realistically so. However, the notion of value works well both from the perspective of the buyer and the seller. Although subsistence customers focus on functionality, they aspire for higher level attributes and are willing to pay a small premium for higher quality. Given the central importance of limited monetary resources, it is difficult for individuals to abstract across other nonmonetary components that they "give" to an exchange, such as time and effort. It is difficult, and perhaps impractical, for individuals to factor in these other components when severely lacking in the financial component. As a result, they often pay little heed to bodily effort and the negative consequences until a breaking point is reached, such as a severe health crisis, that in effect, prevents certain physical activities, such as long periods of walking. Both low literacy and economic constraints may combine to accentuate this approach to judging value. Difficulties with abstractions may lead to a more concrete approach, equating low price with the "give" component. In fact, even quality considerations may not matter with extreme poverty, and low price may be equated with value. For example, with a heavy work schedule of manual labor, the priority may be to fill one's stomach, with quality concerns being pushed aside. Moreover, both low literacy and economic constraints may lead to a feeling of futility about quality, essentially, a feeling that quality is whatever is offered and that is the quality one gets for the price.

For these reasons, the broader notion of value has a number of implications. Businesses need to carefully design the give and get aspects of the value proposition and communicate it in effective ways. It requires careful treatment in educating potential customers and in encouraging them to abstract across the give and get aspects. Also, the elements involved in the "give" component may be limited to time and money. Unanticipated considerations may play a role, such as the need to buy at the neighborhood store. From the perspective of communicating to customers, a fine line has to be traversed between highlighting convenience and being practical, in light of the monetary constraints individuals face. Convenience is desired, time being a precious commodity often needed to seek out livelihood opportunities. Convenience is valued in such situations as when buying key ingredients to cook a meal after receiving daily wages. Quality is very much appreciated, particularly in terms of staple foods, with customers willing to trade up to slightly higher quality. The "get" component is typically evaluated in an experiential sense. However, the give component, where there is very little room for error, is often purely cost focused. With greater exposure to information and products than a couple of decades ago and a greater variety of products, nuances in being a customer are not lost on individuals in the subsistence contexts we studied. In fact, they are often savvy in being entertained by advertisement for unaffordable products while blocking such marketing communications out for purposes of serious purchase considerations.

10.3.5 Product Design

We treat product design at an individual level with limited capabilities when compared to large organizations in terms of products that are used. Key insights here include the link between ingredients and benefits from the buyer's perspective and the link between the product and its costs from the seller's perspective. The capabilities of subsistence entrepreneurs and the nature of product design they engage in, are important for businesses to understand as they seek partners and localize production. Also central here is the need to use the insights that subsistence entrepreneurs bring in terms of designing products that satisfy customer needs, through an understanding of product characteristics and the underlying needs they serve.

10.3.6 Market Research

Market research is also informative in terms of what is relevant at an individual level and the implications that can be derived for businesses. We translate market research into informal conversations that individuals can have with a variety of individuals, such as potential customers and current sellers, as well as observations of the marketplace. Insights are, of course, qualitative in nature with some experimentation with versions of products, again, at an informal level. The goal here, in a sense, is the opposite of aggregation at some larger level. Research translates to a more informal and intuitive sense of gathering and evaluating information for purposes of making decisions. Key issues here include the importance of being unbiased, asking tough questions, seeking out information proactively, testing out ideas and products with friends and acquaintances, observing marketplaces, and systematically enumerating details, such as costs.

Some of the approaches that are appropriate for entrepreneurs in these marketplaces may also have relevance for larger businesses. Unstructured approaches may be central for large businesses to understand these marketplaces. More structured methods may face several obstacles in terms of respondents' being able to complete surveys because of literacy issues or in terms of difficulties in aggregation due to myriad differences. Techniques may need to focus on aggregating from qualitative information in various, distinct neighborhoods or from retailers. A subsequent section discusses this issue.

10.3.7 Customization

Also relevant here from the perspective of small entrepreneurs is the challenging environment for managing small enterprises. From a seller's perspective, there is a fundamental tension between the one-to-one interactional context and the need to adhere to general business principles. The seller carefully manages word-of-mouth through such means as adhering to single price, not writing off loans, not discriminating discernibly on price, managing customer-to-customer communications, not discussing private information about customers, and avoiding family problems. Sellers usually do not price-discriminate on items where price is easily discernible (e.g., packaged goods versus generic rice), but rather on generic items, such as rice, sold by weight. Thus, price discrimination is adjusted for negative word-of-mouth effects and frequent one-to-one interactions. Through one-to-one interactions, understanding personal circumstances of customers, dealing only with certain family members, and allowing some exceptions, the seller adjusts and provides need-based services. Sellers customize based on input from an area or neighborhood. For example, because a neighborhood has many manual workers who have one square meal a day and require more pickle per packet, a seller may adjust the packet size for that neighborhood. Here, the tension in a one-to-one world between customization and the need to adhere to business principles is resolved in favor of customization, presumably because this will not become public knowledge and is done through an intermediary. If customization becomes public knowledge, there needs to be a justifiable reason for it. In this case, interaction among storeowners in different neighborhoods may be less likely than among customers in the same neighborhood. Here again, the practice of offering everyone the same product is crucial to maintaining cordial relationships in an environment where constant communication among customers is the norm. In a one-to-one world, it is important to maintain parity in offerings. Otherwise, word may spread quickly and the businessperson would face consequences. At the same time, there is constant pressure to customize. Each seller finds a unique way to balance these factors.

The constant pressure to customize and the need to adhere to some consistent procedures are factors that businesses need to consider in functioning in subsistence contexts. The ability to customize offerings to different settings is crucial in a variety of business functions and processes, such as product design and marketing communications. Also important is the need to work with intermediaries to provide sufficient flexibility in processes to respond to customer demands, while adhering to some consistent procedures.

10.4 Implications for Marketing[1]

Broader insights about subsistence marketplaces have important implications for marketing. In this section, for illustrative purposes, we summarize some insights about subsistence marketplaces and discuss how elements of marketing should be approached differently in these markets. We describe five elements that are central to this function – market research, product development, pricing, promotion, and distribution. Due to the brief nature of this discussion, we mention but do not elaborate on issues of sustainability in terms of conserving natural resources and minimizing negative impact on the environment. However, the ecological impact of elements of marketing, such as product design, distribution, and disposal, and the need to conserve scarce natural resources are central for marketing for subsistence marketplaces.

10.4.1 The Nature of Subsistence Marketplaces

The one-to-one interactional nature of subsistence marketplaces has been described in detail earlier. This stands in stark contrast to the situation in developed

[1] The section on implications for marketing is reprinted with minor editing from Viswanathan, Madhubalan, Srinivas Sridharan, and Robin Ritchie, "Marketing in subsistence marketplaces," in Charles Wankel, ed., Alleviating Poverty Through Business Strategy, Copyright © 2007, Palgrave Macmillan Ltd., reproduced with permission of Palgrave Macmillan.

markets, where customers' marketplace interactions typically consist of detached exchanges with anonymous employees of chain stores. For businesses seeking to serve subsistence contexts, the importance of these differences is that the relationship between buyers and sellers in these environments extends well beyond their marketplace roles. As a result, economic exchange may be treated as an extension of everyday personal interaction, rather than being divorced from it. This important insight can provide a basis for new marketing approaches, because it recognizes social relationships as a community-owned resource that might be harnessed to add value for that community through market exchanges. Such an approach has considerable appeal, as its underlying philosophy is one of leveraging the strengths of subsistence markets rather than of overcoming perceived weaknesses. Some authors have argued that strategies which fall into the former category will tend to outperform those that fall into the latter (London and Hart 2004; Ritchie and Sridharan 2007).

Whereas marketplace-level phenomena are important considerations when serving subsistence contexts, it is also helpful to consider characteristics of individual customers. Particularly relevant are low literacy, low income, and the consequences that arise from their joint occurrence. As discussed earlier, research on literacy in the USA provides an interesting starting point for understanding these effects. Perhaps most striking is the difficulty experienced by functionally low-literate customers when faced with abstractions, labeled concrete thinking (Viswanathan et al., 2005). A related predilection is pictographic thinking, the tendency to view brand names and prices as images in a scene rather than symbols, and think about product quantities by picturing them rather than using available symbolic information. Functionally low-literate customers develop several coping mechanisms to deal with these limitations, including depending on others, or buying one item at a time from a menu. Central to their marketplace interactions is a need to maintain self-esteem in public settings that could potentially 'expose' their low literacy.

Research conducted in India suggests that concrete thinking and pictographic thinking are also common in subsistence marketplaces, as are coping mechanisms to compensate for individual shortcomings in marketplace proficiency. Self-esteem issues are also widespread, with low literacy leading to fear of interaction, inability to ask or answer questions in conversation, avoidance of unknown products and unfamiliar pricing schemes, and feelings of futility in making enquiries or demands. Subsistence customers we studied in India struggle with many of the same challenges faced by low-literate customers in the USA. However, as discussed earlier, the one-to-one interactional marketplace appears to afford some unique advantages that can enhance coping ability. These marketplace-level and individual-level characteristics are important in that they differentiate subsistence environments substantially from relatively resource-rich markets that most businesses are used to dealing with. This understanding of buyer, seller, and marketplace behavior has important implications for business practices in general and marketing practices in particular. Next, we illustrate some implications for market research, product development, pricing, promotion, and distribution.

10.4.2 Market Research

Market research is conducted in nonsubsistence markets by a large, thriving industry that has built up an impressive array of tools and techniques to elicit consumer and market information for the benefit of competitive players. However, in subsistence contexts, market research remains in its infancy, leading to a consequent lack of knowledge regarding effective practices. At a minimum, it seems clear that many of the tools and techniques found to be useful in resource-rich and literate contexts are unlikely to be as effective here.

An important element of market research is the concept testing that enables companies to refine products before launching them on a large scale. Conventional market wisdom relies heavily on attribute-based approaches to product design, using methods to identify an optimal combination of relevant attributes. However, low-literate customers tend to think of products holistically, perhaps making it difficult for them to express their preferences along abstract attributes. A more effective approach for subsistence markets would, therefore, be to present the product in a more tangible way. Customer-ready prototypes can be helpful in this regard, because they enable low-literate customers to experience the product and develop an overall sense of preference.

Product testing in subsistence contexts should also be adapted to account for the concrete thinking and pictographic thinking of low-literate customers (Viswanathan et al., 2005), as well as their lack of experience as participants in market research. These characteristics suggest a need for more realistic product testing situations, using concrete, visual stimuli, rather than abstract tasks. Because low-literate customers focus primarily on experiential attributes, product testing should represent the product as realistically as possible. Field-testing and observations of products are highly effective but not always possible. As a practical alternative, in our broader research program, we developed a task in which participants sort sheets of paper containing pictorial representations of a product whose various versions differed on several attributes; appearance (different colors), cost (using currency notes), convenience of availability (using pictures of shops located nearby versus far away), familiarity of the vendor, availability of credit for purchase, and whether the product was advertised on television. The sorting task itself provided a means of eliciting responses without overburdening the respondent with an abstract task of completing ratings on different attributes. By the same logic, other forms of market research are also likely to benefit from the use of more concrete, realistic stimuli. Instead of cueing respondents with a list of brand names, for instance, questionnaires are likely to produce more valid findings if they feature images of actual product packages.

Research methods aimed at eliciting customer information should also recognize that self-esteem plays a central role in the decision-making of subsistence customers, and can compound problems of low literacy and unfamiliarity with market research. This argues for personal administration of surveys and other data-gathering exercises, because these methods are more effective in building personal rapport and eliciting trust from participants. In addition, when used in conjunction with a relatively unstructured data collection approach, personally administered methods may help to alleviate some of the anxiety akin to "test-taking" triggered by low literacy. Conventional, structured approaches, which require respondents to rate products from memory using numbered or labeled response scales (such as numbered 7-point scales) can be abstract and, thus, anxiety-inducing for individuals with low literacy and numeracy skills. In our own research, personal interviews have been effective in collecting such data. When employing 7-point scales, we have used a two-stage process that begins by asking respondents whether they are neutral, positively, or negatively-inclined toward the target (or alternatively, neutral, in agreement with or in disagreement with particular statements), and then asking for further discrimination within the positive or the negative side of the scale to determine their overall favorability (agreement) on the scale.

Other pertinent considerations when conducting marketing research in subsistence contexts include the length and language of procedures. Generally speaking, participants should be able to relate to the tasks they complete and have at least a general understanding of the purpose of the research, lest the abstract nature of the task result in inaccurate responses. To avoid placing unreasonable cognitive demands on the respondent, language and procedures should be straightforward, and surveys, if used, should be of reasonable length. In our experience, long interviews are possible, but only if they feature interesting tasks that respondents can relate to, include a sufficient number of planned breaks, and are conducted by empathetic interviewers who are capable of developing a genuine rapport with participants.

Additionally, the fundamentally social nature of the one-to-one interactional marketplace suggests that researchers would do well to think in terms of collectives (i.e., groups, communities) rather than individuals, and conduct their research on such a basis. One approach is to test market, since this makes it possible to capture the effects of natural social networks and most of the vagaries of the broader market. Researchers would then be able to monitor word-of-mouth, with special attention given to the views of local opinion leaders, such as retailers, community organizers, and leaders of local self-help groups. In situations where a test market is not possible, research methods, such as focus groups, can be used to mimic the processes that occur naturally in the marketplace, such as those that relate to buying decisions and word-of-mouth influences.

A final key issue is that market researchers need to develop a deep understanding of the contexts in which subsistence individuals survive, buy, and consume products. Although this is true of market research in any context, its importance is accentuated in these settings where market researchers often lack familiarity and personal connection with the individuals whose lives are being studied. Moreover, deep understanding of life circumstances may be a precursor to designing products that are likely to be used in varied contexts while being included in the restrictive set of products that subsistence individuals can afford to consider. In a broader sense, the process we undertook to conduct research has many valuable lessons relating to such issues as the procedures used, and the composition of a research team.

10.4.3 New Product Development

New product development is an aspect of marketing strategy that has received substantial attention in the literature. From power cuts to water shortages, customers in subsistence markets grapple with substantial unpredictability in their daily lives. When new products are developed for these markets, it is, therefore, important to test them using procedures that can capture this variability in environmental conditions. Such an approach runs counter to the norm for product development processes in developed markets, which are typically designed to produce efficient solutions for specific usage scenarios. For example, the design of home appliances with built-in safety features (e.g., "child-proofing") would need to reflect a wide range of usage conditions of stoves for cooking in subsistence contexts, such as on a mud floor of a hut, with children nearby. In subsistence markets, customers must often demonstrate considerable ingenuity to cope with extreme resource constraints. In such instances, product development techniques that assume a narrow set of usage conditions can be an impediment to the successful development of new products. Understanding the various ways in which subsistence customers might need to use the product can also enable the marketer to avoid situations where a seemingly value-adding feature actually detracts from the overall utility of the product. Prahalad (2005) highlights the often hostile conditions under which products have to perform in subsistence markets, illustrating the point with examples, such as salt that is iodized using an innovative process that ensures it is retained in cooked food, rather than lost during the cooking processes typically used by customers in these environments.

The above discussion of unpredictability of usage context is merely a specific aspect of the more general and basic notion that product design in subsistence contexts should be driven by a deep understanding of customer needs and the environment in which the product will be used – an understanding that is currently lacking when it comes to subsistence contexts. Indeed, genuine appreciation of the challenges faced by customers in low-income, low-literacy environments is likely to be difficult for typical product development teams, which tend to be composed of highly specialized, relatively resource-rich individuals. This argues for a grounded approach in which every step of the product development process includes immersion in the field, and where separation between engineering tests and market tests of a product may become blurred. Examples of such processes exist in high-technology industries – an environment in which uncertainty is also quite common – where cross functional product development teams and lead user teams have been a hallmark of a number of product successes (Sethi et al., 2001). There is reason to believe that similar approaches might be effective in conceiving new product concepts for subsistence environments.[2] Product design should also take into consideration the need to conserve

[2] In a sense, the inherent uncertainty and unpredictability of subsistence settings poses a similar product development challenge as that posed by the market turbulence that characterizes high technology environments in developed markets. As such, useful parallels can be drawn between the two contexts even though the nature and root cause of the uncertainty is fundamentally different – arising from a lack of stable infrastructure in the former case, and rapidly evolving products and needs in the latter.

natural resources and the potential ecological impact of products, e.g., such as through use of recyclable materials and through local manufacture of elements.

Considerable research has addressed the issue of boosting the creativity of product design processes and making ideation more effective. Analogical thinking merits special attention in this regard, since it appears to be a basic mechanism underlying tasks where individuals transfer information from familiar, existing categories and use it in the construction of new product ideas (Dahl and Moreau 2002). What may be needed for subsistence marketplaces is a similar approach, with input from nonprofit organizations, small vendors and retailers, and self-help group leaders. Finally, contrary to assumptions that only product functionality matters to subsistence customers, our experience suggests that product aesthetics and visual aspects of product design play an important role as well. This suggests a similarity with developed market customers in terms of the importance they have been found to attach to aesthetic considerations while evaluating new product designs (Veryzer and Hutchinson 1998).

10.4.4 Pricing Strategy

Pricing is among the most critical aspects of a company's marketing strategy (Monroe 2002; Kotler 1999), being the only element of the marketing mix, that directly influences the inflow of resources, rather than their outlay. For managers involved in setting and managing prices for products marketed to subsistence markets, several important implications arise from careful consideration of the nature of these markets.

Perhaps the most important of these is that the extreme resource constraints faced by subsistence customers imply a very narrow range of acceptable price levels (Dawar and Chattopadhyay, 2002). Our observations suggest that, even if a customer is inclined to consider quality when appraising product value, low income and low literacy can result in a feeling of futility when shopping, i.e., the sense that a particular quality level is all one can expect for that price. However, even within these narrow price levels, subsistence customers still seek out higher quality and are willing to pay higher prices to trade up. In this regard, Prahalad (2005) notes the importance of quality products at affordable prices to serve the needs of discerning subsistence customers. Although this may seem counterintuitive, it can be understood by recognizing the centrality of specific consumption events to subsistence customers' daily life, the severe resource constraints they face, and the consequent consideration of a very narrow set of necessary products. For instance, because paying a slightly higher price often enables an individual to obtain better quality rice (a staple food in South India), the importance of what may be the only square meal of the day can prompt customers to pay more for an upgraded product. Pricing managers should recognize that this tendency may exist across a variety of product categories, including expensive, high-technology products that have traditionally been seen as out-of-reach for subsistence customers. For instance, an interesting consequence of the recent boom in the telecommunications industry in India is that rural fishermen and fisherwomen, even those that are extremely poor, have come to rely on mobile telephones. They use these devices while working at sea, in order to communicate estimated catch sizes and negotiate prices with fish buyers and wholesalers back on land. Such communication demands a high quality phone capable of supporting the fisherman's livelihood-generating activity; as a result, many are willing to pay more for better quality.

A second critical pricing consideration stems from what subsistence customers account for when appraising a product's value as discussed in the earlier section derived from translating concepts for our educational program. In nonsubsistence contexts, customers often consider savings of time and effort in the "give" component (what they give up) when considering a product's value (Zeithaml 1988). In contrast, the lack of monetary resources in subsistence markets makes it difficult for customers in those environments to think beyond price. This is compounded by low literacy, and a tendency to struggle with abstractions. As discussed in an earlier section in this chapter, the result is that subsistence customers tend to consider price as the sole determinant of the "give" component when determining good product value.

In light of the monetary constraints faced by subsistence customers, the preceding discussion suggests that companies should carefully consider the value proposition of their offering when setting pricing strategies. For instance, by recognizing instances where quality is highly valued, even though customers are able to afford only products within a very narrow price range, companies can create a win-win outcome by offering higher quality options and pricing them at an appropriate premium. On the other hand, subsistence customers often focus heavily on monetary cost when assessing the "give" component of product value, while ignoring potential savings of time and effort. For example, they may go to great lengths to pay less for product purchases, even at great risk to their health, or seek to reduce family expenses by skimping on important medical services. However, time is a precious commodity for subsistence individuals for a variety of reasons, such as the need to constantly seek out livelihood opportunities or the need to purchase ingredients to cook a meal after receiving daily wages. Pricing strategies should account for these tendencies by incorporating them into the pricing structure and carefully communicating the relationship between costs and benefits to customers. Costs and benefits beyond the near term, or benefits that may outweigh costs, need to be communicated carefully. This should be done in a manner that is respectful of the value judgments of customers, but also educational in encouraging the formation of new types of value judgments that are beneficial in the long run.

10.4.5 Marketing Communications

Individual characteristics of subsistence customers also have important implications for marketing communications. Chief among these is the lack of informational resources that results from the economic resource constraints faced by these individuals. This is especially important for products that offer unique benefits, because it is critical that companies communicate their value proposition effectively. For example, HLL's (Hindustan Lever Limited) campaign to promote hand-washing has seen the company go to extraordinary lengths to explain the need for hand washing by encouraging customers to 'visualize' the problem of germs (Prahalad 2005). In this case, the "get" component was communicated in a manner that accommodated the distinctive cognitive style of subsistence customers, notably concrete and pictographic thinking.

Aspects of the one-to-one interactional marketplace are also extremely important when developing strategies for marketing communications. The social nature of these environments suggests that subsistence customers may be particularly receptive to the use of spokespersons or characters to personify the brand, because individuals who are accustomed to dealing with people, rather than abstract information, may process such information, more readily. In addition, marketers should strive to develop cultural knowledge, such as popular folklore, since this provides a rich repository of shared meaning that the marketer can draw upon. Particularly germane here are marketing communications that can build on the heavy influence of word-of-mouth in a one-to-one interactional context. Such marketing communications include relying on peer-to-peer contact to spread information. Given the central role of social networks in the one-to-one marketplace, such techniques may be especially effective in subsistence settings.

As has been widely acknowledged, the effectiveness of word-of-mouth marketing depends heavily on the company's ability to identify and influence the right people, i.e., the opinion leaders or "market mavens" (Feick and Price 1987). To be able to exert such influence, a person, for example, the owner of a retail store or the leader of a self-help group, should possess both the respect of others and a sufficient number of social connections to allow the influence of their opinion to spread. Marketers who seek to work with these individuals should thus be sufficiently embedded in the community that they are not only able to identify them, but build a sound and trusting reputation, emphasizing the importance of market research approaches discussed earlier.

In addition, the power of social networks in subsistence markets can be harnessed more directly via efforts to incorporate local individuals into the company's sales network. The social relationships possessed by these individuals can facilitate trial and adoption of products as well as collection of high-quality customer feedback that would be difficult to obtain through other means. A good example is HLL's distribution system in rural India, the Shakti program. By working with women in villages who function as resellers for their health and hygiene products and communicate with rural customers, the company credibly communicates its value proposition. Although the main innovation of this strategy is at the level of distribution, it is also a highly effective communication vehicle. HLL has recognized this in a formal sense by creating two distinct roles within the Shakti program – Shakti Amma for the physical distribution of products and for one-on-one communication, and Shakti Vani for broader communication (Rajan, 2007). Key to the long-term effectiveness of such promotional systems is to safeguard the social capital that makes the local representative a partner in the first place. At the most basic level, this comes from ensuring that products are of high quality, affordable and beneficial, such that the individual's role as a vendor is seen to add value to her relationships, rather than detract from them. Relatedly, companies also need to reinforce the notion that the relationship is indeed a partnership, rather than a conventional employer-employee relationship, by including subsistence customers as genuine stakeholders when designing their marketing goals and strategies.

Perhaps most importantly, effective marketing communications in subsistence contexts requires "out-of-the-box" thinking. Rather than using one-size-fits-all top-down approaches, our findings emphasize the need for marketers to work from the ground up and look for ways to customize their approaches for what are invariably widely dispersed, fragmented markets. For example, village fairs, advertisements on vehicles, and other locally-suited media outlets are often extremely useful. Moreover, the nature of these communications should accommodate the constraints imposed by low literacy as well as the differences in local languages across various subsistence markets. Marketing communications should also expand beyond informational to educational approaches, and take on the challenge of conveying product benefits to low-literate audiences.

10.4.6 Marketing Channels

In developed markets, the norm is to make products available to end users by moving them through formal, centralized distribution channels. In subsistence markets, delivery to market is usually accomplished in a less formal manner, with small merchants obtaining their products from a diverse set of wholesalers, large retailers, and manufacturer representatives. This represents both a challenge for companies, as well as an opportunity to create value through innovation in go-to-market strategies. For example, as Prahalad (2005) points out, customers in many subsistence contexts, urban and rural, are often forced to pay a large premium to local intermediaries for services, such as money loans. This is the result of a system in which doing so is often the only way to obtain a particular product or service, and has the effect of placing intermediaries in a position of unusual power that can lead to unscrupulous practices. An interesting implication, according to Prahalad, is that companies adopting certain types of direct distribution models have an opportunity to alleviate this "poverty penalty." In India, for instance, ICICI Bank now offers rural customers direct access to financial services through microfinancing institutions and self-help groups, demonstrating this potential to innovate through marketing channels. In Bangladesh, one of the key ingredients of Nobel Prize winning Grameen Bank's microcredit programs is the facilitation of direct access to credit and loans for subsistence customers. ITC's e-choupal represents an approach where the supply chain has been streamlined to enable direct interaction between farmers and the company (Prahalad, 2005).

Interestingly, the direct-distribution model that this implies does not always need to be specifically designed to overcome the predicament caused by intermediaries. In many instances, the one-to-one interactional marketplace discussed earlier creates an environment where small, local retailers or service providers enjoy the trust and patronage of local customers. In these instances, a direct distribution model can benefit significantly by securing the cooperation of local individuals rather than bypassing them. As illustrated with the HLL example, individuals from specific communities can work as resellers, giving the company access to previously neglected markets. This is also evident in the distribution of cellular phone services through local entrepreneurial women, a phenomenon increasingly employed by companies in subsistence markets around the world (e.g., Grameen Telecom in Bangladesh, Roshan in Afghanistan). As with marketing communications, approaches to distribution need to incorporate a willingness to work from the ground up and customize, rather than adopt a one-size-fits-all solution.

As noted earlier, one of the key characteristics of the one-to-one interactional marketplace is the willingness of vendors to extend credit and adjust terms of trade when customers find themselves in times of need – two practices that create a form of customer lock-in that is not easily disregarded. In similar fashion, retailers form relationships with suppliers, creating mutual obligations that influence the future actions of both parties. By adopting pricing and distribution practices that make it easier for retailers to extend credit, adjust prices, and vary products to accommodate the changing circumstances of their customers, manufacturers are likely to be more successful themselves. Part of the solution lies in offering products where, at the least, the final stage of manufacture occurs at the retail level, allowing customization. Local production also has potential advantages in terms of improving livelilood opportunities, lowering transportation costs, and lessening negative impact on the environment. Localized production has the added benefit of creating win-win scenarios by offering livelihood opportunities to subsistence individuals and communities. The earlier discussion of customization emphasizes the need to allow flexibility for retailers to meet the varied demands of customers.

Another way that companies can align their distribution systems to the needs of subsistence markets is through the use of information and communication technologies (ICTs) that leverage the strengths of the one-to-one interactional marketplace. A good example is the Inter-City Marketing Network, an initiative of the Chennai-based Foundation of Occupational Development (FOOD). This program gave mobile phones to community-based women's organizations as a means of encouraging the creation of social networks between artisans/skilled workers and individuals who could provide sales and promotion for their products in neighboring markets. Though created to encourage the small-scale manufacture and marketing of locally manufactured products, the program is a good example of a system that takes advantage of connections between individuals to identify and respond to commercial opportunities. Similar approaches could be used for a broad range of products and services.

10.5 Challenges to Business Research and Practice

The mind-frame with which to approach subsistence marketplaces needs some mention. Whether examining this issue as an educator, researcher or practitioner unfamiliar with subsistence contexts, approaching it with a completely open mind is critical.

Mind-frames that there is nothing new here or that this is a special case of things already understood are particularly unproductive. If anything, the opposite mentality is preferable, with a healthy dose of tough self-enquiry about what is new and what is not following in the analysis stage but not impeding the data collection stage. There are, of course, a number of reasons to maintain that there is little that is new here, in light of one's own exposure. For instance, it is perhaps impossible for literate researchers and practitioners to recall the experience of being low-literate. It is similarly very difficult, perhaps impossible, to imagine what extreme poverty and living near subsistence mean for relatively resource-rich individuals. What this calls for is a recognition that these extreme conditions may well challenge conventional notions of theory and practice.

Subsistence marketplaces challenge conventional theory and practice as well as conventional notions of rationality.[3] For example, one of the most rational statements we heard from subsistence customers was in a rural setting in India, when we asked a woman if she planned her purchases and how she spends her income. She said, "Why should I plan?" "Why should I plan when I don't know where my next source of income is coming from?" When people have enough money to buy wholesale at cheaper prices than retail and stock up, they may still not do so. This may be because, down the road, during the next crisis, one option may be to forego consumption. It may be necessary to buy from the usual retail store who offers credit in time of need, out of fear of the next crisis. As mentioned earlier, we asked one woman who patronized a retail store whether she checks prices. She said no, and asked us to consider how the retail owner would feel if she were to do so, after all the credit he has provided in times of need. It is interesting to note the different services offered at a neighborhood retail store. In one sense it is like a bank, securing money for a fee, an important service for individuals who want to keep their money from thieves or alcoholic husbands. In another sense, it is like a credit card company, offering credit and possessing good knowledge of creditworthiness. As discussed, subsistence markets are resource-poor but can be network-rich, a one-to-one interactional world. People may get a prescription from a doctor, buy the medicine from a pharmacy by pattern matching the first letter, and then show the medicine to the doctor again to confirm it is the right one. These are just some examples that highlight the need for a fundamental shift in thinking to understand subsistence marketplaces.

Regarding such contexts as mere variations on traditional markets can easily lead to certain counterproductive tendencies, such as believing that solutions for such markets

[3] This paragraph is reprinted with minor editing with permission from Elsevier from Viswanathan and Rosa (2007). This article was published in Product and Market Development for Subsistence Marketplaces: Consumption and Entrepreneurship Beyond Literacy and Resource Barriers, Editors, Jose Rosa and Madhu Viswanathan, Advances in International Management Series, Joseph Cheng and Michael Hitt, Series Editors, Viswanathan, Madhubalan, and Jose Rosa (2007), "Product and market development for subsistence marketplaces: Consumption and entrepreneurship beyond literacy and resource barriers," 1–17, Copyright Elsevier, 2007.

can and should be "exported" from nonsubsistence contexts.[4] A more effective approach may be to treat subsistence environments not just as markets to develop solutions for, but also as individuals, consumers, entrepreneurs, communities, and markets to learn from. To conduct effective market research and design successful products, companies need to embrace this perspective and learn lessons that may be applicable even in nonsubsistence environments. The Villageherbs brand of herbal remedies and products offers a case in point. Launched by Gram Mooligai, an entrepreneurial venture in South India, this line of products was developed using the traditional medicine and knowledge of rural subsistence communities, and is now being successfully marketed to urban, nonsubsistence markets as well. There is considerable innovation in subsistence markets, at both the entrepreneurial and consumer level, arising from a basic need to survive. Such insights from 'doing more with less' stem from ingenuity in surviving under extreme resource constraints, using available products in innovative ways that cannot be easily anticipated by market researchers not exposed to life in these conditions.

Well-intentioned efforts to conduct research and create solutions for subsistence contexts can also be hindered by subtle assumptions of "knowing what the poor need". An example is the dominant logic of product functionality, which can obscure the reality that subsistence customers may value very different features from those imagined by outsiders – product aesthetics, for example. It is instructive to note, for instance, that some of the world's finest art, handicrafts, and ornamentation are made by individuals living in subsistence conditions – a testament to their traditionally honed skills and appreciation of aesthetics. An approach that is open to learning from buyers and sellers in subsistence can lead to many advantages including opportunities to co-create successful product designs.

Finally, coupled with openness in perspective and a willingness to learn from subsistence marketplaces is the need to strive for accurate understanding despite the impetus to act immediately when confronted with the harsh realities of subsistence. Similarly, there is a need for accurate assessment, despite the temptation to assume that outcomes of programs will benefit people. The desire to ultimately benefit people has to be coupled with accurate understanding of contexts and accurate assessment of possible offerings to generate sustainable solutions that actually benefit individuals and enable businesses to succeed. It is in these contexts as much as anywhere else that tough questions need to be asked about the actual benefit of a product or the prospects for sustaining a business.

10.6 Conclusion

Our research and the development of the educational program have a number of implications for businesses that plan to develop goods and services for subsistence marketplaces. The educational program offers businesses avenues for social

[4] The next two paragraphs are reprinted with minor editing from Viswanathan, Madhubalan, Srinivas Sridharan, and Robin Ritchie, "Marketing in subsistence marketplaces," in Charles Wankel, ed., Alleviating Poverty Through Business Strategy, Copyright © 2007, Palgrave Macmillan Ltd., reproduced with permission of Palgrave Macmillan.

initiatives, for training employees and partners, and for supplementing the value chain, creating win-win scenarios in the process. The actual design of the educational program reflected our explicit and implicit learning in these contexts and its delivery and assessment have afforded additional insights. A reexamination of the educational program and the translation of generic business concepts to a subsistence context explicates our approach and provides additional implications for business. Our approach involved deep understanding of these environments through research, with implications for business. Finally, subsistence marketplaces present unique challenges to business research and practice that require a fundamental shift in thinking. Overcoming these challenges can help empower individuals living in subsistence as consumers and as entrepreneurs, while also improving the effectiveness of management practice, teaching, and research. The lessons learned in subsistence markets can extend to all markets, in terms of doing more with less or finding sustainable solutions.

References

Dahl, D. W. and Moreau, P. (2002). The influence and value of analogical thinking during new product ideation. *Journal of Marketing Research*, 39(1), 47–60.

Dawar, N. and Chattopadhyay, A. (2002). Rethinking marketing programs for emerging markets. *Long Range Planning*, 35(5), 457–474.

Feick, L. F. and Price, L. (1987). The market maven: A diffuser of marketplace information, *Journal of Marketing*, 51(1), 83–97.

Kotler, P. (1999). *Kotler on Marketing: How to Create, Win, and Dominate Markets*. New York: Free Press.

London, T. and Hart, S. L. (2004). Reinventing strategies for emerging markets: Beyond the transnational model. *Journal of International Business Studies*, 35, 350–370.

Monroe, K. B. (2002). *Pricing: Making Profitable Decisions*. New York: McGraw-Hill.

Prahalad, C. K. (2005). *The Fortune at the Bottom of the Pyramid: Eradicating Poverty Through Profits*. Upper Saddle River, NJ: Wharton School Publishing.

Rajan Rohithari (2007). Unilever's business in India's subsistence economies. In J. Rosa and M. Viswanathan (eds.), *Product and Market Development for Subsistence Marketplaces: Consumption and Entrepreneurship Beyond Literacy and Resource Barriers. Oxon*, UK: Elsevier.

Ritchie, R. and Sridharan, S. (2007). Marketing in subsistence markets: Innovation through decentralization and externalization. In J. Rosa and M. Viswanathan (eds.), *Product and Market Development for Subsistence Marketplaces: Consumption and Entrepreneurship Beyond Literacy and Resource Barriers*. Oxon, UK: Elsevier.

Sethi, R., Smith, D. C., and Park, C. W. (2001). Cross functional product development teams, creativity, and the innovativeness of new consumer products. *Journal of Marketing Research*, 38(2), 73–85.

Veryzer, Jr., R. W. and Hutchinson, J. W. (1998). The influence of unity and prototypicality on aesthetic responses to new product designs. *Journal of Consumer Research*, 24, 374–394.

Viswanathan, M., Rosa, J. A., and Harris, J. (2005). Decision-making and coping by functionally illiterate consumers and some implications for marketing management. *Journal of Marketing*, 69, 15–31.

Zeithaml, V. A. (1988). Consumer perceptions of price, quality, and value: a means-end model and synthesis of evidence. *Journal of Marketing*, 52, 2–22.

Chapter 11
Implications for Basic and Applied Research

There are a number of lessons learned and insights generated by this process of moving from basic research to education. A number of aspects of our research are relevant for basic and applied research, including a focus on research across literacy and resource barriers, research methods, treatment of human participants, the iterative process between basic research and the development of an application for societal welfare, and synergies between research, teaching, and social initiatives. This chapter explores these implications for basic and applied research in the social sciences. The discussion is intended to be illustrative rather than exhaustive.

11.1 Research Across Literacy and Resource Barriers

Basic research conducted here and the application developed as a result have a number of implications for research in the social sciences. Our research represents an effort to study consumption and entrepreneurship across literacy and research barriers, whereas previous research, has focused predominantly on relatively resource-rich, literate buyers and sellers (Figure 1). Pathbreaking work in disciplines, such as anthropology, have examined a variety of subsistence contexts. Nevertheless, focus on this area across a number of other disciplines, such as business and psychology, is rare (Viswanathan and Rosa, 2007). There have been a number of trends in recent years ranging from calls to study the base of the pyramid (Prahalad, 2005; Hart, 2005) to increasing literature on social entrepreneurship. For instance, recent efforts in consumer research have focused on the need to emphasize consumer welfare (Mick, 2006). Our experience speaks directly to these calls. Our work provides a bottom-up understanding of buyers, sellers, and marketplaces. Whereas economic approaches tend to be at the macro level and business strategy approaches, such as the base of the pyramid approach, at the medium level, our focus is at the micro level. We derive our insights from this level of understanding and build on them and draw implications. Our findings challenge conventional theory and practice and emphasize the need to incorporate extreme economic constraints into our thinking. They emphasize the need for a fundamental shift in thinking in research and practice.

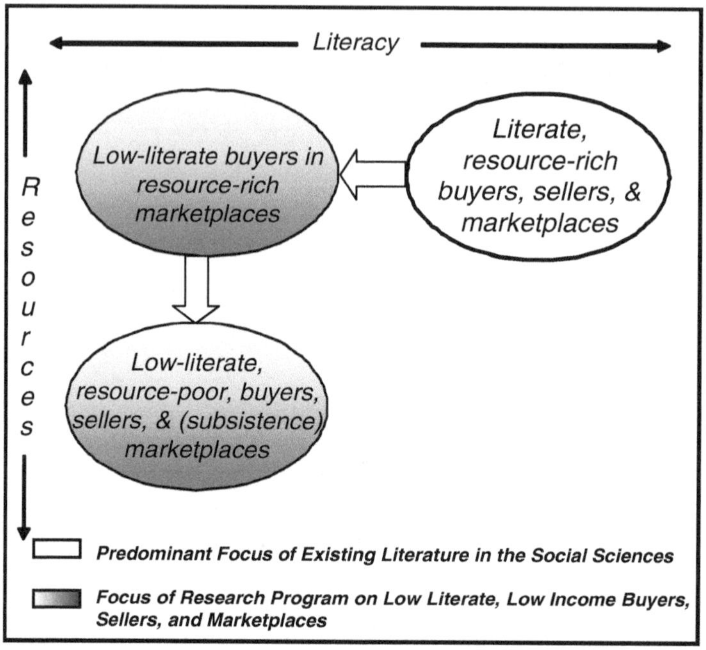

Figure 1 Illustration of New Directions of Research Program on Low-Literate Buyers, Sellers, and Marketplaces

At the broadest level, our research provides understanding of subsistence customers, in terms of the environment they negotiate, the products and markets they interact with, and the interface between their roles as buyers and sellers. The process of moving from basic research to the development and implementation of an educational program served to strengthen our insights in several ways. The process was iterative, with feedback and observation of participants in the educational program serving to guide subsequent research, which, in turn, led to modification of the educational program. Our experience has implications for the conduct of research in the social sciences and the development of applications to enhance individual and societal welfare.

11.2 From Basic Research to Application

There were a number of elements to our work that informed our effort to move from research to practice. Foremost was the importance of systematic research in designing interventions. A research focus permeated our entire approach and was invaluable in designing an educational program that would lead to maximum benefit. This research process extended beyond deciding content and teaching methods to gathering feedback and adjusting aspects of our program, and to documenting our work. A second striking issue was the power of education. We met many dedicated individuals working in nonprofit organizations and delivering educational programs, essentially involved in remarkable work in these settings. We were also overwhelmed by the extreme adversities that individuals living in poverty face, which often leads to feelings of futility about interventions of any kind. However, a research-based educational program such as the one we developed does have the power to transform lives by enabling people to learn how to learn and by increasing their confidence as well as awareness of their rights. Our experiences and the feedback we have received have been extremely rewarding and uplifting. A third issue was the need to innovate in the design of the educational program. Counterintuitive as it may seem from the notion of equating subsistence with low technology and a flashback to yesteryears, the reality that subsistence customers face intertwines the old with the new in terms of the products, marketplaces, and technologies they encounter. Our program attempted to reflect the complex realities that subsistence customers face in the era of globalization. Moreover, despite the difficulties with abstractions associated with low literacy, we focused on conveying basic concepts that tapped into individuals lived experiences. Such an approach, distinct from a coverage of a concrete list of business activities as we observed in other programs, served to enable individuals to learn how to learn, and, hopefully, provided lasting benefits. Fourthly, innovation has to extend beyond content to delivery as well. This is reflected in the program in terms of designing picture sortings and role-plays for low-literate individuals. But it is also true in terms of scaling the program to reach a larger audience, such as through the use of an e-educational approach. Finally, the close interlinkages between research and application and the synergies they afford point to a somewhat expanded role for the researcher beyond what may traditionally be envisioned. Such an expanded role strengthens research and practice, while also enabling the researcher to guide dissemination and application of basic research in socially responsible ways. The educational programs we conducted enabled us to test our findings and make new observations in a live setting where individuals were actively engaged in the assigned activities. Ongoing educational programs provide continuous feedback that enables us to avoid premature closure in our ideas and thinking.

11.3 Research Methods and the Role of the Researcher

Several issues relating to research methods are noteworthy here based on our experiences. Some issues have been discussed in the chapters on implications for education and for business. In our qualitative research, we used unstructured approaches, allowing individuals to relate their stories to us. This gave us a big picture understanding of the lives and struggles of people living in subsistence. Our sampling was deliberative, to maximize the amount of information we could gather. Our research was conducted over several years, allowing us to absorb the insights we gained and adjust the method. The research was appropriately broadly construed in terms of lives and struggles, while emphasizing aspects of the economic realm. Critical here was the need to approach the phenomenon without preconceptions. We deliberately began with a grounded approach aimed at educating ourselves. Labels, concepts and categories only go so far and the localized knowledge we gained was invaluable in developing understanding. We approached the phenomena with an open perspective, allowing for the possibility that everything we learned could be new. Whether this is the case or not is perhaps best addressed through comparison and contrast after the fact, but for purposes of research, we found this openness to be invaluable. Also central to our approach was that our research associates (the second and third authors of this book) have experienced the subsistence context first-hand and possess decades of experience in social work and community development in subsistence contexts.

Our interviews were, first and foremost, sincere conversations. Individuals broke down as they told us their life stories. Central to this process was the sincere intent to listen and learn with empathy. Both from a research and an ethical standpoint, it was important that we not use the interview to exploit the situation, whether it was in finding interesting "quotes" or dwelling on aspects that emphasized the respondents' problems and vulnerabilities. Again, invaluable here is the need to be open and not seek preconceived outcomes either for the interview or for the research.

In terms of conducting research in these contexts, the notion of using subsistence individuals' insights for research without the possibility of any real benefit in return is particularly difficult. In many ways, our ideas of developing the program outlined here were very helpful in explaining the goals of our research. Individuals seemed to appreciate the possible benefits of the research even when they were explained early on in relatively abstract terms. There was an openness and a willingness to share their troubles with others who seemed to care enough to talk to them.

As discussed in Chapter 10, coupled with openness in perspective and a willingness to learn from subsistence marketplaces is the need to gain accurate understanding of contexts and accurate assessment of possible offerings to generate sustainable solutions that actually benefit individuals. Subsistence individuals have strengths and vulnerabilities; central to one's research orientation is the need to be accurate in this regard. It is important to avoid romanticizing about the harsh realities of poverty or painting a rosy picture that does not reflect reality. At the same time, it is also important to be open to the unique strengths that individuals in these contexts possess, stemming from the impetus to survive under the worst of conditions.

In the context of the marketplace literacy educational program, despite the temptation to assume that benefits to participants are sizable or the impetus to act immediately to help individuals living in subsistence, the need to constantly assess the program through different means and to continuously modify it is critical. Tough questions need to be asked about the actual benefits of the program and of ways to scale it in a sustainable manner. Moreover, the specific means to benefit individuals living in subsistence that one is invested in can take on a life of its own and become *the* most important element of any solution. This is all the more reason to adopt and maintain a research orientation that enables one to step back and view the larger picture. The challenges in adopting multiple roles are sizable as are the synergies that emerge, as discussed in a later section in this chapter.

11.4 Treatment of Human Participants

Procedures relating to the treatment of human participants pose some interesting issues. The overriding temptation in subsistence contexts is to ignore approved procedures and there is certainly much encouragement to do so. We were often encouraged to go ahead with research without covering informed consent procedures or without incentives. The general notion was that there were many individuals available to talk and there was no need to provide them with incentives. Informed consent procedures that were important in a western context were not considered necessary in the South Indian context. However, this is precisely where it is all the more important to carefully adhere to approved procedures and provide appropriate incentives. The intent to follow procedures is often tested. One arena where this may happen is in conducting confidential interviews, say, in a village. When talking to one person, many spectators may gather and some may volunteer to answer "accurately" on behalf of the interviewee! Here, it is very important to make every effort to conduct the individual interview in a confidential manner and treat group interviews separately, the latter being another very useful forum. Confidential interviews are difficult to implement and the controlled interview environment that one envisions in many western settings is very difficult, sometimes impossible, to create. There are myriad human interactions going on in a short time that cannot be prevented, or controlled in most situations. Procedures used for conducting interviews and, more generally, for collecting data should also stem from an understanding of cultural norms and should be respectful of local beliefs and practices.

A related issue that is germane to proper treatment of participants as well as effective research is the need to truly assume the role of being an equal, rather than someone of privileged status who has the solutions to the problems that individuals face. This is easier said than done. However, it is critical to strive to understand and realize that it is actually the participant who has privileged information about the subsistence context, even though it is the researcher who is likely to be perceived as occupying much higher status. A large barrier in this respect is the perception of participants that they have little to offer and that the researcher knows much more. Such a perception is compounded when researchers, despite their good intentions, have a sense of possessing the solutions and being more knowledgeable than the participant.

In summary, perhaps the most rewarding aspect of our research was in the feedback we received that our participants were happy to have participated in our research. This, more than anything, was centrally important. Our participants were at the lowest level of the power structure in so many ways and our intent in every interaction was to respect the inherent dignity of every human being, no matter what we can do or can "get away with".

11.5 Developing Synergies Between Research, Teaching, and Social Initiatives

This program represents an example of actual dissemination of research into applications to benefit society. This represents an extremely rewarding intersection of research, teaching, and social initiatives. Although knowledge dissemination and public service can be viewed as being distinct from scholarly research, this work represents one of many examples of a proactive model bridging academic research with practice. This approach creates valuable synergies between research, teaching, and social initiatives, strengthening all three elements along the way. For instance, our experiences have led to a one-of-a-kind course on product and market development for subsistence marketplaces (http://www.business.uiuc.edu/~madhuv/submktcourse-mainpage.html) in addition to several independent study projects with students. We are also piloting a module for first year undergraduate students in business on developing sustainable businesses for subsistence marketplaces. Our work with students has, in turn, enriched the research and social initiatives. Synergies across research, teaching, and social initiatives, as well as between a methodological orientation and a substantive focus are illustrated in Figure 2, further emphasizing the importance of a research orientation.

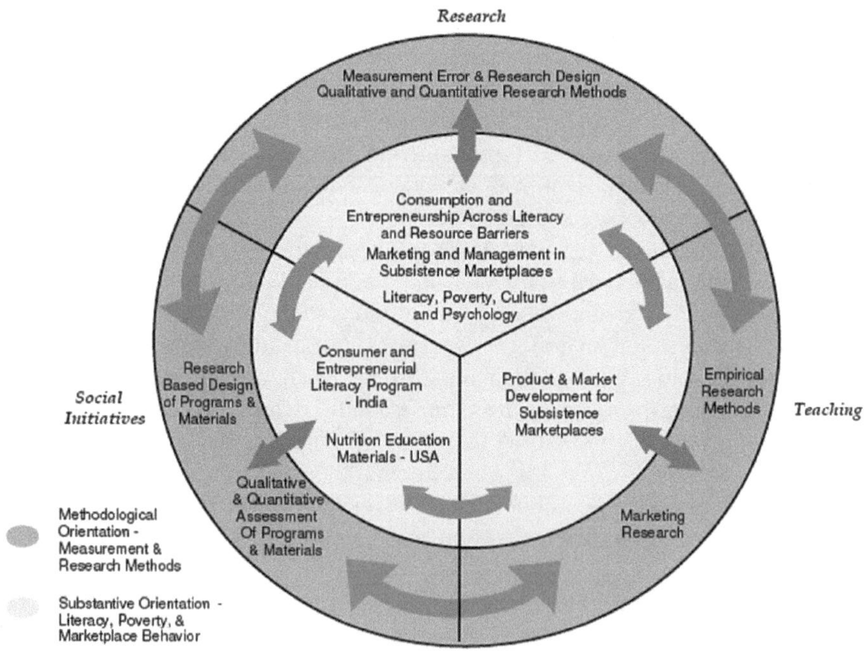

Figure 2 Synergies Between Research, Teaching, and Social Initiatives[1]

[1] The synergies represented in this figure reflect the experiences and impressions of the first author and cover programs of methodological and substantive orienatations.

The synergy between research and social initiatives occurs at a number of levels. At the broadest level, it occurs in terms of the need to educate oneself through immersion in a radically different context, suspending prior beliefs and preconceptions. This is no small task for researchers who have not experienced subsistence firsthand, and do not recall what it means to be low-literate. It also occurs in having a research orientation that guides all the aspects of the development of the educational program in terms of the content and the instructional methods as well as assessment. A research orientation is also reflected in careful documentation of the work, such as through this book, which in turn modified the educational program and provided new insights. Although our development of the educational program was at a practical level, it built on the implicit beliefs we had developed about subsistence marketplaces as well as about customizing business concepts to a one-to-one interactional marketplace. The process of documenting the work and articulating our rationale uncovered insights as well. Also central here is a methodological orientation that allows for the use of diverse methods in basic research underlying the education program as well as in its assessment.

At a more specific level, our work provides new insights on consumption, entrepreneurship and management that are not addressed in a sustained manner by the existing literature. The one-to-one interactional marketplace and inherent social skills of the subsistence individuals we studied provide insights into coping mechanisms that are employed by buyers and sellers. Such understanding has social relevance, such as through leveraging these skills in designing and implementing educational programs, as demonstrated with our marketplace literacy program. Insights about entrepreneurship include the adaptivity of subsistence entrepreneurs and their ability to seamlessly move between personal and business realms. Insights at the management level relate to the need to fundamentally reexamine the definition of a business in subsistence contexts. At the broadest level, implications for research relate to the need to learn *from* subsistence marketplaces. Implications extend to education, as outlined in Chapter 9, and to other disciplines, such as psychology, which have not focused in a sustained way on human behavior at the confluence of culture, poverty, and low literacy.

Noteworthy here is that the basic elements for such an approach relate to research and the development of an educational program, both central to the academic career. Our approach demonstrates the power of research and the power of education. Academic researchers have a unique vantage point to pursue broader approaches that develop synergies between research, teaching, and social initiatives, in light of their experience with research and education. Although there are several starting points that can lead to such synergies, we began with purposeful research, which has the potential to improve individual and societal welfare.

11.6 Conclusion

This book begins and concludes with a focus on basic research. The potential for marketplace literacy educational programs is large, as is the potential for researchers to study subsistence marketplaces and develop solutions that enhance individual and societal welfare. The key is to develop solutions that are based on a deep understanding of subsistence marketplaces, to systematically assess such solutions, and to constantly modify solutions to varying circumstances. Underlying all these aspects is the need for a research orientation that leads to valuable insights, accurate assessment, and constant learning and modification. Our research-based approach to marketplace literacy represents but one of a variety of educational programs that can benefit individuals and communities in subsistence, while providing insightful lessons for nonsubsistence contexts as well. Our work aims to enable progress toward marketplaces charcterized by sustainable production and consumption that conserve natural resources and enhance individual and community welfare. In conclusion, we hope that this work contributes in a small way in enabling a large proportion of humanity currently functiong in subsistence marketplaces to participate in sustainable marketplaces.

References

Prahalad, C. K. (2005). *The Fortune at the Bottom of the Pyramid: Eradicating Poverty Through Profits*. Upper Saddle River, NJ: Wharton School Publishing.

Hart, S. (2005). *Capitalism at the Crossroads: The Unlimited Business Opportunities in Solving the World's Most Difficult Problems*. Wharton School Publishing, University of Pennsylvania.

Mick, D. (2006). Meaning and mattering through transformative consumer research. In: Cornelia Pechmann and Linda L. Price (eds.), *Advances in Consumer Research*, Vol. 33. Association for Consumer Research.

Viswanathan, M., and Rosa, J. A. (2007). Product and market development for subsistence marketplaces: Consumption and entrepreneurship beyond literacy and resource barriers. In: J. A. Rosa and M. Viswanathan (eds.), *Product and Market Development for Subsistence Marketplaces: Consumption and Entrepreneurship Beyond Literacy and Resource Barriers*. Advances in International Management Series, Joseph Cheng and Michael Hitt (Series Editors), Elsevier.

Author Index

Subject Index

Education in the Asia-Pacific Region

1. J. Fien, D.Yencken and H. Sykes (eds.): *Young People and the Environment*. An Asia-Pacific Perspective. 2003 ISBN 1-4020-0944-5
2. M.W. Charney, B.S.A. Yeoh and T.C. Kiong (eds.): *Asian Migrants and Education*.The Tensions of Education in Immigrant Societies and among Migrant Groups. 2003 ISBN 1-4020-1336-1
3. Y.C. Cheng, K.W. Chow and M. Mok (eds.): *Reform of Teacher Education in the Pacific in the New Millennium*. Trends and Challenges. 2004 ISBN 1-4020-2701-X
4. S. Alagumalai, D.D. Curtis and N. Hungi (eds.): *Applied Rasch Measurement*. A Book of Examplars Papers in Honour of John P. Keeves. 2004 ISBN 1-4020-3072-X
5. C.-H. Ng and P. Renshaw (eds.): *Reforming Learning*. Issues, Concepts and Practices in the Asian-Pacific Region. 2005 ISBN 1-4020-3002-9
6. Y.C. Cheng (ed.): *New Paradigm for Re-engineering Education*. Globalization, Localization and Individualization. 2005 ISBN 1-4020-3619-1
7. W.J. Campbell, N. Baikaloff and C. Power (eds.): *Towards a Global Community*. Educating for Tomorrow's World. 2006 ISBN 1-4020-3960-3
8. C. Bjork (ed.): *Educational Decentralization*. Asian Experiences and Conceptual Contributions. 2006 ISBN 1-4020-4356-2
9. P. Hughes (ed.): *Secondary Education at the Crossroads*. International Perspectives Relevant to the Asia-Pacific Region. 2006 ISBN 1-4020-4667-7
10. Y. Nagata (ed.): *Alternative Education*. Global Perspectives Relevant to the Asia-Pacific Region. 2006 ISBN 1-4020-4985-4
11. L. Joubert (ed.): *Educating in the Arts*. The Asian Experience: Twenty-Four Essays. 2008 ISBN 1-4020-6386-2
12. M. Viswanathan, S. Gajendiran, and R. Venkatesan: *Enabling Consumer and Entrepreneurial Literacy in Subsistence Marketplaces*. 2008 ISBN 1-4020-5768-7

Kolibri 360 GmbH
Ferdinand-Jühlke-Straße 7
99095 Erfurt, Deutschland
produktsicherheit@kolibri360.de